Gres

The Anatomy of a Disaster

Gresford
The Anatomy of a Disaster

STANLEY WILLIAMSON

LIVERPOOL UNIVERSITY PRESS

First published 1999 by
LIVERPOOL UNIVERSITY PRESS
Senate House, Abercromby Square,
Liverpool L69 3BX

British Library Cataloguing-in-Publication Data
A British Library CIP record is available

ISBN 0–85323–892–8 *cased*
     0–85323–902–9 *paper*

Set in Plantin by
Wilmaset Limited, Birkenhead, Wirral
Printed and bound in the European Union by
Redwood Books, Trowbridge, Wiltshire

If one ponders well the course of human affairs it will be seen that many events happen and many misfortunes come about against which the heavens have not been willing that any provision at all should be made.

Machiavelli ('Discourses', trans. Walker)

You've heard of the Gresford disaster,
The terrible price that was paid;
Two hundred and sixty-two colliers were lost,
And three of the rescue brigade.

Down there in the dark they are lying;
They died for nine shillings a day.
They have worked out their shift and now they must lie
In darkness until Judgement Day.

Farewell our dear wives and our children,
Farewell our dear comrades as well.
Don't send your sons down the dark dreary pit,
They'll be damned like the sinners in hell.

Anon.

'THE PICTURE IN THE FIRE. [The Gresford colliery disaster on September the 22nd was the worst which has happened in our coal-fields for many years. More than two-hundred-and-fifty imprisoned miners lost their lives, and the consequent distress and destitution demand far more to relieve them than local funds can supply. Readers of *Punch* are earnestly entreated to contribute so far as they may be able to the Mansion House Fund, opened by the Acting Lord Mayor of London.]' *Punch*, 3 October 1934 (reproduced by permission of Punch Ltd)

Aerial photograph of the disaster scene at Gresford Colliery. *The Illustrated London News*, 29 September 1934 (reproduced by permission of The ILN Picture Library)

Rescue workers, with gas masks and breathing apparatus, arriving at the pit-head during the night. *The Illustrated London News*, 29 September 1934 (reproduced by permission of The ILN Picture Library)

The Chief Inspector of Mines, Sir Henry Walker—in front, in overalls—joined in the rescue work and is seen here returning to the surface after spending several hours in the pit. *The Illustrated London News*, 29 September 1934 (reproduced by permission of The ILN Picture Library)

Watchers at the pit-head (reproduced by permission of the Liverpool Daily Post and Echo Ltd)

A family group waiting for news at the pit-head. *The Illustrated London News*, 29 September 1934 (reproduced by permission of The ILN Picture Library)

Five of the only six survivors of the explosion [l to r: Burt Samuels, Thomas Fisher, Davy Jones, Jack Samuels, Ted Andrew] (reproduced by permission of the Flintshire Record Office)

Sir Stafford Cripps, seen here as the victorious Labour candidate in the East Bristol by-election on 16 January 1931. *The Illustrated London News*, 24 January 1931 (reproduced by permission of The ILN Picture Library)

The Gresford Memorial (photo: Vic Cleveley)

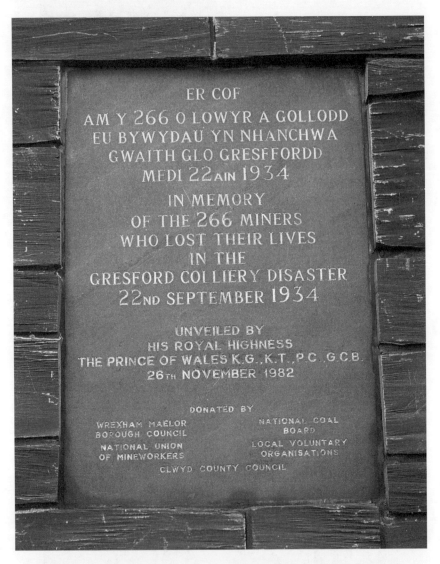

ER COF
AM Y 266 O LOWYR A GOLLODD
EU BYWYDAU YN NHANCHWA
GWAITH GLO GRESFFORDD
MEDI 22ain 1934

IN MEMORY
OF THE 266 MINERS
WHO LOST THEIR LIVES
IN THE
GRESFORD COLLIERY DISASTER
22nd SEPTEMBER 1934

UNVEILED BY
HIS ROYAL HIGHNESS
THE PRINCE OF WALES K.G., K.T., P.C., G.C.B.
26th NOVEMBER 1982

DONATED BY

WREXHAM MAELOR
BOROUGH COUNCIL

NATIONAL COAL
BOARD

NATIONAL UNION
OF MINEWORKERS

LOCAL VOLUNTARY
ORGANISATIONS

CLWYD COUNTY COUNCIL

Inscription engraved on the Gresford Memorial (photo: Vic Cleveley)

Contents

Acknowledgements

For their kindness in assisting me with research, granting me interviews and answering personal inquiries I should like to thank:

the staff of Clwyd County Record Office, the Health and Safety Executive, Manchester Central Library, Wrexham Public Library, the Library of the National Coal Board, the Library of the National Union of Mineworkers, and the Working Class Movement Library, Salford; the Editor of the *Wrexham Leader*; Sir Geoffrey Wilson KCB CMG; Lady Jones; Tom Ellis MP; Professor W. H. G. Armytage; Mr Josiah Ellis; Mr R. T. Ellis; Mr E. Frow; Mr R. Page Arnot; Mr Edward Jones; Mr J. A. Jones; Mr J. Idwal Jones; Mr Ithell Kelly; Mr E. Roberts; Mr L. Salisbury; Mr T. B. Saunders; Mr Harry Tomlinson.

The extracts from the 1954 Mines and Quarries Act on pages 206 and 208 are reproduced with the permission of the Controller of Her Majesty's Stationery Office.

Finally, I must thank Mildred Marney for her meticulous scrutiny and impeccable typing of the unsightly first draft I presented her with, and Dr Robert Houlton, without whose advice, assistance and encouragement the typescript would not have attained the status of a book.

CHAPTER 1

The Disaster

The night shift in the Dennis Section of Gresford Colliery began at 10.00 p.m. On Friday 21 September 1934, David Jones, the fireman in 29s district, arrived at the colliery office at 9.30 and descended the shaft with some of his men at 9.45. At the pit bottom he called at the office of the overman and received his instructions: 'fill coal on all faces, in order to have the place secured for the week-end'. He then walked 'inbye' (into the pit) as far as a junction known as the Clutch, along a road known as 142s Deep, and so to his own cabin, or 'station', just inside the turning that led to 29s (see page 41, Fig. 2). Here, in accordance with the regulations, he inspected the safety lamps of all the miners entering the district to see that they were properly adjusted and searched a sample of about 12 men for contraband—matches or other inflammable material. The haulage started up at 10.35 p.m. and soon afterwards he set out on the first of his routine inspections of the district, testing for gas wherever he went, until he arrived at the coalface.

There were men at work on most parts of the face and in the three roads that led to it. Some were filling coal into wagons, others setting supports for the roof, others cleaning up the coalface. At the bottom end of the face the coal-cutter was being turned round; elsewhere a man was drilling holes for shot firing.

At about 2.00 a.m. most of the men were having their 'snapping', the mid-shift meal break. Jones was standing with a boy in the road junction at the bottom end of the face, entering the men's times in a book, when he heard a loud blast like the sound of a burst pipe, and was thrown off his feet. Their lamps went out, the air became suddenly warmer and they were hit by a shower of dust and small stones. He remarked to the boy, 'Well, we're in a right mess, aren't we?'

Two of the men turning the cutting machine round were brothers, John Edward Samuel and Albert Samuel. They heard a thud, and a heavy gust of air sent them staggering. 'What the hell's up?' Albert asked. His brother replied, 'It's the bottom end gone.'

1

Albert took this as a matter of course as a reference to the adjacent 14s district.

The blast and the gust of air had been felt at the pit bottom. Edward Williams, the attendant of the haulage engine for the Dennis Section, who had just left his cabin to try to discover why the haulage had stopped for longer than usual, heard a distant rumbling: 'It came nearer until it was like thunder, and a big bang, and then the place was all black—you couldn't see anything.'

Some way along the haulage road Isaac Williams, a young lad, was 'minding slaughters'—watching for derailed tubs. As the deafening bang from the depths of the pit reached the refuge hole where he was sitting a whirlwind lifted dense clouds of dust that obscured both of his lamps. A few minutes later it began to subside and he reached for his scarf, poured water over it and wrapped it round his face to prevent himself from suffocating.

Henry Tomlinson, a rope-splicer, had been signing reports in a cabin. Rushing out at the sound of the explosion he found several men apparently amused by the state of their faces and clothing and did his best, with some success, to wipe their smiles away. Telephoning the Dennis Section and getting no reply he crossed over by way of some ventilating doors to collect stretchers from the return airway. It was filled with thick fumes and dust.

The night overman thought at first that the noise had been caused by one of the cages dropping out of control. As soon as the dust had subsided he telephoned the surface with an urgent message to the manager and under-manager: 'Something's happened down the Dennis—I think it's fired' (i.e. exploded).

In 29s the men had been assembling and debating what should be done. There was no panic and John Samuel seems to have unobtrusively taken command. Their first thought was to make for the main haulage road, which was also the air intake, and a party of about 30 men, including John's brother Albert, set out from the top end of the face, but at a junction they heard groaning and discerned a man lying in the crossroad just to their left. The road was full of gas but one of them crawled in to the injured man and some of the others linked hands, forming a chain to pull the pair of them out. By the time they had succeeded the man was dead, and his rescuer now collapsed and had to be revived.

There was then discussion as to the best route to try. When a door between themselves and the main haulage road was opened a strong smell of burning came through, borne on a warm wind, and they hurriedly closed it. A collier remembered that there were doors in the roadway which led from the junction near where they were standing to the main Martin return: if they could get past these doors they would be safe. The plan was put to the deputy who agreed, and a party of six set off in that direction, calling on the main body to follow closely and fanning the air in front of them with anything they could lay hands on. When they were a short distance along the road, which led for 40 yards up a gradient of 1 in 3, Albert Samuel looked back but could see no one behind him.

Between the men and their objective there was a series of faults forming steps to a height of 20 feet, which had to be negotiated by a set of ladders. The party had three lamps which had not been extinguished but the road was long, and narrow in places, and they had not travelled it before. Their journey was later described by John Samuel.

> We put the deputy, David Jones, down on his hands and knees and Fisher took the lead. We kept wafting these bits of rag and our caps and things round our faces. It was very hot, and a lot of gas there. We carried on until we came to a slight bend in the road, and David Jones said something about being done, but I said 'stick it', and we kept carrying on until we came to the bottom of the ladders. The going had been heavy and it was hot, and David Jones again said he was done. Fisher and Challoner had started up the ladder by this time, and I said to my brother 'take your time, don't be in a hurry. We won't leave Dai here'. We got him to the foot of the ladder, and he got his hands on the rungs, and I got my shoulder underneath him and pushed him up. As we were going up the ladder he seemed to revive and the air was clearer.[1]

On reaching the top of the ladder they were able to make better progress although one or two of the weaker men fell behind from time to time and Samuel had to stop and help them. At last, as they were approaching a junction there came 'a big gust of wind'.

> I said, 'thank God, they've reversed the wind. We're all right now'. We continued out against the wind along this junction road, and we came to a man who was dead, and then we carried on a bit further and I heard my brother shout, 'we're by the Clutch'. So I was all right then, I knew where I was.

These six were the only men to come out of the Dennis Section alive. John Samuel was subsequently awarded the King's Medal for his courage and skilful leadership during their hazardous journey.

While they were struggling to safety all the men working in the

Slant Section of the mine, which was unharmed, had been called to the pit bottom and the manager and under-manager had arrived from the surface. A preliminary inspection by two workmen had revealed a fall of rock about 200 yards along the road between the pit bottom and the Clutch which appeared to block the road completely, but as the under-manager and Tomlinson the rope-splicer were working their way down to inspect it they were met by the survivors from 29s who had found their way round the obstruction. They also came across the first and only accessible victims of the explosion in that part of the mine—six men killed instantly at their work on the roadway: one on his knees with his head in his hands as the 'afterdamp', or carbon monoxide gas, had caught him, another stripped naked, even to the hair on his head, by blast, a third pinned under the body of a dead horse which was still attached to the shafts of a tub. Most were severely burned but in every case, according to the evidence of the Medical Inspector of Mines who later examined the bodies, death had been caused by carbon monoxide poisoning: a mere two or three gasps would have been sufficient.

The return airway from 29s which the six survivors had used for the first part of their escape was now full of smoke and the smell of burning; a canary put into it with the aid of a stick at once showed signs of distress, and it was obvious that no more men would come out of 29s alive.

Back on the main road down to the Clutch, and along 142s Deep, there were more falls of rock, and about 20 yards short of the normal entrance to 29s the roadway was on fire. The flames were being fanned by a jet of air from the compressed air main which had burst nearby, and the smoke was too dense to be penetrated. No one would emerge from the Dennis Section that way, but efforts had to be made to get the fire under control. According to the first eye-witnesses it was not unmanageably large at that time and might have been put out if water and the means of throwing it 30 or 40 feet had been available; but they were not, and as dust from the road made no impression on it the fire rapidly gained a strong hold.

There were fully trained rescue men at every pit in the area but later accounts suggest that there was some delay in getting them to the scene, a reflection of the general disorganisation and confusion at management level which became more apparent as the night wore on. It was two hours, the miners' agent later complained, before he had word of the disaster. The captain of one of the rescue teams from Llay Main Colliery was called from his bed at 4.30 a.m. By 5.00 a.m. his team of five men had assembled and, jumping into a lorry, were soon at Gresford. The Gresford team was already down the pit and the Llay Main men expected to follow them, desperate to get below and do what they could for their mates, for whom by this time nothing could in fact be done. But no call came. Worse, they had no proper place to wait in and their rescue equipment was dumped in an old cabin, 'being knocked and kicked about by all and sundry', as the captain later recalled in a vivid narrative of the night's events.[2]

> My life is going to depend on that apparatus, and I'm in no mood to see it jumped on. This is not good enough, nerves on edge, it is essential that my team are settled or there is going to be difficulties when we are needed.

After an interview with their own colliery manager, who was by now on the scene, they were moved to the general office and given tea and coffee. They were moved out again when the general office was taken over as a temporary mortuary for six bodies brought out of the pit. By 8.20 a.m. all 18 men of the Llay Main rescue team were present, some of them straight off the night shift, and still there was no summons from below. 'This waiting period is far worse than the actual work. Good Lord, when are they going to call on us?'

Volunteers had been arriving from the moment when word of the disaster began to spread round the area; they were sent below to help with clearing the rock falls and doing the little that could be done to contain the fire. A manager from another colliery who went down at about 4.30 a.m. described the scene:

> The heat was intense. Our method of fighting the fire was to throw sand wherever we could, and stone dust ... We were working with fire extinguishers. You had to bore a bit of a hole in the falls, which were burning underneath, and then discharge the contents of the extinguisher in the place as best you could.

At 8.40 a.m. the call came at last to the surface for the No. 1 Llay Main rescue team and they were sent down with a Gresford man who was to show them the way around the pit. On arrival their task was explained to them, but with tragic imprecision. Thought had at last been given to a return airway on the west side of the Dennis Section. That anyone should be left alive in that part of the mine six hours after the explosion had sent afterdamp coursing through all the airways of the pit was out of the question. The airway could not be approached from the main Martin return with which it communicated, because that too was full of smoke and fumes, but the manager had given instructions for a dirt barrier, leading from the main intake, to be pierced. On learning at about 7.00 a.m. that this had been done he passed a message back that rescue men would be wanted to ascertain 'the state of the airway', but that they were not to go in until they had definite instructions from him, because he was convinced that it was so full of carbon monoxide that there was no chance of getting men out by way of it. Arriving back at the break-through point he found that a further tragedy had occurred. For some reason his message, passed to them by the deputy who had been left in charge, had been interpreted by the rescue men to mean that they were to find out 'the state of the *air* in the airway', and that they were to try to get along it. There was no plan of that part of the mine available but the Gresford volunteer had said he knew the way, and without waiting for the manager's instructions he and three of the team had gone in, leaving behind one member whose apparatus was not functioning properly.

There was a high concentration of gas which killed a canary at once but they pressed on, Williams, the captain, first and the others following at 20 yard intervals. After about 120 yards they found that the roof of the airway, which was supposed to be a route for men to travel, had sagged and the walls had caved in, leaving a space which the captain estimated at three feet high by three feet wide. Soon afterwards, crawling on hands and knees, he saw that further progress was out of the question; it was equally impossible to turn round in the confined space with his apparatus on so he worked his way backwards to the wider section. Gathering his men together and risking a dose of lethal gas he pulled aside the mouthpiece of his breathing apparatus and told them what the conditions were like and that they must retire. An extraordinary and uncharacteristic development then occurred.

> Lewis and Bill Hughes [the Gresford volunteer] seemed to get alarmed and kind of jostled for supremacy of leadership to get out. I called to them not to be alarmed but to take their time. They didn't take much notice of that ... I saw one, he would be about forty yards away, and he fell ... it was Lewis. When I came up to him ... I stopped to have a look at him. He had ceased breathing. He had no pulse, and I lifted his eyelid and tapped the ball of his eye, and there was no response. His mouthpiece was

> in, and his nose clip was on, and his apparatus was working, but he was
> dead ... I left him and proceeded on. I got up close to Bill Hughes, and I
> could see he was lying down ... Dan Hughes was a few yards in front of
> him, and from what I could see of Dan Hughes he'd apparently been
> assisting Bill, to try to get him on. I examined Bill Hughes. His nose clip
> was off, and he was apparently dead.

Williams left Bill Hughes and went to help Dan Hughes, who
was very unsteady on his feet, but almost at once he was in trouble
himself.

> When I examined my apparatus the feed pipe from the oxygen cylinder
> had become disconnected off the barrel, and that's what had brought me
> down, and I was practically exhausted ... my only alternative was to push
> the pipe in my mouth, to save myself. I then had to leave Dan Hughes,
> and Dan was alive at the time; on his knees, crumpled up, but alive. I
> could see lights at the top end of the airway, a matter of forty or fifty yards
> away. I signalled for help. Someone whistled, I signalled again, and
> waited about four or five minutes. I couldn't see anyone coming down. I
> made my way out.

Some time later Dan Hughes was brought out dead.

When the captain had signalled for help the message was passed
to the surface, where his mates from Llay Main were still chafing at
their enforced inaction. Suspecting from the form of the message
that a mishap had occurred they stepped out of the cage at the pit
bottom to be met by men carrying the body of Dan Hughes, and by
an official who, distracted by the situation, seemed to be trying to
rush them into the same death trap. Naturally they wanted to know
why the earlier team had been sent into such a lethal atmosphere,
but on learning that some of them were still lying in the airway they
at once put on their own apparatus and made their way in. They
fetched out the body of William Hughes, the Gresford man, and
were preparing to return for Jack Lewis, whose lamp they had seen
burning further in still, but the Gresford manager and the Mines
Inspector who had now arrived forbade them to go. In spite of their
pleas—'Don't let us leave him—the reputation of all rescue men is
at stake'—they were ordered out of the pit and the roadway was
fenced off. Gresford had claimed three more victims in addition to
those killed by the explosion. In the opinion of an inspector of
mines who later investigated the whole incident, some of the most
vital provisions of the General Regulations relating to rescue had
been disregarded. 'There does not appear to have been any organization of the rescue operations—nothing save chaos.'

A further indication of something seriously amiss with the running of the pit was that, in spite of stringent regulations designed to enable a tally to be kept of every individual going into or coming out of it at any time of the day or night, it was some time before the likely number of casualties was known. A telephone message passed to the Department of Mines at 8.15 on Saturday morning referred to an explosion 'involving approximately 100 men'. The figure given to the press was 102, and according to the *Manchester Guardian* special messengers had to be sent to the homes of all the men who worked at the pit to find out who was missing. This sounds somewhat improbable in view of the wide area from which the men came, but whatever the method adopted may have been a revised and accurate figure was finally arrived at. Two hundred and sixty-two men remained unaccounted for, and no one with any knowledge of conditions in the pit entertained the slightest hope of seeing any of them alive again. The immediate task was to subdue the fire and clear the atmosphere of the pit so that at least their bodies might be brought out.

Throughout Saturday and the following night work continued on clearing the rock falls, pulling overturned tubs and twisted girders aside, and trying to contain the fire. When the Llay Main team reported for duty again at 5.00 a.m. on Sunday they found the main fire fighting force nearing the entrance to 29s junction which was blocked by one huge fall, with the fire still smouldering under it. After an hour's work the entrance was revealed.

> What a sight! The whole of the level is just one mass of flame, the coal sides of the roadway burning in one white mass, and the more stones we moved to one side, the more air we put on the flames, and the fire roaring away.

Working in two teams of six, protected by goggles and breathing apparatus, never going more than a few yards ahead of the rest so as to remain within speaking distance, and even then often hidden from view by smoke, they could only remain in front of the fire for two or three minutes before falling back to let others take their places.

When they returned to the surface after the four-hour shift, which was as much as a man could stand in the front line of fire fighting, they met representatives of the miners who asked what the position was. 'We told them it was no hope, and that it would be better to call out all the men, as the pit looked to be on fire, and there were grave possibilities of further explosion.'

The warning was not heeded at this stage but later on Sunday afternoon those in charge were forced to take it seriously. The manager from a neighbouring colliery who was helping to fight the fire was discussing the situation with a group which included the son of the managing director, the Chief Inspector of Mines, two inspectors for the division and the secretary of the Lancashire and Cheshire miners when an explosion deeper in the pit lifted them off their feet. The visitors went back towards the pit bottom for a conference while the fire fighters continued working.

> About 5.15 there was another noise, and I called for silence. It was a low rumble, like distant thunder. It increased in violence and then died down again ... We all stood very uneasy for about five minutes. I could see the men were getting nervy, and who in God's name could blame them? Somebody said, 'Hadn't we better withdraw?' But I said, 'No, carry on—more sand, more sand.' We carried on, and I never felt more proud of the men in my life. In about ten minutes there was another loud sound, and the whole place trembled. The men could feel the vibration.

This time there was no room for doubt. Over 200 men were working between the pit bottom and 29s turning, every one of them at risk. After a final consultation all the rescue workers were withdrawn from the pit and in the manager's office a statement was drafted, signed by the responsible officials and handed to the waiting press.

> The attempt to overcome the fire in the main road has gone on continuously since yesterday, but in spite of very strenuous efforts, and although some progress has been made in this road the fire has got a further hold in a road to the right, through which it was hoped access might have been got to any possible survivors.
>
> Today several explosions inbye of the fire in the main road have occurred, and this afternoon they became more frequent and closer to where the men were working on the fire.
>
> The air in both main returns is carrying carbon monoxide in dangerous quantities, and it is with great reluctance that all parties—management, miners' representatives and H. M. Inspectors—have come to the conclusion that no person can be alive in the workings.
>
> In these circumstances, and in view of the grave risk to the men engaged in combating the fire, it has been decided that it would not be right to continue to expose these workers to such serious risk, and all persons have been withdrawn from the mine.

Since the small hours of Saturday morning cold, drenching rain had been falling, but thousands of people had gathered at the pit, not only relatives of the entombed men but sightseers from miles around, straining for a glimpse of a returning rescuer, or a body on a stretcher; clogging the roads with their cars, hindering the passage of vehicles bringing volunteers and supplies and calling forth unheeded pleas from the police to keep away.

With the publication of the official bulletin there was a sudden change. The crowds melted away in the rain, the pit-head gear, the fans, the blowers, slowed down to silence, and in the words of an eye-witness, 'an eerie peace descended on Gresford Colliery'.

NOTES

1. See Chief Inspector's report, p. 93.
2. See Davies, P. (1973).

CHAPTER 2

The Village

When the compilers of William the Conqueror's Domesday Survey arrived in 'Cesterscire' they recorded, five miles south of the city of Chester, a manor called 'Gretford'. The property of three Normans, Hugh, Osbern and Rainald, it contained 'a church, a priest and seven villans and twelve bordars [husbandmen] and one Frenchman'.

The Domesday spelling of the name has no significance and was modified as time went by. Both King Offa and his shadowy predecessor Wat placed the lines of their great dykes to the west of the village that developed on the site, making it part of the Anglo-Saxon kingdom of Mercia. A local historian in the early twentieth century rejected suggestions that it had once had a Welsh name: in all the surviving documents, he insisted, it is always referred to as 'Gresford', which is 'evidently English'.[1] But whatever name it went under its history was chequered.

Before the Norman conquest, control of the 'debatable lands' along the Welsh border had been effectively in the hands of trusted noblemen. William continued the system, creating an Earldom of Chester for one of his followers, but this seems not to have saved Gresford from harassment by Welsh Britons. The same historian writes

> For two hundred years and more after Domesday, a dark veil rests on the parish and district, and when it is raised we find all the lords of the land are Welsh-speaking. The English have either been driven out or have been absorbed and assimilated.

When Edward I finally completed the conquest of Wales the Marcher lordships were left in possession of their powers and privileges, but under the Acts of Union, in the time of Henry VIII, they were abolished. A new county, Denbighshire, was created, incorporating most of the ancient parish of Gresford: for so long in the front line of Anglo-Welsh conflict; Welsh-speaking but bearing an English name; situated barely four miles from the boundary with England, and sharing far more of the characteristics of that lowland landscape than of the bare uplands to the west;

subjected for decades to a steady process of anglicisation, yet now for administrative purposes firmly and finally in Wales.

For 400 years after the passing of the Acts of Union Gresford seems to have led an undisturbed life. It was not too far off the beaten track to attract visitors, even when communications were at their most primitive. Its remarkably handsome church, whose bells were widely acclaimed as 'one of the seven wonders of Wales', owed its magnificence, according to a writer in 1543, to the fact that pilgrims from 'divers parts of the Realme' had come to visit it, bringing with them the wealth from which it 'was strongly and beautifully made erecte and buylded, as also all manner of ornaments wer bowght and provyded'.[2]

With the long overdue improvement in the road system which was begun in the mid-eighteenth century, and the coming of the railways in the nineteenth, North Wales was opened up to tourism, and a flood of topographical literature poured from the presses, in which the awe-inspiring grandeur of the mountains of Snowdonia did not wholly overshadow the gentler charms of the lowland landscape. The Vale Royal of Cheshire impressed one anonymous early nineteenth-century traveller as:

> a tract of country remarkable for the richness of its soil, the beauty of its scenery and the pleasingly diversified views which it presents. The little Vale of Gresford is one of the most lovely in the Principality, abounding with pleasing and interesting objects, enlivened by the wandering of the River Alyn through its meadows, and finely varied with richly wooded eminences, on one of which stands conspicuously its beautiful Church . . .

Another traveller, John Jones, passing the same way in the 1850s, was equally delighted with what he saw.

> The scenery of the vale of Gresford is beautiful beyond description. The little River, Alun, winds playfully through it, here and there glancing through the foliage like a coy beauty through her curls, then tripping to its sylvan retreat. The bold background of the Welsh hills, and the affluent dairy lands of the vale royal of Cheshire, with the quaint old city in the distance, give grandeur, profusion, and picturesqueness to the view.

A different aspect to this idyllic scene revealed itself under the probing of the stern and highminded commissioners who investigated the state of education in Wales in the late 1840s. The parish of Gresford, they ascertained, consisted of a number of townships, extended over 12,000 acres and contained 3,928 inhabitants, all of whom spoke English. The population of Gresford itself was very much smaller, having risen from 392 in 1801 to 614 by 1851. The next decade saw a twofold increase to 1,356 and by 1871 it was 1,792.

In 1847 there were two schools 'provided for the poor', a church school in the village itself and an infants' school at Rossett, two miles away towards Chester. The church school was an old-established institution conducted at the time of the inspection by a master and mistress who were husband and wife; 'neither of them was ever trained to conduct a school'. When the commissioners arrived at 10.00 a.m. 'we found the master in the public house'; the 66 boys were in the school meanwhile, 'playing with all their might'. The mistress was 'near her confinement and incapable of much activity in the discharge of her duties'.

In the infants' school at Rossett they found one mistress teaching 50 girls and boys, more than half of whom did not know their alphabet. Rossett, the commissioners found, had an unusually high number of children among a population which was itself expected to rise, as the village had become a first-class station on the Liverpool to Shrewsbury Railway. Schools were greatly wanted by the inhabitants 'who, being employed in agricultural labour, would allow their children to remain much longer in school than in the neighbouring coal and iron districts'. Here was another aspect of the Gresford scene which was mostly passed over in silence by admirers of its pastoral attractions, although occasional hints were given. 'Coal is found within the parish, and mines are worked to a considerable extent in Gwersyllt township, where are also some mills for drawing wire, which afford employment to a small number of persons.' The picturesque heart of Gresford village, which survives almost untouched today, was spared these unsightly intrusions because it had the good fortune to lie on the right side of, literally, a great divide known to geologists as the Wrexham Fault and one of the determining factors in the later history of this part of North Wales.

NOTES

1. Palmer (1903–05), refuting Jarman (1899).
2. See Fishbourne (1924).

CHAPTER 3
The Coalfield

The North Wales coalfield extends in a shallow arc from the Point of Ayr, at the north-western tip of the Dee estuary, southward through Clwyd (formerly Flintshire and Denbighshire), and ends a mile or so inside the boundary of Shropshire, near Oswestry. It is about 45 miles long and 9 miles across at its widest point. The geological strata in this corner of Wales dip steeply eastward, producing a sharp and dramatic landscape, as limestone outcrops north of Llangollen give way to the rounded sandstone mountains which present their long eastern slopes to the Dee Valley and the rich pasture-lands of Cheshire. The coal-bearing measures, reaching the surface on the sides of Esclusham and Ruabon mountains, the hills of Flint and the Dee estuary, disappear to a great depth beneath the Triassic sandstone of the Cheshire Plain and re-emerge at a workable level in Lancashire and north Staffordshire. The seams are much broken by faulting and discontinuities. The Great Bala Fault, following a line running roughly north-east to south-west, effectively cuts off the Flintshire coalfield (to use the old names) from that of Denbighshire, which itself is divided into several large sections by faults, some running transversely, others from north to south. This pattern largely determined the development of the mining industry in the coalfield. The earliest exploitation occurred for obvious reasons where the seams lay nearest the surface: in Flintshire, along the shores of the Dee and in the hills immediately behind it, and in Denbighshire among the outcrops a thousand feet above sea-level. As the more easily accessible supplies gave out, the search, concentrated chiefly to the south of the Bala Fault, moved steadily eastward, at ever increasing depth and in the face of growing hazards and more formidable technical problems.

The earliest references to the mining of coal in North Wales occur in Flintshire in the fourteenth century: at Mostyn on the Dee estuary in the time of Edward I, at Ewloe in 1322 and at Hope in 1358. Denbighshire comes into the picture a little later with the inhabitants of Holt, on the banks of the Dee, receiving a charter

14

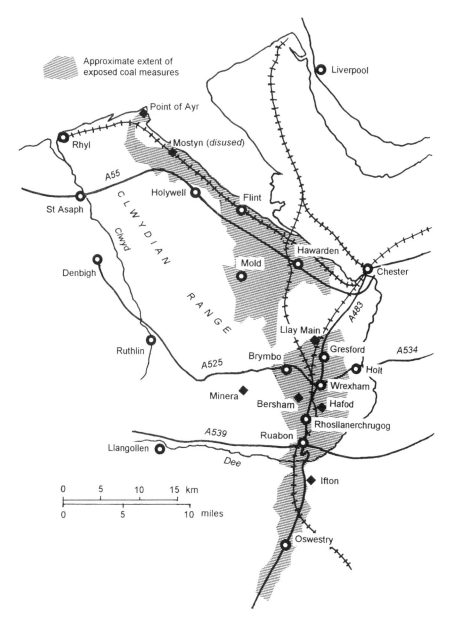

Fig. 1 The North Wales coalfield (loosely based on *The History of the British Coal Industry*, Vol. I, 1993, pp. 129–35)

from the Earl of Arundel in 1410 permitting them to dig coal and turf at Brymbo on the slopes of Esclusham mountain. By the end of the next century there had been a small but steady growth. When Leland visited North Wales he found 'se-coles' being got at Harwood, now Hawarden, and a place called the Mines, evidently the Roman site at Minera, and 'cole pittes at three quarters of a mile from Molesdale toune', i.e. Mold.

The impetus to make a more systematic exploration for coal came in the sixteenth century, with the necessity for finding a new source of fuel to replace the nation's depleted forests; and it might have gathered stronger momentum in North Wales if it had not been hampered by lack of population and capital, poor communications and a general backwardness traceable chiefly to centuries of strife along the border. There was no large-scale industry near at hand and little possibility of building a market for coal outside the area. Epitomising the way in which progress seemed to be by-passing North Wales the Dee shifted its channel, leaving the ports on the Flintshire side to become silted up and useless. By the early 1700s the small coal-pits of the county, among the earliest to be worked, were in many cases exhausted.

By the mid-eighteenth century advances made outside the area and the demand created by wars on the Continent and in America enabled North Wales once again to get back in the race. The lead industry flourished, the rich copper deposits of Anglesey were heavily worked and the great reserves of fire-clay on Buckley mountain became the basis of an expanding pottery industry. The demand for coal rose, new pits were sunk, and as long as the prosperity of the mineral industries lasted, coal in Flintshire enjoyed a hey-day. By the 1840s, however, the boom years were over and coal fell back into the doldrums, to be rescued by events in the neighbouring county.

Denbighshire, which shared to some extent in the prosperity of the lead industry, owed much more to Shropshire-born Abram Darby who passed the details of his process for smelting iron with coke to his friend Charles Lloyd, the tenant of an estate at Bersham, near Wrexham, where he set up a small furnace. Some years later the estate was taken over by the Cumbrian ironmaster Isaac Wilkinson, who in due course handed it on to his two sons, William and John.[1] William made less impact on events than his elder brother who, taking advantage of the demand for armaments, made Bersham into a supremely successful munitions factory. 'A great foundery [sic] for cannon', was how Thomas Pennant described it in 1778, adding in a much-quoted comment that John Wilkinson 'supplies many parts of Europe with this *ratio ultima regum*; and in the late war between the Russians and the Turks furnished both parties with this species of logic'.

From the point of view of the North Wales coal industry Wilkinson's most significant step was taken in 1792. A few miles from Bersham was the estate of Brymbo where the men from Holt had been granted the right to 'dig coals' 350 years earlier. Wilkinson was able to buy Brymbo and began to pillage it for its abundant supplies of coal and iron ore. By the time he died some 40 pits had been sunk, and his successors added at least another 50, leaving the ground honeycombed with abandoned, often flooded and potentially dangerous workings. The last pit at Brymbo, called the 'Smelt', was sunk in 1790, reopened in 1934 after a brief period of disuse, and not finally closed until 1968.

The years of prosperity considerably changed the face of large parts of Flintshire and Denbighshire. From being sparsely populated they had seen an influx of workers, many of them coming from coalfields elsewhere in Britain, others migrating from the agricultural districts of West Wales where even at the best of times life was harsh enough to make the poor wages and primitive living conditions of the coalfield seem attractive by comparison. As they flocked to the manufacturing areas, towns and villages expanded to meet their needs. Among those which prospered was Wrexham, first mentioned in the twelfth century, although its origins probably pre-date the Norman conquest.[2] Situated uncomfortably close to the Welsh-English border—the line of Wat's Dyke[3] passes though it—it suffered the many changes of ownership and influence which accompanied alternate Welsh and English domination. After centuries of makeshift administration its growth finally earned it the status of a borough in 1857, but although it was the chief town in a mining area it was never a purely mining town. There were collieries on its doorstep, but by far the greater number of pits in the coalfield were scattered along the 45-mile arc from north-east Flint to the Shropshire border, and although there were concentrations in certain localities they were seldom the hemmed-in, isolated, inward-looking communities found in the mining valleys of South Wales or in north-east England. Possible exceptions were to be found in areas such as the parish of Ruabon, which acquired an unhappy notoriety in the mid-nineteenth century.

Coal and iron had been mined in the Ruabon area from the late eighteenth century, with results that were summed up in a *Topographical Dictionary* published in 1833:

> ... a great part of the parish is now occupied by pits, charcoal hearths and mineral works of various kinds, and is intersected in different directions by railroads ... there are also numerous blast-furnaces and forges in other parts of the parish for the manufacture of iron ...

These developments were largely due to the rapid and uncontrolled speculation which hit the area in the 1820s and which, when it collapsed, left a trail of temporary ruin and a lasting legacy of decline. Much of the damage was done by outsiders from London and elsewhere, but a share of the blame must lie with the local gentry who had tried to cash in on the boom, like the ironmaster and coalowner who sank 30 pits in his immediate neighbourhood before going bankrupt in 1823.

The 1840s in North Wales were a watershed in more ways than one,[4] for by the time an economic revival had taken place the main current of industrial development had, like the channel of the Dee, shifted its course. The iron industry had largely moved away to areas such as the Black Country and South Wales, where better communications offered easier access to larger markets. Fortunately for North Wales its untapped coal resources included the profitable Main Seam which was well suited for gas manufacture and household purposes and for which local outlets could be found; it is no coincidence that towns in Denbighshire and Flintshire pioneered developments such as the use of gas for street lighting. But whatever dreams and ambitions the success of Wilkinson and his associates may have prompted the North Wales coalfield was clearly destined never to play a major role in the national economy. In 1892 a correspondent to a local newspaper pointed out that North Wales contributed a mere one-and-a-half per cent of the output of all British coalfields. It is against this perspective that the events of the succeeding half-century must be viewed.

By the 1840s the ruthless exploitation of the more easily accessible deposits on the western upland of the coalfield had exhausted them, and technical problems, chiefly flooding, had brought production at other pits to a halt. The next phase of development depended on the sinking of new and far more costly pits to the east. Excepting a few survivors from the eighteenth century and one or two from even earlier times, most of the collieries on which the continued activity of the coalfield came to depend date from a period of about 20 years, from the mid-1850s to the mid-1870s; most were in Denbighshire and most passed from the scene through exhaustion or economic factors in the 1920s.

The sinking of these pits and the technical problems they presented once again called for skills and outlay which it was for the most part beyond local resources to provide, but there were still enterprising men elsewhere who saw enough scope in North Wales to encourage them to try their hand there. Prominent among these immigrants was an engineer from Cornwall whose name became associated long after his death with the greatest tragedy ever to befall this coalfield, and one of the greatest in the history of British mining.

Henry Dennis was born in Bodmin in 1825.[5] After training as a surveyor he began his working life with a local railway company and moved in about 1850 to a firm of mining engineers, who gave him his earliest contact with North Wales by sending him there to build a tramway from the Llangollen Slate Quarries to the Shropshire Union Canal. He left Wales for a short time to work in the lead mines in Spain but returned to Denbighshire to manage Bryn-yr-Owen Colliery, which had been sunk in the early part of the eighteenth century by the owner of Erddig, the great house near Wrexham which has now passed into the care of the National Trust. The colliery lay just off the road from Wrexham to Ruabon, on the line of Offa's Dyke, filling the ditch with its mine tip. Dennis remained manager until 1857, when he left to form his own firm of surveyors and mining engineers and to become a captain of industry in true Victorian style.

For the next 40 years there seem to have been few developments in the industrial life of North Wales with which he was not profit-ably associated. He reached the pinnacle of his profession in 1901, becoming President of the Mining Association of Great Britain, and although, as his biographer deprecatingly remarks, 'immersed in commerce he found little time for local government', he was elected one of the first aldermen of Denbighshire County Council, 'in recognition of his wonderful business aptitude'. He did find time to breed Shropshire sheep and sell them to Bismarck, with whom he may have felt some affinity, although his chief hero seems to have been Napoleon, whose achievements were portrayed in huge paintings hung on the walls of his home at New Hall, near Ruabon.

When Dennis died in 1906, 5,000 people are said to have attended his funeral. He had seen and assisted in the transformation of the North Wales coalfield. When he first arrived there were 25 collieries in Denbighshire and 30 in Flintshire, accounting for 150 pits (the words 'pit', 'shaft' and 'mine' occur indiscriminately in contemporary accounts, making it difficult to be sure which is meant).[6] These mines were by modern standards almost puny. A qualified observer in 1851 put the total underground area worked by a pair of shafts at no more than five acres, at a correspondingly shallow depth. Working conditions were also still primitive:[7] in spite of legislation inspired by appalling accidents in other coalfields it was still possible for a mine in North Wales to be worked from a single shaft, divided in two by a brick wall only nine inches thick, leaving a downcast pit no more than three feet in diameter. Scientific ventilation in mines everywhere was still so experimental that the appearance of an 'air pump' at Westminster Colliery and that of a ventilating fan at South Mostyn Colliery, both in North Wales, were sufficiently novel to secure for themselves a mention in most histories of British mining. The North Wales coalfield had only recently caught up with the railway age with the completion of a line from Chester to Shrewsbury, which connected with private local tramways of the kind which Dennis had come to Denbighshire to build. In these conditions fewer than 5,000 underground workers in the coalfield raised just short of a million tons of coal a year at a cost of one life for every 46,000 tons.

By the turn of the century many of the old-established collieries had finally gone out of production (although usually not from the landscape), to be replaced by a dozen or so large newcomers, worked by 12,500 miners and producing in the peak year 1899 over 3 million tons of coal. British mining in general had never known better days, and North Wales appeared to be riding as high as the rest.

Yet there were clouds on the horizon. Observers noted that throughout the nation as a whole employment in the coalfields had doubled, output had doubled, wages had increased rapidly, but productivity had declined. From the vantage point of the 1920s, J. W. F. Rowe, an early historian of wages in the coal industry, explained the apparent prosperity of the pre-war years in terms of higher demand for coal enabling producers to pass on the cost of declining productivity to the consumer. To a contemporary, the inspector of mines for the North Western Division, the prosperity itself appeared less obvious. In North Wales between 1870 and 1900, while the work-force was doubling output rose by scarcely half a million tons, and profitability was dangerously low.

'It is somewhat remarkable', the inspector wrote in his report for 1897, 'that with an almost continual annual increase in the demand for and consumption of fuel the trade should still continue un-remunerative.' The explanation, he suggested, lay in the self-defeating policy adopted by individual colliery owners of trying to reduce the cost of getting coal by raising far more than they could hope to dispose of: '... hence supply is always in excess of demand and what has been saved over the cost is more than lost when the coal has to be sold'. It was a diagnosis of which much more was to be heard in years to come.

In the meantime what should forward-looking owners in North Wales do? Advances in mechanisation offered the possibility of reduced production costs but could only be justified in collieries with a reasonably long life in prospect, and this could seldom be assured. Of those still working some were approaching exhaustion, while for others the exceptionally faulted and discontinuous geo-logical structure of the coalfield put their long-term future in doubt. The Royal Commission on Coal Supplies in 1904 estimated the reserves in North Wales with remarkably confident precision at 1,736,467,829 tons, but even when rounded out to a reasonable figure this clearly included much coal which for practical reasons was unlikely to be mined by way of the existing outlets. The future must lie with the opening up of a new part of the coalfield.

With the exception of reserves brought within reach by the opening of Point of Ayr Colliery, Flintshire had virtually nothing further to offer. In Denbighshire the limit of practical mining was long thought to have been defined by the Wrexham Fault, which followed a gentle curve from the Bala Fault southward towards Ruabon. West of this line the coal-bearing strata shelved steeply towards the fault itself; beyond it they disappeared to great depths under later deposits. But exploration showed that this was not the whole story. Further east a parallel line of faulting brought the Main and other seams nearer to the surface again, though still at a greater depth than at any point in the long-established mining areas. It was to these hitherto untapped resources that North Wales must presumably look for future developments, and it was here that after 20 years of deliberation and preparatory work a start was made on what was seen as a new lease of life for the coalfield.

The first step was the formation of a new limited company, incorporated on 14 July 1905, of which Henry Dennis became managing director. On his death in 1906 his son Henry Dyke Dennis took his place. The setting for the new operation was a property called Acton Grange,[8] which was part of the estate of Sir Robert Cunliffe, Bart, of Acton Hall, a large residence on the outskirts of Wrexham, long since demolished. Here on Wednesday 6 November 1907, on a site about two miles north of Wrexham, sandwiched between the main road and the railway line to Chester, in the presence of distinguished guests, the first sods were cut for the two shafts of a new colliery: one by the chairman of the company, Sir Theodore Martin, of Onslow Square, London, and Bryntisilio, Llangollen, 91 years old, solicitor, parliamentary agent, translator of the classics and German poetry, author of a five-volume life of the Prince Consort and in the following year of *Queen Victoria as I Knew Her*; the other by Mrs Dyke Dennis, wife of the managing director. The shafts, 50 yards apart, were named appropriately 'Dennis' and 'Martin'. The most obvious name for the colliery itself might appear to have been Acton Grange but for reasons which are now beyond recall this course was not adopted. For a short time, while the sinking of the shafts was in progress, it was known (at least to the local division of the Mines Inspectorate) simply as the United Westminster and Wrexham Colliery. By the time it was in production it had borrowed the name of the attractive and unspoilt village of Gresford, a mile or so away across the fields.

The sinking of the shafts took a little over three years. The Dennis shaft, penetrating to depths previously unknown in the coalfield, reached the Main Coal Benches, which were the object of the search, a little short of half a mile below the surface. The Martin shaft came to rest slightly higher.

According to some accounts sinking was completed on 11 June 1911, after which a considerable amount of work remained to be done on both shafts; but a later manager referred to a tradition that the first coal was wound a mere eight days later, on Derby Day,

19 June, and there were certainly urgent reasons beyond the natural desire to produce some saleable coal for setting the colliery to work at the earliest possible moment.

While the shafts were being sunk Parliament was engaged on a massive overhaul of the law relating to mining. The resulting Coal Mines Act was dated 16 December 1911, and under the heading 'Travelling Roads and Haulage' (section 42 [1]), it was specified that 'For every seam in a mine newly opened *after the commencement of this Act* [author's italics] ... there shall be provided ... two main intake airways ... one of which shall not be used for the haulage of coal'.[9] The existing practice was to provide only one intake airway (a passage-way below ground, not to be confused with the vertical shaft), and compliance with the new requirement would have cost the promoters of Gresford a great deal more money. It was clearly a matter of urgency to have the colliery operating before the Act came into force, and they appear to have succeeded, so avoiding the obligation to provide a second airway and unwittingly sowing more seeds for the tragedy which overwhelmed them 20 years later. In most other respects they built their mine to good standards, using the best brick to line the shafts and in general not sparing expense where it could be justified.

Coal-getting at the colliery was barely under way when it was brought to a halt by the national strike of 1912, the first of its kind to be called by the Miners' Federation of Great Britain, as the climax to its campaign for a minimum wage. The strike lasted from late February until early April and ended in partial victory for the miners.

By the end of the year there were 375 men working underground at Gresford and 126 on the surface, and a branch, or 'lodge', of the North Wales Miners' Association had been formed, with a membership of 21. By 1913 this figure had increased to 561, and Gresford was one of 14 North Wales collieries which in August successfully threatened to withdraw their labour if the new rates of pay were not paid with arrears by an agreed date.

From one point of view the new colliery had begun operating at a particularly propitious time. With the outbreak of war in 1914, demand for coal rose sharply to a level which kept every mine in the land working at full stretch. Trade was brisk, wages were high, and government control, freeing the industry temporarily from the normal market pressures, commercial rivalries and inequalities of pay, kept disputes to a minimum. In Lancashire and North Wales, the divisional inspector reported in 1919, employment had been better than during any similar period.

By the end of the war Gresford had acquired a new manager. In 1917 the man who had been in charge since it opened retired and was replaced by the assistant manager, William Bonsall, who had arrived from Hinckley in Leicestershire in 1914. There had been difficulty in finding sufficient manpower while the war was on and the end of hostilities did not greatly improve the position. Gresford was deeper and hotter than anything the local colliers were used to; the pit, being new and in a previously unexplored part of the coalfield, had no traditional source of labour to draw on, and there was unwillingness to work in it even when the company built a Garden Village on the outskirts of Wrexham as an incentive. As the 1920s unfolded the situation eased, at least from the point of view of the owners. Following the policy foreshadowed by the decision to sink Gresford they closed two other pits which had given their names to the company—Westminster (1925) and Wrexham and Acton (1924)— and a third, Gwersyllt (1925), which had been used for some time simply as a pumping station. These closures forced many men on to the labour market but not necessarily into Gresford Colliery. United Westminster and Wrexham Collieries now owned only one enterprise, but they had been joined in their pioneering venture into the new area of the coalfield by a second new colliery a mile or two away, called Llay Main. The promoters, Hickleton Main Colliery Company from Yorkshire and a firm of coal exporters from Liverpool, began operations in 1914, but after three years, while sinking was still unfinished, they were compelled by wartime conditions to break off and were unable to resume until 1919. Coal production from shafts even deeper and seams even thicker than those at Gresford began in 1923, but within little more than a year nine lives were lost in the only explosion of any magnitude which the coalfield had known for more than 25 years. An inquiry was conducted by the recently appointed Chief Inspector of the Mines Department, Henry Walker, whose conclusion, not seriously disputed, was that the firing of a charge in the roof of a gallery had ignited firedamp and that

> if the requirements of the Explosives in Coal Mines Order had been strictly complied with, i.e. if no shot had been fired in the presence of firedamp, the accident would not have occurred ... In this respect we are

hampered by the human element, which no amount of legislation or regulation can overcome.[10]

NOTES

Full descriptions of the North Wales coalfield will be found in: Geological Survey (1924); North (1931), pp. 128–33; Ministry of Fuel and Power (1945). See also Rowe (1923), p. 20; Dodd (1929); *The History of the British Coal Industry*, Vol. I (1993), pp. 129–35; Lerry (1968).

1. Palmer (1893); Dodd (1951); Chapter V.
2. Dodd (1957).
3. Fox (1956).
4. See report of Children's Employment Commission (Mines) 1842, p. 7:

> North Wales [is] a large coalfield, heretofore possessed of considerable ironworks, which however, seem now to be sinking before the competition of those in the West of Scotland, and other districts; it still, however, supplies with fuel nearly the whole of North Wales and a large portion of Cheshire and Shropshire.

5. Lerry (1952).
6. The Royal Commission on Mines (1909) commented that some of those who had given evidence seemed to be confused as to the precise requirements of the law 'owing to the indiscriminate use of the terms "colliery", "mine", "pit" etc.' (p. 37).
7. The great Victorian scientist Lyon Playfair quoted a number of examples from his own experience in his *Memoirs and Correspondence* (1899). He was one of a group of scientists, which included Faraday and Lyell, who were called on from time to time to investigate and report on accidents in coal mines. On one occasion Playfair had inspected a mine which was apparently quite free from gas, and congratulated the owner, who confessed that he had only shown him the good parts of the pit. Taking him to another place he extinguished Playfair's candle and lowered his own nearly to the ground.

> We both sat down, while the owner slowly raised his candle till the flame elongated and a blue flickering fire-damp burned round its edges. Holding it perfectly steady, he calmly said, 'One inch higher and you and I would be blown to the devil!!'

In 1845 Playfair was asked to investigate the causes of an explosion in a very deep and extensive pit in Jarrow which had resulted in 39 deaths.

> There had been no ventilation since the accident [so] a stream of water was turned into the shaft to push air down by its descent ... There was only one shaft, and the lining had been destroyed by the blast so that neither a platform nor a basket could be lowered ... I confess my courage

> required screwing up when a rope with two loops was produced, and I was asked to put one leg through the lower one, while the viewer put his through the one above. This is a mode of descent well known to miners but I had never seen it and was not comfortable in its use ... we were very slowly lowered down the mine, which was about twice as deep as the height of St Paul's Cathedral ... It was a dreary downward journey, with a cascade of water dashing over our heads and the darkness made more dense by the feeble light of our two Davy lamps ... (p. 95–96)

As a result of this and similar investigations, Playfair was able to establish the composition of firedamp.

8. See *Wrexham Advertiser* and *Chester Chronicle*, 9 November 1907 (in both cases). Lerry (1968), p. 54.

9. See the report of the Royal Commission on Safety in Coal Mines, Cmd. 5890, p. 108.

> Gresford Colliery was not a mine *newly opened* after the coming into force of the Coal Mines Act, 1911, but it is necessary to consider whether, if it had been and, accordingly, two main intakes had been provided in the Dennis Section of the mine, any of the persons who were killed might have escaped.

10. Reports of Commissioners: Explosions in Mines: Llay Main Wrexham 1924–25 (Cmd. 2365), xii 509.

CHAPTER 4

The Industry

By the end of the war Gresford Lodge was, in terms of membership, the second largest in North Wales, but the coalfield of which the colliery was one of the major hopes was not in good shape. During the war the government had set up the 'Pool', an arrangement under which the proceeds of the more profitable coalfields were used to support earnings in the less profitable—as the agent of the North Wales miners later reminded his members, 'to make it impossible for one miner in Nottingham to receive a minimum of 16s.3d. per shift while the miner in North Wales can only get 8s.8¼d.' But the Pool failed to remove all the anomalies, as another message from the same agent to his disgruntled members in 1917 makes plain.

> The reason ... that South Wales and Yorkshire miners are better paid than you are is first (I am sorry to admit) that they have better pits: secondly, Yorkshire started off in the year 1898 with 1s.6d. per day more than you ... If it had not been for the war, South Wales would possibly have to suffer a reduction in wages. It was the Government that came to the rescue of both Northumberland and South Wales, or they would very likely be worse off than you.

There were thus many on the trade union side of the industry who had benefited in one way or another from government control and were hoping to see it continue indefinitely. There was therefore consternation when, following a sharp but shortlived boom in the immediate post-war years, the government announced early in 1920 that it proposed to hand the mines back to the owners.[1] The consequences for North Wales were starkly spelled out by the agent:

> This coalfield is in a very precarious position. If this precious Government (which a large number of you have gone out of your way to create) mean what they say, viz, to decontrol the coal industry on 31st March this year, and financial control on August 31st, who knows how serious it would be. I am told there is a loss on every ton raised in this coalfield. I leave it to you to imagine whether one half of our collieries can be carried on for one week at a loss.

To the solution proposed by the men in the pits—'make the public pay more for their coal'—the agent had an unwelcome reply.

> I admit that in time gone by coal has been too cheap, to the detriment of both colliery owners and miners, but if ... you increase the price for coal how can you, *with an inferior coalfield* [author's italics], compete with the best coalfields in Britain in the markets of the world? I am afraid that the summer months will bring with it [sic] such a state of affairs that will surprise some of us.

With this uncompromising assessment of their position to brood on, the North Wales miners could do little more than sit by while the more powerful and militant areas fought the great battles of the 1920s and the industry slid into the decline which the slump of the 1930s converted into a major and chronic sickness. Supplying a mainly inland and predominantly local market, North Wales was in some ways less hard hit than coalfields such as South Wales which relied heavily on exports and were crippled by state-subsidised foreign competitors undercutting them to win larger shares of a contracting market. Employment in the pits in North Wales in 1929, standing at 16,000, was only a few hundred less than it had been in 1913, and production by the same year had fallen by barely 50,000 tons from the 1913 level of 3.5 million tons.

But output is by itself no index of prosperity, and North Wales, never among the more prosperous coalfields, suffered correspondingly in hard times, especially during the lock-out of 1921, and even more during the prolonged, crushing and ultimately fruitless agony of 1926. In retrospect not all of those who were called on to stop work in North Wales were convinced that the strike was wise or justified as far as their own coalfield was concerned. Early in 1926 one of their leaders informed them bluntly once again that if their wages were to be based on the ability of the district to pay, the only alternatives would be a reduction in wages and an increase in hours (in direct contradiction to A. J. Cook's slogan 'Not a penny off the pay, not a minute on the day!'), or a continuation of the subsidy with which the government had hastily but temporarily bought off the threat of a strike in 1925.

The immediate consequences of the miners' capitulation towards the end of 1926 were a return to district instead of national negotiations and an increase in the length of the working day, and it would be difficult to decide which was the more bitter pill for the men to swallow. They had never expected a standard minimum wage to apply to every miner in the industry but they expected the minimum, although it might vary from district to district, to be 'national' in the sense that it could not be reduced in any district without the consent of the industry as a whole; in this way the poorer districts would not be made to suffer at the hands of the more prosperous. With the return of something like a free-for-all in 1926 the districts were at the mercy of the same cut-throat competition as that which characterised dealings between individual companies.

The extension of the working day, which again meant the surrender of a hard-won and dearly-prized victory, was achieved by an Act of Parliament passed some months before the strike was called off. The original '8 Hour Act',[2] as it was popularly called, was passed in 1908 and allowed the eight hours below ground to be exceeded on not more than 60 days a year. In 1919, in the first flush of their post-war power, the miners succeeded in having seven substituted for eight on the same terms. The Act of 1926 achieved a return to eight hours by the roundabout method of returning to a seven-hour day which could be exceeded on any day of the year, thus allowing the miners to keep the shadow of their former victory while losing the substance.

The defeat sustained by the men was plain to see but the victory apparently gained by the owners proved hollow. The economies they had forecast from the lengthening of the working day appeared to materialise; the considerable loss of production due to the eight-month stoppage had to be made up; more men were taken on and output rose above the level of 1925. But it was a false dawn. Employment rose more rapidly than the demand for coal and had to be checked. By the spring of 1927 output was being cut back, prices were falling, short time was being worked.

The story throughout 1928 was much the same—output down, employment down, even greater irregularity of working hours, excess of production costs over proceeds twice as great as in the previous year. An exceptionally severe winter and a tendency to build up emergency stocks against a possible recurrence produced a semblance of a revival in 1929 but even this reprieve had its disadvantages. Faced, as they believed, with a return to 'normality' the owners lost the mild interest they had begun to show in those modest 'schemes to secure greater cooperation' in the industry which the Baldwin Government had half-heartedly initiated in the aftermath of 1926. In North Wales no proposals for reorganisation were reported.

Midway through 1929 the second minority Labour Government took office with the problem of unemployment in general, and the plight of the coalfields in particular, at the top of its agenda. Within a month the President of the Board of Trade announced that the government intended to take

> ... powers to compel colliery owners to conform to the rules of a district organization inaugurated with the approval of owners of collieries producing the majority of the output of the district, ... power ... to initiate a scheme in any district which fails to constitute an organization ... and power to set up a central co-ordinating authority, if one is not constituted voluntarily.

Notice was thus served on the industry: obstruction and procrastination were out; if it could not, or would not, put its house in order the government would step in and do the job.

The measures proposed were embodied in the Coal Mines Act of 1930, a composite piece of legislation which by pursuing mutually exclusive objectives did more credit to the hearts of its sponsors than to their grasp of the problems that faced them.

Part 1 of the Act dealt with the production, supply and sale of coal, and was designed to limit the overproduction and suicidally competitive price-cutting which kept profits, and hence wages, at unacceptably low levels. A Central Council was to assess from time to time what the nation's requirements were likely to be for a given period. The Council would then allocate a fixed proportion to each coal-producing district, which an Executive Board elected by all the owners in the district would divide up among the various collieries. There were provisions for penalties for exceeding the quota, and for the maintenance of certain minimum prices.

Part 2, carrying the strategy further, set up a Commission whose function was 'to further the reorganisation of the coal-mining industry and ... to promote and assist amalgamations where they appear to be in the national interest'. Owners could be required to put forward their own scheme for reorganisation; if they failed or refused, the Commission could draw one up for them, and if the scheme proposed satisfied the provisions of the earlier Acts it could be enforced.

Part 3 of the Act was inspired partly perhaps by the determination of the miners to recover ground lost in 1926, and partly as a token attack on the problem of unemployment. The extension of the working day by one hour on any day of the year was replaced by an extension of only half an hour. The eight-hour day thus became a seven-and-a-half-hour day, and it was intended that when the 1926 Act expired in 1931 the maximum should once again become seven, as in 1919. The owners accepted the first reduction with a bad grace but stood firm against the possibility of the second unless a corresponding reduction in wages was agreed.

Part 4 of the Act was a half-hearted and ultimately unsuccessful attempt to remove the other bone of contention left over from 1926, the insistence by the owners on district rather than national negotiations on wages and conditions of work. A compromise worked out to meet their objections was simply disregarded in practice and the government plainly felt disinclined to try to enforce it.

Even if the Act had been better designed for its purpose it would have availed little in the face of the storm which had been gathering since the Wall Street crash of 1929 and which burst over Britain while the Bill was completing its passage through Parliament. The slight improvement in the coal trade which 1929 had brought was short-lived. By the middle of 1930 output in Britain had fallen back to the 1928 level and abroad the position was even worse as the world-wide industrial depression deepened and demand for coal declined.

Districts supplying the home market, although spared the misfortunes of the exporting districts, had to contend not only with the fall in demand for their own output but with competition from hard-hit exporters searching desperately for buyers at home for coal they could no longer sell abroad. As stocks piled up at the pit-heads, work, even for those with a job, was so irregular that in some coalfields as many as 16 weeks were lost during the year. For more than 300,000 miners there were no jobs at all.

The sufferings inflicted on the industry by the depression were intensified by two developments which had been gaining ground since the end of the war—the onward and irresistible march of mechanisation, which had to be paid for by improved productivity, and an irreversible trend towards a declining demand due to the more efficient use of coal in many industries, notably steel and railways, and to its replacement by oil in one of its former principal consumers, the world's shipping. It was a reluctant recognition of these trends which had prompted both Conservative and Labour governments to introduce their modest measures aimed at the reorganisation of the industry. Responsibility for their failure rested partly on the miners, who had no choice but to fight in defence of their already abysmally low living standards, but much more on the owners who, hating each other rather more than they distrusted their labour force, resisted all attempts to persude them to collaborate and preferred instead to put their faith in a blind and self-destructive individualism. 'I should have thought that the miners' leaders were the stupidest men in the kingdom', Lord Birkenhead is reported to have said in 1926, 'if I hadn't met the owners.'[3] Their recipe for survival in the declining markets of the post-war decades differed little from the policy which the inspector of mines for the North Wales area had noted at the turn of the century—chasing markets by cutting prices, cutting prices by reducing costs, reducing costs by increasing output, and thereby adding to the glut of coal which could only be disposed of, if at all, by cutting prices still further.

In this descending spiral the ultimate losers were inevitably the miners. In a pamphlet entitled *The Position of the Coal Miner* published in 1933, the Miners' Federation quoted figures to show that, since 1920, while the miner's output had increased by over 50 per cent, his wages had been reduced by over 50 per cent and he worked a longer day. Many miners and their families were living on less than £2 per week, and some on less than 30 shillings; the allowance of cheap coal and the low rents which were held in some quarters to offset the low wages were valued, according to figures from government sources, at no more than four pence three farthings a day. The real sacrifice, it was often pointed out, was made by wives and children, who stinted themselves so that the men could be adequately fed for their long and hard day's work at the pit.

While acknowledging the effects of adverse trading conditions, the miners laid heavy blame for their plight on the chaotic internal structure of the industry, and independent investigators mostly supported their analysis.

In 1934 there were in Britain something like a thousand colliery owners operating more than 2,000 separate mines which produced 220 million tons of coal. Twenty-five of these mines were responsible for a third of the total production; only about 20 of them produced more than two million tons per annum; many were very small, employing a handful of men in what were scarcely more than surface workings.

To transport the output of the mines, many of which were located in inaccessible parts of the country, there were 750,000 wagons of widely differing types, many of them reaching the end of their useful life, many of them too small. They belonged to more than 5,000 different concerns, made on average two round trips of 42 miles each per month and spent two-thirds of the time standing still, whether empty or full, waiting to be shunted. Transport charges in some cases added 60 per cent to the pit-head value of coal.

The retail trade was in the same state of anarchy. There were more than 27,000 retail coal merchants of whom less than eight per cent handled as much as 2,000 tons per quarter and 30 per cent handled barely five tons a week. The domestic consumer paid more than he need have done to keep in being this huge, ramifying and inefficient distribution system, which provided a precarious living for numbers of largely unnecessary middlemen. Giving evidence to the Samuel Commission in 1925 a former Chief Inspector of Mines, Sir Richard Redmayne, remarked, 'if you endeavoured to follow a sack of Derby Brights from the colliery to a London cellar you would arrive there a shattered wreck from the number of hands you had gone through'.

The Act of 1930, renewed for a further five years in 1932, was agreed to have played a modest part in tiding the industry over the immediate crisis but its shortcomings as a solution to the underlying problems were widely recognised. It curbed the worst excesses of the earlier free-for-all but the structure of minimum prices was increasingly evaded by middlemen and by the owners who, as their president Euan Williams admitted, were still placing more coal on the market than they could sell.

The recognition that markets for much of this unwanted coal were never likely to be won back carried with it the acceptance of an even more alarming prospect—that the severe unemployment of recent years would never be wholly cured. Few of the men who had lost their jobs between 1924 and 1934 would get them back, and for a number variously estimated at between 200,000 and a quarter of a million there would never be permanent work in the industry again. Some were men who had been attracted to it during its brief spell of post-war prosperity and were not genuine coalminers; some had drifted away to other occupations and no longer appeared on the books as unemployed miners; but the very large proportion who remained constituted a problem which, as the *PEP Report on the British Coal Industry* (1936) insisted, had 'long ceased to be a purely industrial problem and ... assumed the position of a national problem of the first magnitude'.

Various remedies were proposed, some of which met with a warmer response than others. One which was generally favoured was that Britain should fall into line with other nations and raise the age at which boys might enter the industry to 15 for surface workers and 16 for underground workers. At the other end of the scale there was widespread recognition that mining was not 'an old man's industry', and that an earlier retirement age would be in everyone's interests. But in the absence of a pension scheme a man in his fifties who lost his job at the pit and was too old to find one elsewhere, and almost certainly had no savings to fall back on, either became a burden on the younger members of his family or struggled to live on the meagre allowances of the Unemployment Assistance Board or the Public Assistance Committee until he qualified for an equally meagre old age pension at 65.

A third proposal, that hours of work should be reduced, over-looked the development which more than any other was changing the face of the industry at an accelerating rate and to the growing bewilderment, alarm and resentment of the miners. Increased efficiency, through reduction in costs and improvement in output per man shift, was linked largely to increased mechanisation, which called both for fewer workers and for harder work from those who remained.

The application of machinery to coal-getting had a long history, with the emphasis on ways of bringing the coal down from the face and conveying it to the pit bottom.[4] All the early devices gave rise to problems and the growth of mechanised cutting was slow, being confined for a long time to narrow seams where the weight of coal would not so frequently put the cutter out of action. Thereafter its advance throughout the country became more rapid, as did the realisation of its implications for the colliers. In the beginning they had passed resolutions welcoming it, 'as it might tend to diminish loss of life',[5] and also because the men who were sufficiently skilled to handle the unfamiliar machines could command high wages. Fifty years later they were changing their tune. Wages were cut to accommodate the high capital cost of mechanising and the machine seemed to be forcing a change in the miner's pattern of life,[6] in much the same way as the advent of power-looms had affected handloom weavers a century earlier. By the 1930s, with 50 per cent of coal in Lancashire and North Wales and over 80 per cent in some coalfields being cut mechanically, and around 40 per cent of it being conveyed along the face by endless belts or incredibly noisy vibrating troughs, the miner had become both the slave and the victim of the machine, as Joseph Jones, vice-president of the Miners' Federation described graphically in *The Coal Scuttle* (1936).

> The machine cuts the coal at lightning speed and the conveyor brings it out to the wagons in an endless stream: to feed the conveyor adequately the men have to work at the highest pressure and without a moment's respite ... The whirr of the coal-cutting machines, the hammering of pneumatic picks, the crash of the conveyor pans make a deafening noise.

To the complacent assurances of authorities such as Sir Richard Redmayne that 'to the workers the mechanization has proved a veritable *Deus ex machina*',[7] and that 'the avocation of a coal miner is a very healthy one—short hours spent in an even atmosphere',[8] more perceptive observers responded with a long list of the new hazards which machinery had introduced into the miner's life. The weight and vibration of the cutters placed extra strain on the strata, adding to the difficulty and danger of preventing rock falls. In the race to keep up with the machine the men were tempted to take risks, neglecting safety precautions, with a consequent rise in the accident rate. There was an enormous increase in the amount of overtime demanded. In order to squeeze the maximum use out of the machinery and step up production, managements would make the coalface so long that the 'cut' could not be completed or the face cleared within a normal shift. The law permitted them to require men to stay on and 'deal with any emergency or work uncompleted through unforeseen circumstances ... in order to avoid serious interference with the ordinary routine of the mine', and this provision was regularly invoked to keep men underground long beyond the end of the statutory shift period.

When the machines were working the quantities of dust generated brought greatly increased risk of silicosis, the crippling disease of the lungs which had barely been known in pre-machine days, and nystagmus, damage to the eyes caused by straining to see in darkness barely relieved at the best of times by the inadequate light of a safety lamp and now rendered nearly opaque: there was often so much coal dust in the air, it was said, that the miner's sense of sight was almost lost to him

No less important were the psychological implications of mechanisation. For the man at the coalface, W. D. H. Stewart pointed out in 1936, the conditions of work were so much changed as to mean almost a new trade to him.

> For the first time in coal-mining the coalface miner was compelled to forego his hitherto privileged position of being the 'superior' man in the mine. The machine eliminated the most skilful part of his work, namely, the holing or undercutting of the coal, thus making it possible for unskilled men to enter the mine freely ...

and worse still to earn better wages, for 'although physical strength had always played a part in the making of wages in a coal mine, it had now become paramount.' Worst of all, from the point of view of status and pride in workmanship: 'there [was] now a greater degree of supervision than was ever known before, with the result that the miner—the skilled miner—hitherto one of the most independent workmen in the country [was] now reduced to a living tool'.

This, then, was the position of the miner as the 1930s unrolled: reduced to despair by the defeat of 1926, the prisoner of an industry in a state bordering on demoralisation, increasingly at the mercy of voracious machinery, and condemned by a cruel paradox to scrape a steadily deteriorating living, when he was lucky enough to have a job at all, by producing more and more of what appeared to be needed less and less.

During this period, from 1926 to 1934, four more of Denbighshire's old-established collieries closed: Wynnstay (1927), Vauxhall (1928), Vron (1930) and Gatewen (1932). Flintshire, with the loss of two, was reduced to only one of any consequence, at Point of Ayr in the far north of the county, where 432 men were employed in and about workings which lay mostly under the sea. Elsewhere there were five minor concerns of which the largest employed 20 men and the smallest three. Denbighshire retained 18 collieries, ranging in size from the diminutive Poolmouth Level with four workers and Glascoed with eight to Hafod with 1,457, Gresford with 2,200 and the giant Llay Main with 2,900. The last-named, which reached an output of more than a million tons in the relatively prosperous year 1929, was now owned by the Carlton Main Company and among the most progressively managed; it was, for instance, the only colliery in North Wales at this time to possess pit-head baths, put up by the company at a cost of £35,000 with accommodation for 3,000 men. Miners at the other leading collieries in the coalfield had to wait several years, in some cases until after the Second World War, to enjoy this elementary amenity.

The detailed history of Gresford has largely gone beyond recall with the agreed destruction by the trustee of all its records when the protracted negotiations resulting from nationalisation had been concluded, but from a few balance sheets and terse statements to shareholders which survive it is clear that the early 1930s were, as might be expected, a period of some anxiety.

The nominal capital of the company, United Westminster and Wrexham Collieries Ltd, was 400,000 shares of £1 each, of which just over 300,000 were issued. The principal shareholders in 1933 were the chairman, Henry Dyke Dennis, with 86,000, or about 35 per cent, and his son, Henry M. P. Dennis, with 29,700. Five other shareholders, including J. A. Harrop, the company secretary, accounted for about 65,500 shares between them and the remaining 119,000 were distributed among a little under 200 shareholders.

The pits, its principal assets, with their buildings, machines and plant, were valued in 1929 at just under £220,000, freehold land, houses and minerals at £42,700, and railway wagons at approximately £12,000.

In view of the many devices by which a colliery was enabled at least partially to cover its tracks, it may not be wise to take published trading accounts too readily at their face value, although there is no surviving evidence to connect United Westminster and Wrexham Collieries with any activities of this kind. The bare facts as published show that in 1929, when income included sales at £258,000, there was a trading loss of £5,543. By September 1930, as a result of the slight improvement in the early months of the year, this loss had been converted into a minuscule net gain of £715, and the chairman, confessing that 'the new Coal Mines Act is a source of anxiety to your Directors', warned the shareholders that the outlook for the next 12 months was 'extremely precarious'. In spite of this the accounts for 1931 showed a profit on the year's working of £4,841 with a net gain to the company of £3,551. The chairman's report, recalling an interim dividend of two per cent declared out of reserves a few months previously, and announcing a final dividend of two per cent less tax from the same source, described the result of the year's working as 'disappointing, particularly after the strict economy which has been exercised in every department of the Colliery'.

By 1932 the recession had begun to bite deeply and the company balance sheet, published in June, revealed the extent of the wounds. There was a net loss on the year's working of £9,489, and the directors decided to 'pass the payment of a Dividend'. They had come to the decision with regret but felt it was the prudent course to adopt in the present state of trade. Reporting the renewal for a further five years of Part 1 of the 1930 Act the chairman announced that the owners had guaranteed to maintain the existing rates of wages, which in 1929 had cost the company just short of £200,000.

In June 1933 the year's working showed a loss of £7,116, and prudence could presumably only have suggested a further decision to 'pass the payment of a Dividend'. But equally it seems to have been felt that something must be done for the deprived investors.

> In accordance with a Special Resolution of the General Meeting held on 10th March last, £45,008.2s.0d. of the undivided profits standing in reserve was capitalised for distribution among the Shareholders ... The Warrants for the first half-yearly payment of interest at 5 per cent. per annum, due on the 10th of this month are being sent.

The corner, not only for Gresford Colliery but for the British coal industry, was about to be turned. In spite of a mild spring, followed by an exceptionally warm summer which reduced domestic consumption, there were definite signs of an improvement in trade, thanks chiefly to a revival of demand in the heavy industries. The decline in employment had been arrested; working was slightly less irregular. The upward trend in demand continued in the early months of 1934, though less satisfactorily in North Wales, where the improvement in output, at around 3 per cent, was the lowest of any district, contrasting with 11 per cent in Northumberland and Durham.

The moderately brighter prospects must have been greeted with relief at Gresford, where some organisational changes had taken place. A new under-manager had been taken on, a well-qualified local man who had recently spent some years in South Wales. The agent, Mr Cockin, who had been with the company since the days, 25 years previously, when he had supervised the sinking of the shafts, retired in October 1932 and, perhaps as one of its economy measures, the company decided not to replace him but to hand over his responsibilities to Mr Harrop, the company secretary, who had no training or experience as a mining engineer but was very sound on the commercial side. Another new face seen in and around the pit at various times was that of a junior inspector of mines, recently transferred from Scotland and residing, as did a number of his predecessors, in Chester, from which he could most easily exercise his responsibility for the North Wales coalfield and parts of Lancashire.

NOTES

For accounts of the coal industry from the end of the First World War, see: *The History of the British Coal Industry*, Vol. 4 (1987); PEP, *Report on the British Coal Industry* (1936); Court (1945); Keynes (1925); Griffin (1977).

1. See Appendix A: Mining Industry Act 1920, 10 and 11 Geo 5 C 50 (4).

2. The Coal Mines Regulation Act 1908. 'I (1) Subject to the provisions of this Act a workman shall not be below ground in a mine for the purpose of his work, or of going to and from his work, for more than eight hours *during any consecutive twenty-four hours*' (author's italics). The Coal Mines Regulation Act 1872, 7.(2) stated that 'A period of a person's employment begins at the time of his leaving the surface and ends at the time of his return to the surface.' In Gresford a man working on one of the more distant faces could spend at least an hour of his 'working time' walking to and from the district.

3. Quoted in Young (1952) p. 90.

4. According to Boyd (1879), 'the first patent for coal-cutting machinery dates from 1862 . . .'.

5. See Boyd (1879), p. 172.

6. For a summary of the arguments for and against mechanisation see the Royal Commission on Safety in Coal Mines (1938), p. 68: 'Effects of Modern Methods of Work'.

7. Redmayne (1942), p. 150.

8. Report in the *Colliery Guardian*, 16 November 1934.

CHAPTER 5

The Colliery[1]

A coal mine is a three-dimensional maze which changes its topography daily, expanding in one direction, as the men burrow deeper and deeper in pursuit of the coal, stopping short in another as the coal seam, displaced by some catastrophe in geological time, ends against a wall of rock, perhaps to be rediscovered many yards below or above the fault, perhaps to be given up as lost for ever. Within this maze roads are made and abandoned as the tide of battle moves on; others, no longer needed for the passage of coal, are kept open for the passage of air; others again, still needed for working purposes, may become blocked by falls of rock and be temporarily or permanently replaced by diversions. The older the colliery the more intricate and, to the outsider, the more bewildering its geography becomes.

Parts of the Dennis Section of Gresford Colliery were less up-to-date than others. In the districts known as 20s and 61s coal was still got by hand. A small group of miners went to their allotted 'stall', bringing the coal down and wheeling it away, leaving a substantial pillar of coal untouched to support the roof and moving on to open out a new stall. The other districts had been mechanised and were worked on the longwall system. The coalface, which might be well over a hundred yards long, was undercut by the machine to a depth of five feet or so and shots were fired to bring down the coal, which was then 'filled', i.e. sent out of the pit by means of conveyor belts and tubs; the cutter was moved across the cleared space to the face again, and in the worked-out area behind the scene of operations the props were withdrawn and the roof was allowed to collapse and form the 'goaf', or waste. Ideally the cycle would begin on the night shift, with the cutting and shot firing, and be completed within 24 hours by the morning and afternoon shifts, but on some faces in Gresford the sequence of operations did not always keep in step with the shift pattern.

Many factors might contribute to this situation. The steady advance of the face further and further from the pit bottom required

40

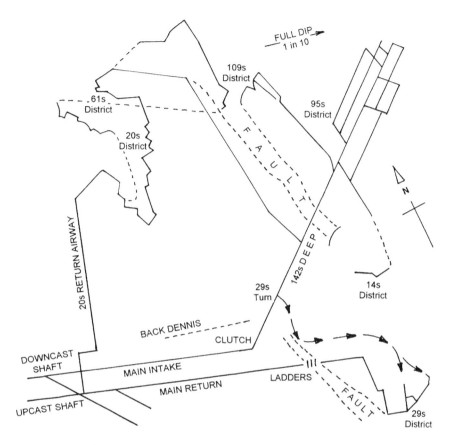

Fig. 2   Plan of underground workings: the Main seam of the Dennis Section at Gresford Colliery, 21 September 1934

new roads to be driven and maintained through the goaf or through virgin rock; mechanised equipment, continually being manhandled under cramped conditions, took a battering and had constantly to be repaired; rock fell when it should not have done, killing and injuring men; a thousand and one mishaps and unforeseen obstacles could disrupt the smooth running of the pit.

The colliers, descending the Dennis, or 'downcast',[2] shaft at the start of their shift, emerged from the cage at the pit bottom to face a roadway running for 1,000 yards in an easterly direction down a gradient of 1 in 10. This was also the main 'intake' road along which air passed on its way into the workings. Parallel with it some way to the south was the main 'return' road, which carried the air back, much depleted, hotter and full of the accumulated pollution of the mine, to the bottom of the Martin, or 'upcast', shaft.

Not far from the shaft bottom a road branched off to the south-east, leading to a section known as the Slant which, apart from sharing the common shafts to and from the surface, was completely self-contained and plays no part in this story.

At the end of their first 1,000 yards' walk (there were no riding trains in Gresford) the miners working in the Dennis Section arrived at the point referred to as the Clutch, from which another road, 142s Deep, branched off to the north-east and led to the various districts. There were five of these, each one representing a separate campaign to win coal from the Main seam, which was the only one the Section was currently concerned with. They had not been started simultaneously and were at varying stages of development, but rather than describe them in chronological order it will be less confusing to picture them as being distributed, so to speak, round the face of a clock.

At about 11 o'clock were 20s and 61s, two interlinked districts which were not mechanised. To reach them the colliers proceeded northwards along 142s Deep for about 400 yards and then, at a junction, struck off to the north-west for perhaps a mile or so.

Ignoring this turning to 61s and continuing along 142s Deep the colliers would come shortly to a place where a small fault interrupted the line of the Main coal seam. Beyond the fault, at about 12 o'clock, was 109s district, reached by another left-hand fork from 142s Deep.

Passing by the turning to 109s, and pressing steadily northwards along 142s Deep, the miners would arrive at 95s district, which for practical purposes was treated as part of 109s. It would be located at approximately 2 o'clock. By this time the men would be something like a mile and a quarter 'inbye' from the bottom of the Dennis shaft and, because of the steady dip of the coal seam, about 200 yards deeper into the earth than when they had stepped out of the cage: well over half a mile below the rich farmland lying between the Wrexham–Chester road and the River Dee.

To locate the remaining two districts it will be simpler to return in imagination to the Clutch and follow another group of miners. They would set out along 142s Deep, like the other men, but very shortly some of them would turn at an acute angle to the right, making for 29s, which lay somewhere around 4 or 5 on the clock face. The final group would continue along 142s Deep as far as the fault mentioned above, beyond which they too would turn sharply to the right into 14s district, at approximately 3 o'clock on the imaginary dial.

To understand the way in which air was circulated through these complex workings it is better to exchange the image of a clock face for that of the outline of a somewhat lopsided heart (but not its mechanism). Air is not pumped into a pit but drawn through and out of it by a fan situated near the top of the upcast shaft. To prevent the flow from being reduced by any downward pressure from the atmosphere there should be an airlock at the top of the shaft, but this was another feature on which the first builders of Gresford had economised, and the omission had still not been rectified by 1934. As it reached the surface the cage, bearing men or coal, simply pushed open two wooden doors which fell back into place beneath it when it had passed.

The air, drawn down the Dennis shaft and along the main intake to the Clutch, travelled along 142s Deep, past the entrance to 29s, which it was in theory prevented from entering by doors which had to be opened and closed every time men or coal needed to pass through. It continued along 142s Deep until it reached the first important junction, where some of it was headed off to the left, winding its way through the workings into 61s district, then to 20s district, then by way of a series of zigzags through old workings until it reached a long passage, an old road, which delivered it almost to the bottom of the Martin, or upcast, shaft.

The remainder of the air, keeping straight on at the junction, followed an even more circuitous route, all the way up to 109s and back, all the way through 95s and back, all the way through 14s and much of the way back, and further south still into 29s, before being finally allowed to join the main return airway for the long straight run back to the Martin shaft. The strong inducements urging it to take short cuts or lose itself in abandoned workings were countered at crucial junctions by doors and canvas sheets known as brattices, but these were not always as efficient as they might have been, which was perhaps as well for the men working in 29s at the far end of the chain, although paradoxically nearest to the pit shaft. If air had not reached them by unauthorised routes they might at times have been rather short of it. The owners appeared at some stage to have grasped this fact, and also the unsatisfactory quality of the air which was reaching 29s, for a special intake known as 'Back Dennis' had been begun from the pit bottom parallel to the main Dennis in the direction of 29s, but it had petered out somewhere in the neighbourhood of the Clutch and work on it had never been resumed.

There were, in 1934, about 2,200 men working at Gresford, 1,850 below ground and 350 on the surface. The underground workers were of course distributed over three shifts, with fewer during the night than on the other two shifts. In practice the numbers at work at any given time could be, and frequently were, higher because of what the men saw as the management's cynical exploitation of the clause in the Act which permitted them to demand work beyond the normal period of the shift in order to deal with an 'emergency', real or manufactured.

Resentment aroused by this practice, common to all coalfields, found expression at many a union meeting, private and public. On 8 May 1933 the executive committee of the North Wales Miners' Association passed a resolution strongly protesting against the amount of overtime being worked in the coal mines at that time. 'The Coal Mines Act ... owing to the increase in machinery ... fails to control this growing evil.' The Association returned to the subject in the following April, when the annual delegate meeting carried unanimously a resolution from Bersham Lodge:

> Believing that the overtime worked at the coal face, which is now too prevalent throughout North Wales, is a direct contravention of the Coal Mines Regulation Act, and also that it constitutes the greatest menace both to employed and unemployed miners, we call upon the Executive Committee to take every possible step to put an end to this illegal and inhuman act.

On Saturday 15 September 1934, following a resolution from Hafod Lodge, the Association called a special delegate conference in Wrexham, presided over by Alderman Jones, who described excessive overtime, including Sunday labour, as one of the most dangerous things that had crept into the industry.[3] Their fore-fathers had made great sacrifices in endeavouring to reduce the hours of work. They had worked 12 hours and only saw daylight on Saturday in the winter. A commission, the majority of whom had no interest in the coal mines, had thought that seven hours should be the maximum worked in a pit in one day, and the government of the day had agreed and legislated accordingly. Since that time another half an hour had been added, but men were not working 7½ hours only—they were working 10½, 12, and even 15 hours, and so, it was reported, were boys of tender age. During the discussion which followed a number of specific examples were quoted: of two brothers, treated for exhaustion after excessive overtime while a third brother was unable to get work; of three men working 50 hours each in a period of three days, being too exhausted to work on the fourth day, and being suspended for absenteeism when they showed up on the fifth day. The conference adopted a resolution protesting strongly against 'the colossal evils of overtime and Sunday labour in the mines of North Wales, reducing miners to a condition of slavery'.

Unfortunately the official union stand on the subject was weakened by the action of a proportion of the membership. While allowing for the miner's shift to be extended beyond the statutory period, Parliament had expressly forbidden any man to work more than one shift in 24 hours.[4] In some collieries, of which Gresford was one, this rule was knowingly broken. In certain circumstances men who had completed one shift would voluntarily remain below ground for another one, a practice known as 'doubling', or return after only eight hours' absence. The most probable incentive was that the men had for some reason missed a regular shift or were likely to miss one some time during the week but couldn't afford to lose the money. An inspector, sent in July 1933 to investigate complaints made by the union, went through the books, checking the amount of overtime worked. At Gresford there seemed, judging by the records, to be nothing amiss. He was not informed, or failed to spot, that the books had been adjusted so as not to reveal the amount of doubling that went on.

During the week in September 1934, when the North Wales Miners' Association discussed overtime at its special conference, Wrexham held its annual carnival in aid of a local hospital. Many miners missed work in order to attend with their families; Gresford brass band took part in the festivities. On the following Saturday Wrexham Football Club were to play a home match against their local Third Division rivals Tranmere Rovers during what would normally be for some of the men their sixth legitimate afternoon shift of the week. There were therefore that week for one reason or another perhaps 40 or 50 Gresford men looking for an opportunity to put in an extra shift and well aware that Friday night would provide it, for on Sundays and Fridays at Gresford the night shift was operated as a coaling shift, when a few extra hands were always unofficially welcomed by the management. Some of the afternoon shift would simply stay on; others would come back having done a morning shift, like the two men who were leaving to go to another colliery on Monday and wanted to fetch their tools out before the weekend.[5]

It was estimated that on the night of Friday/Saturday 21/22 September there were 478 men in the mine. Between 40 and 50 of them were 'doubling'—that is to say that at the time of the explosion, somewhere in the Dennis Section, at 2.00 a.m. on Saturday morning there were men who had been down the mine since 2.00 p.m. on the previous Friday afternoon in the dust-laden, deafening darkness, either working the coal-cutting machinery or sending the coal on its way to the surface.

NOTES

1. A full technical description of Gresford Colliery appears in *The Geology of Wrexham*, Part II, pp. 64–65. For a list of the seams worked see Ministry of Fuel and Power (1945), p. 70.

2. The terms 'downcast' and 'upcast' refer solely to the direction of the air flow. At Gresford coal was raised by way of the Dennis shaft, and materials were sent down the Martin shaft; men travelled up and down both shafts.

3. *Wrexham Leader*, 21 September 1934.

4. See note 2 to Chapter 4.

5. A bewilderingly complex provision of the 1908 Act Section 15 (1) seems to imply that these men were not breaking the law; the men who had already worked an afternoon shift certainly were.

CHAPTER 6

The Aftermath

The news of the disaster at Gresford broke too late for the national press to do much about it on Saturday 22 September beyond rushing out single-page news-sheets for limited circulation in London, and most people in other parts of the country probably first learned about the accident from local evening papers or from wireless bulletins. By Sunday it was front page news, temporarily displacing the forthcoming wedding of the Duke of Kent and Princess Marina, the warrant for the extradition from New York to New Jersey of Bernard Hauptmann, charged with the murder of the Lindbergh baby, the typhoon in the Far East which had caused 20,000 deaths, and the dispute in the South Wales coalfield which if not resolved by the following weekend would bring 137,000 men out on strike.

The leader writers, anxious to articulate the nation's sympathy and condolences, slipped easily into gear. 'Coal-mining', said the *Sunday Times*,

> is a trade in which danger is ever present. In a sense the men at the coal face are on constant active service, as soldiers are in time of war. Moreover, like soldiers ... they are directly serving their country ... To the miners who daily risk their lives to provide us with this precious 'black gold' the whole community owes a profound debt of gratitude.

The *Daily Worker* later pointed out, 'to avoid misunderstanding', that this paragraph, which it quoted, referred solely to the Gresford disaster and 'must not be taken by the South Wales miners as supporting their demand for something more than a subsistence rate of seven shillings per shift in token of profound gratitude'.

By Monday, when it was known that attempts to control the underground fire had been abandoned, the *Daily Telegraph* wished to pay its tribute to the heroism and devotion of the rescue parties.

> ... This is the temper which makes Britons proud of their country. The men in the pit were the rescuers' mates; therefore, whatever endurance, pluck and indomitable will could do to save them was done. The miner

> takes such work as part of his trade, an incident of the normal occupational risk ...

—in much the same way, the *Daily Worker* again commented, as the directors and shareholders took the profits sweated out of the miner as part of their trade, without 'normal occupational risk'.

For its own part the *Worker*, while pouring scorn on all the crocodile tears which, it predicted, would be shed for the heroic miners and their brave wives, and 'the sad-eyed children who wait for fathers who will never return', could not resist plucking a few heart-strings on a similar note.

> Death has entered hundreds of Welsh homes where fond fathers will never more fondle their babies on their knees, where children will ask for fathers who will never come back, where families are plunged in grief which is so deep that only workers can understand ...

—the children of 'non-workers' being notorious for not crying when their fathers die.

While the fires of polemic and recrimination were being stoked up elsewhere, officials at Gresford were exercised by the problem of what to do about the very real blaze in the pit. The immediate need was to cut off the supply of air from above that was feeding the flames. On Sunday evening, before the rescue parties were finally withdrawn, discussion took place on the advisability of trying to seal off the main roadways underground, but apart from the risk to the men who would have to do the work, analyses of the atmosphere in the main airway revealed as much as six-and-a-half per cent of gas and it was thought doubtful that seals of sufficient strength could be built underground to withstand further explosions. A decision was therefore taken to seal the shafts at the pit top and this work was completed during the early hours of Monday. On Tuesday the worst fears expressed about conditions in the pit were realised when, at about 1.30 p.m., violent explosions blew the seal off the Dennis shaft, sending out volumes of dense smoke and scattering debris which killed a surface worker some distance away. After yet another explosion at midnight more effective seals were built. The pumps, halfway down the shaft, had stopped working earlier in the day, leaving water to pour into the pit at the rate of 75 gallons a minute.

Some time on Monday the managing director, Mr Henry Dyke Dennis, seen by a reporter as 'an old man, leaning on a walking stick, watching the final touches being given to the sealing up of his pit', made a statement on the question which was in most minds—when would it be possible to reopen the pit? It was impossible to say exactly, he told pressmen; it might be two months, it was more likely to be as long as six.

> We have fixed two pipes connecting the surface with the mine, and from these we can ascertain the exact condition of the atmosphere below ground. As soon as the tests show that it is safe to go down we shall reopen the shaft and descend.

It might be possible to have 1,000 men at work in two or three months, with the affected areas bricked up and work resumed in the others.

Little else can have been expected, but this was grim news for Wrexham which, although not regarded as suffering from exceptionally high unemployment by the standards of the time, was in no position to withstand a blow of this magnitude. Gresford had provided jobs for about 10 per cent of the working population of the town and for slightly less than 20 per cent of all the miners employed in the North Wales coalfield. On Monday 24 September 1,100 men from the colliery signed on at Wrexham employment exchange. Throughout the industry as a whole there had been a slight fall in unemployment in recent months, with 83,000 more men at work than in September 1933. The improvement continued and by mid-October the *Colliery Guardian* was able to report that a considerable number of the younger men and boys from Gresford were finding work at other pits, all of which were working full time, and that some had moved to Yorkshire where there was a steadily growing colony of migrants from North Wales. This left a hard core of older men, some of them in their sixties or even seventies, who were not an attractive proposition to other employers, or were unable or unwilling to uproot themselves from the familiar surroundings of a lifetime. One hundred and sixty were said to have failed ever to find jobs again. For them, and much more for the 800 or so dependants of those killed in the explosion, the outlook was bleak.

In spite of the poor wages they earned some of the men who died had managed to set a little money aside for small insurance policies on their lives, from which it was reported that something like £10,000 would be due to their dependants, although this may have been indirect benefit from the war which the mass circulation dailies were waging among themselves at the time. When free sets of the works of Dickens and other literary inducements failed to do down the opposition, several papers had offered the bait of free insurance schemes. On completing an order form for the regular daily delivery of the paper by a recognised newsagent the customer became a 'registered reader', entitled without further payment to lodge claims in accordance with a fixed scale of payments in respect of a variety of mishaps ranging from broken bones to death. The schemes were shrewdly and selectively drawn up, so that, for instance, a broken arm qualified for payment but the much more common broken wrist did not. At the other end of the scale the disparities in payment were enormous and reflected both the true purpose of the exercise and the actuarial realities on which it was based. The victim of a rail crash, like the one which killed 12 people near Warrington on 29 September, if he had been a registered reader of both the *Daily Mirror* and the *Sunday Pictorial*, would have been worth £1,000 from each source. For the *Daily Herald* reader, death on the railway was worth £5,000. For a fatal accident at work, on the other hand, the maximum sum payable from any newspaper was £50, which was also the rate of recompense for being knocked down and killed by a car, or killing yourself while practising for the Isle of Man Grand Prix.

Among the newspapers operating insurance schemes were the *Daily Express*, the *Mirror*, the *Herald* and the *News Chronicle*. The *Worker*, sliding into one of its recurrent financial crises, and pleading with its readers to rescue it, was in no position to offer them free insurance in return and contented itself with disparaging accounts of its rivals' efforts to get in first with the biggest list of registered readers among the Gresford victims. The totals reported were in the event unimpressive, and reference to the subject was soon dropped.

Apart from these incidental and relatively insignificant sums, and the meagre compensation which might ultimately be screwed out of a reluctant management, the family deprived of its bread-winner had little to fall back on in an emergency. Thrift and provision for the future were virtues difficult to practise in the coalfields in the 1930s, and nowhere more so than in North Wales. In the immediate aftermath of the disaster the urgent problem for many families was simply where to lay their hands on ready cash, because the men had 'risen their pay'[1] before they went down the pit that night and the money was buried with them. Few of the pay packets would have contained more than £2, and perhaps the bitterest line in the anonymous 'Ballad of Gresford', written to commemorate the disaster, asserts that 'They died for nine shillings a day'—an over-estimate in more than a few cases. A correspondent from the *Daily Herald*[2] claimed to show on the basis of his own inquiries, which were corroborated by statistical evidence from other sources, that hundreds of men in North Wales, including perhaps nine out of ten of the Gresford men, had been taking home after a week's work barely two shillings or half a crown more than they would have received in unemployment benefit.

Miners' wages, as many students of the subject remarked, were the despair of any outsider trying to understand them, varying greatly from district to district, from pit to pit, from job to job, from bad times to worse times; and calculated according to a formula so arcane as to be almost designed to foment disputes.

The basic principle (quoted from the 'Agreement as to the Regulation of Wages in the North Wales Area', operative in 1934) was that

> The wages payable in this Area during any period shall be expressed in the form of a percentage of the basic rates then prevailing in the Area, and shall be periodically adjusted in accordance with the results of the industry as ascertained in the Area.

The basic rates were in the main those prevailing in 1911, at the time of the passing of the Coal Mines Act, although even here there tended to be variations from coalfield to coalfield. The percentage addition, known for obvious reasons as 'the ascertainment',[3] was arrived at by a complicated calculation based on the performance of the industry (i.e. the proceeds from the sale of coal) in the area during the relevant period 'as ascertained by returns made by the Owners ... checked by joint test audits carried out by independent Accountants appointed by each side ...'. There were provisions designed to ensure that the area minimum percentage did not fall below 22 per cent, and that all 'adult able-bodied daywage workers' earned a minimum of six shillings per shift.

Speaking in the House of Commons on 25 July 1935 the Secretary of State for Mines reported that although the total number of colliers on the books continued to fall, there was 'some consolation ... to be found in the average cash earnings per year', which showed that the miners were much better off than they had been in the depth of the depression. But this averaging out of figures for the whole country concealed some striking and disagreeable anomalies. Conditions varied so much between coalfields that comparisons could be misleading, but there seems to have been some substance in the claim, heard on and off for a century or more before the Gresford disaster, that the North Wales miner was among the worst paid in Britain. Less often stressed was the fact that, on the evidence, and discounting the possibility that his working conditions below ground may have been exceptionally difficult, his average output per shift was in general the worst in the country.

Wages were seldom mentioned at the inquiry into the accident but there was an illuminating exchange when a representative of the Miners' Federation was questioning a collier.

Q What was your minimum wage?
A 7s.10d. I used to get. That's what I've had off 14s.
Q Working under the conditions you were working in in 14s, do you feel that that was a proper wage for a man to get?
A I thought I ought to have had more.
Q When you'd used all your vitality and energy in 14s to produce as much coal as you could, and you hadn't earned the minimum, you had to humiliate yourself to go to the colliery company to apply for the minimum, hadn't you?
A Yes, sir.
Q How many times would you be on the minimum?
A Very often. It was left to them whether I got anything extra.
Q ... Working under the conditions you were working in in 14s, what do you think is a reasonable wage to pay for mining?
A I don't know; I couldn't say.
Q Let us know, because we're going to have it now. You tell me what you think is a reasonable wage.
A What we earn. What we deserve ... 15s. to £1 a day.

By contrast another man, also working in 14s, to which he had been transferred from 29s at his own request, was earning 10 shillings a day there and expressed himself as satisfied with his wages.

But 'earnings' did not reveal the whole story for there were of course various deductions to be made—health and unemployment insurance, union dues (for the minority who paid them), hospital fund, etc.—amounting on one reckoning to 2s.6d. a week. Colliery workers in North Wales worked 11 shifts a fortnight, six one week, five the next. A surface worker or a man on the haulage on the basic rate of six shillings a shift, of whom there were said to be many, would thus be left after a six-shift week with 33s.6d., and at the end of a five-shift week with 30s. If he had a wife and three children his unemployment pay would be 32s. Unless he could make a little extra on overtime, in some weeks he would be marginally better off on the dole than working; in alternate weeks it would be just about worth his while to work.

On the evening of Sunday 23 September some 800 women, children and old people were deprived of even this meagre source of subsistence. In many homes there were scarcely the resources to buy a meal, and the battle to recover not only the bodies of their menfolk but also the week's pay they had taken into the pit with them had been called off indefinitely. The only solution for many families, until formal official provision could be made for them, lay in an appeal to charity, which was made and met on a scale unparalleled, with the possible exception of the rather different circumstances of Aberfan in 1966.

Within hours of the announcement of the disaster appeals for funds were launched—by the Mayor of Wrexham, the Lord Lieutenant of Denbighshire, the *Daily Mirror*, and eventually by the Lord Mayor of London, on whose behalf Alderman Sir Louis Newton broadcast on Wednesday 26 September.[4] The Mansion House, he assured the nation, 'held no shutters of silence when assistance was needed'. A fund had been opened and had received a magnificent lead from the King (who had given £50), the Queen and all the members of the Royal Family.

> How shall we follow that lead? We have read of the indomitable bravery of the scores of miners and rescue workers in the face of appalling danger ... This is the true English type of courage and calmness. Always steadfast in moments of great shock and calamity; always dependable ... I know the country desires to help ... Will you stretch out a hand—the hand of sympathy and understanding which can weld a world, that shall do something to soothe a great sorrow?

To this and other appeals the nation responded with a ready generosity that threatened to overwhelm the organisers, and suggests the prompting of something more than mere sympathy. The public had perhaps a conscience about the miner—the dirt, darkness and danger of his work, the pitiful reward he received for it, the apparently hopeless plight of much of the industry. Distress at the unending unemployment, the dereliction, the poverty and malnutrition of the mining areas; a guilty suspicion that the 'victory' of 1926 and its outcome reflected no credit on a civilised nation; genuine shock at the discovery that accidents of this magnitude, which the Secretary of Mines had only recently claimed were a thing of the past, could on the contrary still happen; all these strands of perception and emotion seem to have come together to distract public attention, briefly, from the bitter squabbles that had broken out following *Rainbow*'s defeat of *Endeavour* in the America's Cup race, Princess Marina's ministrations to the Duke of Kent, who had a slight cold, the second highest total of road deaths in one week (161) since returns were issued, Don Bradman's acute appendicitis, and the triumphant and long-delayed launch on Clydeside of '534', the largest liner afloat, now named, in defiance of Cunard tradition, *Queen Mary*. For nearly two months, as these and graver matters chased each other in and out of the headlines, donations flooded in from every quarter in response to the Gresford appeals, every one, however small, scrupulously recorded on page after page of the local newspaper.

To avoid confusion and simplify administration the various local appeals which had been opened in all the principal towns and cities in the country were eventually consolidated into two funds, the Lord Lieutenant of Denbighshire's and the Lord Mayor of London's. When they finally closed on 15 November the former had received £291,166 and the latter £275,380, a total of £566,546, worth many times more at present-day values.

Some of the money was used to give immediate relief. Within a matter of days provisional weekly allowances were being made on the scale of widows 10s.; each child under 14 6s.; motherless children 10s. for the first, 6s. for the others; dependent parents 7s.6d. for one, 10s. for two, with deductions if they were in receipt of the old age pension. The committee administering the funds was also prepared to assist those thrown out of work by the disaster, their grants being determined 'according to the difference between the unemployment benefit received and the average earnings of the pit, as ascertained from the colliery books'. A version of the New Poor Law principle of 'less eligibility' seems to have been invoked: no victim of the disaster, alive or dead, must be better off than he would have been if it had not happened. Nor must things be made unnecessarily easy for claimants:

> Applicants should, when attending for unemployment grants, take with them a slip of paper authorizing the Unemployment Officer to inform the Committee of the amount of unemployment grant received by the applicant ... The slip of paper can be obtained at the County buildings

(i.e. the headquarters of the relief fund).

When the relief work had been in progress for a fortnight, with the Mansion House Fund standing at £102,000 and the Wrexham Fund at £77,800, the Acting Lord Mayor of London, Lord Wakefield, paid what was for him obviously an emotional visit to the area to see the colliery and meet members of the relief committee.[5] After inspecting the work in progress at the pit-head he was introduced, at his own request, to David Jones, the fireman from 29s who was one of the survivors. The local newspaper reported:

> Taking him warmly by the hand, Lord Wakefield said 'Let me have the honour of shaking hands with you. I feel I am a better man for having done it ... It is men like you who inspire people in all circles. You have done a greater thing than you know, and your example should encourage others.'

Later the vicar of Gresford took him to the village, where there were several bereaved families within a stone's throw of each other. In one cottage a woman had been left a widow with five children. When she was called to the door Lord Wakefield shook hands with her and told her she was 'a very brave woman'. After meeting a woman who had lost two married sons, and then the widows of the two brothers, he 'indicated that he was so affected that he could not continue with any further visits'.

His next call was at the County Hall where several hundred miners from Gresford were waiting to draw money from the relief fund. On being told who was among them 'the men immediately removed their caps', and Lord Wakefield addressed them from the running board of his car. His heart, he said, had been greatly troubled by what he had seen. He could say with all sincerity that he was a better man for having seen the fortitude which had been shown by men, women and children.

> I sincerely hope that a little sunshine will come into your district. Words are cold and inadequate to try to express the feelings in one's heart on such an occasion as this. God bless you, every one of you. I shall go back to London inspired by your great example and courage.

In the meantime there was to be a meeting with the relief committee at which the mood was markedly more hard-headed.

As they watched the vast sums pouring into the disaster funds and noted the sudden interest being shown by London in the affairs of their comparative backwater the local officials' suspicions were aroused. It was perhaps a little early, one miners' leader told Lord Wakefield, for them to be given an indication as to how the fund would be invested and controlled, but he hoped that the application of the fund would be under local control: those who lived among the bereaved would 'wisely and generously meet the requirements of the people'.

In addition to local pride and patriotism there was behind this attitude resentment over what was described elsewhere as 'the scandal of frozen funds' subscribed for the relief of victims of colliery disasters. According to one estimate £408,000 subscribed on various occasions during the preceding years remained undistributed, and the money was used mainly to provide salaries for officials. Miners' leaders were said to be urging the government to legislate for all the available funds to be pooled and used wherever they might be needed after an accident. The Yorkshire miners, having decided to subscribe £1,600 to the Gresford Fund, withheld payment until an assurance was given that any surplus from the fund would be available for the relief of distress in the coalfield.[6] Herbert Smith, the Yorkshire Miners' president, wrote

> We are not wishful to subscribe any money that is going to be 'locked up' indefinitely when there is need for it, as in many instances we know of in the country—while women and children are starving whom this money ought to be utilised for.

The arrangements first proposed for the management of the fund came under bitter attack from Cyril Jones, the Wrexham solicitor who had handled the affairs of the North Wales Miners' Association for many years, and who had insisted on being allowed to go down the pit himself after the explosion, returning in tears at what he had seen. He pointed out that there was in the fund about £2,000 per family dependant, and that many subscribers had expressly stated that their contribution was for immediate distribution, whereas the scheme proposed to accumulate a Surplus Fund which would be set aside for quite other purposes.

As drafted, he commented, it was based on the theory that relatives of the deceased must not be 'a single penny better off than when the breadwinner was alive'. Clause 4 stipulated that payments and allowances must be 'determined with due regard . . . to the earnings and other means of the victims and also to the extent to which the claimant was dependent on the victim . . .'. Under Clause 6 if a dependant received, or became entitled to, an old age pension, 'the allowance theretofore paid to him or her shall be reduced accordingly'; reductions would also be made in respect of any other income other than earned income, and also in respect of any lump sum received by a dependant by way of insurance effected by the deceased on his own life. Clause 6(a), which proposed that 'the allowance to a widow (whether wife or mother of a victim) shall cease on her re-marriage', was in Jones's view 'void as being against Public Policy as being in restraint of marriage'; it would, he was sure, result in 'avoidance of marriage' so as to preserve rights under the scheme.

These criticisms must have had some effect because in the scheme as it was finally approved the provisions to which Jones had objected were much modified.

A breakdown of the allowances finally agreed for the dependants of the men who died conveys more sharply than all the press stories the blow which the explosion had dealt to the mining community of North Wales. The complete list of casualties contains addresses from 43 localities, and there is scarcely a place-name associated with the history of coal-mining in North Wales which does not appear.

The greatest number of casualties—64—came from Wrexham, with a heavy concentration from the poorer streets near the town centre and a scatter from the new housing estates, but surprisingly none from the Garden Village built by the colliery company before the 1914–18 war for its own employees. There were 13 men from Gresford itself, a high total for so small a village. There were men from Brymbo, Minera and Coedpath, names associated with the great days of Wilkinson. There were men from Holt, five miles east of Gresford and well beyond the boundary of the known coalfield, and a large number from Ruabon, 20 miles or more away on the other side of Wrexham. In the absence of public transport these men, from Acrefair and Pen y Coe to the south, and others from Bwlchgwyn among the hills to the west, and Buckley in Flintshire to the north, had made the long journey to work every day or night in privately owned lorries, and an anonymous letter in the *Wrexham Leader* plaintively asked for help for the proprietors whose livelihood had gone with the closure of the colliery.

In spite of the more than ample resources which it had to

dispose of the relief committee laid down stringent conditions for the award of grants, and a number of claims were held to be 'not sustained', including five from brothers, three from daughters, two from mothers, and others from 'a landlord' and 'a landlady'. One hundred and sixty-three widows received assistance. One had seven children, ranging in age from fifteen to five, and received a total grant of 69s.6d. per week; another with five children, the eldest a boy of 17 at technical college, the youngest one year old, received 66s.6d.; five widows, each with four children, were awarded 51s.6d. Fourteen grants were made to expectant mothers, two of whom were tactfully listed as 'fiancées'; one widow, whose child was born a month after the disaster, already had children of four and two years old. There were 30 grants to mothers and fathers jointly, 35 to mothers, 15 to fathers, and 11 to sisters; there were grants in respect of orphans, of an invalid son 34 years of age, of an invalid daughter aged 47 years; there was a grant to a woman with a son aged 15, an adopted daughter aged nine and a crippled relative aged 32 to support; there was one to a woman who had already lost a daughter aged five and a son of five months. Altogether 238 children under 16 lost fathers; 19 of them were one year old or less.

The satisfactory working out of these arrangements took many months, and long before they were completed the atmosphere of grief and commiseration generated by the first impact of the disaster was soured as concern for victims and dependants gave way to speculation about the cause of the explosion and allegations of negligence and malpractice at the colliery.

Some charges were specific. Joseph Jones, vice president of the Miners' Federation, said

> This disaster, like many others, has been described as an Act of God—meaning, I suppose, that it could not have been prevented by human foresight. Yet there is a lamp which could have been installed which would have given ready warning to the men.

This was an alarm which would automatically indicate the presence of firedamp. If it had been installed, Jones claimed, 'it is likely that the men in the mine ... would have been withdrawn'. The Mines Department responded with an assurance that 'automatic firedamp protection' was under consideration but that the device in question was not regarded as being of greater value than others already available.

Emanuel Shinwell, who had held office in the Mines Department during the short-lived Labour Government of 1924 and had lost his seat in the landslide election of 1931, asked in a speech at Durham why a series of safety conferences which he had instituted during his time in the Department had been discontinued: was it on grounds of expense, and was the trifle of a few hundred pounds to stand in the way of the advancement of safety? In his opinion there was no need for such disasters, and, setting a match to a controversy which was to smoulder for several years to come, he urged that the official inquiry into the accident should be presided over by an independent chairman, not by someone in the Mines Department. This was indignantly challenged by the current Secretary for Mines, Ernest Brown, as an unjustified reflection on the Mines Inspectorate, implying that they wittingly permitted unsafe conditions to continue.

The notion of the accident as an act of God was being called into question in other quarters. While some newspapers were assuring their readers that Gresford was 'a modern pit, equipped with all the latest plant', and even 'remarkably up to date in its equipment ... largely electrified', reporters with an ear for something other than the conventional disaster stories of sobbing women, orphaned children and grim-faced rescuers had been on the track of more sensational material. Wrexham and the surrounding villages, they discovered, were 'full of rumours, some of them wild—and others perhaps not so wild'. There were suggestions which 'even go to the length of questioning whether there should have been a disaster at all'.

The man from the *Daily Worker* had heard of ventilation so bad that for months a lot of men 'worked naked except for their clogs', and of gas present in such quantities that only two days before the catastrophe workers near where the explosion occurred 'had to be pulled out of the mine in a hurry'.

The man from the *Daily Herald*, forecasting that the forthcoming inquiry might prove as dramatic as the tragedy itself, summarised some of the questions that might be asked. 'Had certain parts of Gresford Colliery, especially Dennis Deep, a bad reputation? Was the presence of gas ever alleged? ... Had old miners ever said "Something is bound to happen down there one day, and if it does, everyone will be finished"?'[7]

In view of the rumours already circulating, and the likelihood of possibly damaging disclosures, all parties took steps to have their interests adequately safeguarded at the inquiry. The owners of the colliery were in a position to hire legal representation. The usual practice as far as the workers were concerned was for senior officials of their professional bodies and trade unions to appear for them, compensating for any lack of forensic skill by their exhaustive knowledge of working conditions in the industry. The North Wales miners were apparently not satisfied that this time-honoured arrangement, which would require them to place their affairs in the hands of the Miners' Federation, would be in their best interests. The Labour Party was due to begin its annual conference in Southport on 1 October. Some time during the conference a small party from Wrexham, including the recently appointed agent for the North Wales miners, Edward Jones, travelled to Southport and secured the reluctant consent of the leaders of the Miners' Federation to seek an interview with Sir Stafford Cripps KC MP, one of the most successful and expensive barristers of the day and a rising star of the Labour Party. They persuaded him to represent them, and in so doing they unwittingly ensured that the inquiry into the Gresford Colliery disaster would be transformed from a routine investigation into an accident into one of the most influential events in the history of British coal-mining.

NOTES

1. Griffiths (1969), p. 41.
2. *Daily Herald*, 25 September 1934.
3. Griffiths (1969), p. 39.
4. *The Listener*, October 1934.
5. *Wrexham Leader*, 12 October 1934.
6. *Daily Herald*, 3 November 1934.
7. *Daily Herald*, 25 September 1934.

CHAPTER 7

Sir Stafford Cripps

Richard Stafford Cripps was born in 1889 into a solidly upper-middle-class family. His father, later given a peerage by Asquith, was a lawyer, his mother one of the famous Potter sisters, themselves the daughters of a prosperous Manchester merchant. Another of the sisters, Beatrice, married to Sydney Webb, provided a link with politics, but until Cripps's father accepted office in Mac-Donald's first Labour Government the environment which Cripps himself knew best was comfortably and undemandingly conservative. The deepest shadow on an otherwise happy childhood was the death of his mother when he was five years old.

Sent to Winchester, he proved a brilliant scholar with an unexpected aptitude for chemistry, and won the first scholarship ever offered in the subject at New College, Oxford. His examination papers were so outstanding that they were sent to Sir William Ramsey at University College, London, with the result that Cripps was invited to study and work with him. At 22, being already the inventor of a device for measuring the density of liquids and gases, he became the youngest student ever to read a paper, of which he was co-author, before the Royal Society.

This, however, was not the prelude to a scientific career. Following his father's example he read for the Bar, passed his finals in 1912, and was called to the Middle Temple in 1913.

On the outbreak of war in 1914 he spent a few months in France as a Red Cross lorry driver, but was soon recalled to put his scientific training to good use, somewhat unexpectedly, in the national cause. At Queensferry on the Dee estuary the government had built, at a cost of £7 million, the largest explosives factory in the British Empire, incorporating the two finest sulphuric acid plants in the world. After a brief spell of training Cripps was sent there to be assistant superintendent, with responsibility among other things for the cost accounts of the factory. Not a single person on the staff, either management or operatives, he later told the House of Commons, had ever worked in a chemical or explosives factory before, but the plant was so successful that it had to be dismantled at the end of the war, 'to prevent the commercial manufacturers [of sulphuric acid] going out of business'.

He had been at the factory for two years when a combination of overwork, constant exposure to noxious fumes, and the aftermath of an illness he had picked up during his service with the Red Cross caused his health to collapse, and although he recovered from the immediate effects, he was never a wholly fit man again.[1] After a long convalescence he resumed his legal career in 1919 and soon built up a flourishing practice and a high professional reputation. He specialised mainly in patent law, compensation cases concerning the purchase of land by public authorities, and the Parliamentary Bar, where he was much occupied with private Acts of Parliament promoted by local authorities and public bodies of all kinds.

In these fields he became known as a formidable protagonist. It was said of him that 'he always knew more about his case than anyone on the other side ... he was often able to correct his opponent's prepared speech ... and to refer the judge to documents which no one else could find'.[2] He once reduced a distinguished witness to helpless silence during a cross-examination based on the man's own writings; on another occasion his opening speech on a compensation case took five days, at the end of which, before a word of their own argument had been put, the other side surrendered and settled out of court.

Two developments important to his career occurred during these years: in 1927 he took silk, becoming the youngest KC at the Bar; and he met and greatly impressed Herbert Morrison, the Labour leader of London County Council, for which he appeared in an extremely complex piece of litigation. Throughout these years, also, a political awareness and conviction were quietly germinating within him, ready for a sudden and typically urgent flowering in the next decade.

Cripps was not by birth or upbringing a politically-minded man. As a boy and an adolescent he took his immediate world as he found it although, like any sensitive and inquiring young man, he was aware that others were less fortunately placed than himself and was puzzled that such contrasts in fortune should exist side by side. His formative years were in any case too busy and absorbing to allow time for much searching analysis of political and social issues. But during his illness and convalescence he had time to read and reflect:

on the causes of the war which had just ended; on his perhaps limited contact with the working classes at the munitions factory; on the disruptive political and industrial forces unexpectedly unleashed by the ending of hostilities. As time went by his latent idealism, the Christian principles imbibed from his family background, the example of his father, whose progressive outlook had led him from an orthodox conservatism to acceptance of office in a Labour administration—all these influences, coupled with ferocious energy which even poor health could not wholly quell, impelled Cripps towards movements aimed at reform.

They found expression first in work for the World Alliance of Churches. The aim of the organisation, which his father had helped to found, was to promote peace and international friendship through the practical observance and application of Christian principles, and the breaking down of those prejudices and misunderstandings which set one nation against another. The Alliance represented, in the words of Archbishop Temple, 'the consequence of a spiritual movement in the Church, prompted by loyalty and hope, and a spiritual movement in the world, prompted by disillusion and despair'.[3]

Cripps became very active in the affairs of the British Council of the Alliance, helping it financially, addressing meetings up and down the country and eventually filling the post of treasurer. He also became a member of the House of Laymen in the National Assembly of the Church of England and was an early and keen supporter of the League of Nations, which became a special interest of his father, Lord Parmoor, on his appointment as Lord President of the Council in the Labour Government of 1924. To his legal and managerial skills Cripps was now adding experience of public affairs and of advocacy outside the rarified atmosphere and closely prescribed conventions of the law courts.

He was also becoming disillusioned, not with the ideals of the Church but with its failures in practice. Accustomed to vigorous argument and action, leading to clear-cut solutions, he grew impatient with what seemed to him the absence of a sense of urgency in the Church's approach to the problems confronting society. 'What contribution [has] Christianity made to world affairs during the last twelve months? ... Nothing.' In this situation, searching for a practical outlet for his zeal for reform he turned to politics, to which his thoughts had been directed not only by the active participation of his father and his uncle, Sydney Webb, in Mac-Donald's government but also by direct experience of the kind gained through his own professional work in connection with the acquisition of land for municipal housing schemes and so on. This, he wrote, 'took me to slum areas, of the meaning of which I had been completely unconscious, though I had lived and worked in London all my life'.[4] As a countryman he had always known about the 'disease-ridden hovels ... and the tragically low wage levels' of the agricultural workers; now he began to realise 'what the urban slums really signified in terms of suffering, starvation and ill-health'.

In this frame of mind, although he at first rejected the notion of going into politics, he finally became favourably disposed to the suggestion put to him by Herbert Morrison, who was cannily foreseeing the future needs of the Labour movement, that he should join the party. He became a member in 1929, just before the election of that year which led to the formation of MacDonald's second minority Government. Almost immediately he was of service to the party when, without fee, he defended the successful candidate for a Plymouth constituency on a charge relating to election expenses and won an easy victory.

The next step was to prepare him for entry into Parliament and it was agreed that he should become the candidate for West Woolwich, not a very promising choice for a political unknown, for the sitting member was the prominent and popular Tory Sir Kingsley Wood. Before the matter could be put to the test the contingency occurred against which Morrison had been hoping to provide. The Labour Party had always been short of lawyers and in 1930 the resignation on health grounds of the Solicitor General, Sir James Melvill, left a vacancy which the Prime Minister was only too delighted to ask the party's new recruit to fill. Cripps accepted and received the customary knighthood. It was now a matter of urgency to find him a seat in the House, and there was no doubt relief mixed with sadness in Westminster when the member for the safe Labour constituency at East Bristol conveniently died. The local party was understandably not happy at the idea of taking on an upper-middle-class intellectual and political novice as its representative but was finally prevailed upon to make a sacrifice for the common good. At the by-election Cripps won the seat easily, in spite of the apparent disapproval of 5,000 loyalists who refused on various grounds to turn out and vote for him.

Thus the outstandingly successful lawyer, virtually unknown to the public at large, familiar through his work at the Parliamentary Bar with the machinery of government, but in practical terms a political novice, found himself by a swift turn of fortune not merely in the House of Commons but on the front bench, and plunged almost at once into the task of drafting and piloting through all its stages, to general acclaim, a highly technical financial measure, the brain-child of the Chancellor of the Exchequer Philip Snowden, who was too ill to look after it himself.

Cripps's arrival in the House in January 1931 coincided with the first rumblings of the world-wide storm which before long toppled the government he had just joined and much else besides. When MacDonald, driven by the logic of events and his own quixotic sense of what was required of him, shattered his party by making common cause with his opponents, Cripps was abroad, recovering from an illness. Pressed by MacDonald to join the new National Government, he declined and went into opposition with the bulk of his Labour colleagues.

Within weeks his status had undergone another remarkable transformation. As a result of the election which temporarily crippled the Labour Party as a parliamentary force, Cripps became one of only 46 of its members, and one of only three occupants of the former front bench, to survive the landslide. His own majority was almost derisory—a mere 429 votes—but along with George Lansbury from Poplar, and Clement Attlee from Limehouse, Stafford Cripps from East Bristol, barely one year old as a Member of Parliament, led the opposition to the National Government for the better part of four years, until the election of 1935 allowed some of the party's stalwarts (other than those who had defected with MacDonald) to resume what they no doubt regarded as their rightful places in the front line. Neither Cripps nor Attlee was even a member of the National Executive of the Labour Party in 1931 and Cripps was scarcely known to the rank and file, but the years when, as incomparably the best mind available, he was in the forefront of so much parliamentary skirmishing soon changed all that. By 1935 he might have been a serious challenger for the leadership of the party; in the event he was some way down the path, deliberately chosen by himself, which led in 1939 to his expulsion. He was in the thick of these disagreements with many of his political colleagues when in October 1934 he

responded to the appeal of the North Wales miners to represent
them at the Gresford Inquiry. His conduct of their case, a forensic
triumph even by his own standards, occupied him concurrently
with some of his bitterest battles for political survival, which were
themselves the product of his uncompromising temperament.

For Cripps, who had already acknowledged disillusionment
with the Church as an instrument for reform, his introduction to
the working of parliamentary democracy must have been even more
disenchanting. Within a year of his entry into the Commons he and
the party through which he had presumably counted on being able
to achieve better results were reduced to almost total impotence,
crushed at every turn by the overwhelming majority on the benches
in front of them. His response, unfamiliar to those who knew him
only in the restrained surroundings of the court room, was characteristic of another side of him—impulsive, aggressive and rather
wild. It was this that began to antagonise and occasionally to alarm
his more experienced colleagues in the Labour movement, even
those well-disposed towards him, like Herbert Morrison, who was
chiefly responsible for his being there and now discovered that 'the
quixotic remarks and actions, so improbable in a man with a trained
legal mind, indicated that Cripps was not quite the unassailable
asset to the Party I had thought he would be'.[5]

The contrast between Cripps the brilliant lawyer and Cripps the
erratic politician perplexed many people to a greater extent than it
perhaps need have done. The trained legal mind was accustomed to
dealing in fact, rational argument, clear-cut decisions, and these are
poor preparation for the cloudiness, the emotional rhetoric, the
devious compromises of politics. The evidence suggests that Cripps
took a long time to discern the difference.

In a rare but illuminating reference to his Queensferry days he
described for the Gresford Inquiry one of his rooms at the explosives factory, the walls of which were covered with graphs. It
was a timely reminder that he was well qualified to cross-examine
on the techniques of management; it also pointed to his faith in the
ultimate authority of the facts, from which there could be no appeal.
This faith coloured many of his dealings with others. A former
colleague remarked of him that once he had secured an admission
from you he thought he had convinced you; and having as he
thought convinced you he expected you to behave as though you
were convinced.[6] In a legal context there might be no choice: in

politics, or in business, there might be considerations such as expediency or party loyalty which must be allowed to weigh more than intellectual conviction.

One of his biographers wrote that he was 'quick to take up any idea that seemed worthy of further consideration, and he was equally quick to modify his own in the light of criticism'.[7] This may have been true of some compartments of his life but no one could accuse him of pliancy in his politics. In the early years of his novitiate he took up certain ideas very rapidly, but far from modifying them under criticism he defended and elaborated them with an obstinacy that drove him temporarily into the wilderness.

His reading of the trend of the 1930s, reinforced by contact with the philosophy of new-found associates on the left of his party, was that the forces of reaction were in the ascendant everywhere. Their names were capitalism and fascism, and the urgent task was to confront and overthrow them. The existing social and political institutions were too deeply corrupted by them to be relied on in the coming struggle. On the other hand there was a blue-print called socialism which guaranteed a future free from all the ills and injustices of the contemporary world. No thinking man or woman, having examined it, could deny its excellence or conceivably wish to obstruct its immediate adoption, to which all men of goodwill must forthwith dedicate themselves. Those who, for their own selfish ends, did so obstruct must be told that they no longer counted and be swept aside if necessary. 'He scorns compromise plans and the long tortuous process of getting part of your own way by diplomacy and negotiation', wrote the political correspondent of the *Daily Herald* in October 1934. 'He wants to cut right through red tape, and the law's delay, and to achieve in five short years what virtually amounts to a social revolution.'[8] Like many left-wing theorists of his day he would have preferred to bring about the revolution by peaceful and constitutional means but, as he made clear in 1932, he was quite prepared in certain circumstances to countenance 'a temporary dictatorship' by a socialist ministry, but only, of course, in pursuit of the aim of 'an efficient and rapidly acting democratic machine'.[9] It was not, his apologists insist, that he favoured dictatorship or sought power for himself. He was simply a man of profound intellect and transparent honesty who had reached certain conclusions and believed he had a duty to lay them before the public unequivocally. A socialist government, he asserted, 'must not be mealy-mouthed about saying what they think'.[10]

Cripps, the recent convert to socialism, was certainly not mealy-mouthed. The official Labour Party programme at the election of 1931 had declared that the capitalist system had broken down and that socialism was the only remedy; '... banking and credit must be brought under national ownership and control, and power, transport, steel re-organised as public services ...'. Cripps's gloss on this in 1932 was that the first step for a socialist government on taking office would be to introduce an Emergency Powers Bill, wide enough to deal with attempts to foster panic, particularly by taking control of the machinery of banking and finance. It was unlikely, he wrote in a pamphlet, that a socialist party would be able to retain control without adopting some exceptional means 'such as the prolongation of the life of Parliament for a further term without an election'.[11] Accused of virtually proposing to subvert the constitution he replied that 'a change in the economic and social structure of our country ... can never be brought about under the existing parliamentary forms'.

To those, especially in the trade unions, who had struggled for years to achieve their ends, and to convince the electorate that they could be achieved, by gradual evolution through the time-honoured parliamentary machinery, this was wild and unacceptable talk and, in Walter Citrine's phrase, 'a very grave electoral handicap upon the Labour Party'.[12] Others spoke out in the same vein. 'I don't like emergency powers,' Ernest Bevin complained, 'even when they are operated by my friends.'[13]

There was a much stronger outcry in January 1934 following Cripps's forecast that when the Labour Party came to power 'we shall have to overcome opposition from Buckingham Palace and other places as well'.[14] He wriggled out of that one with an assurance that he was 'in favour of a constitutional monarchy',[15] but it sounded to some as though he might be at heart a republican. To far more observers the whole performance looked merely ridiculous, and an exasperated Hugh Dalton demanded an end to these 'streams of oratorical ineptitudes'.[16]

Throughout these years, while keeping up his law practice, and shouldering the immense burden of helping to sustain the Labour opposition in the Commons, he was devoting to the wider cause of socialism the energy and zeal he had formerly put at the service of the World Alliance of Churches, writing, speaking and organising meetings to propagate the socialist gospel. Most weekends he would visit a different part of the country, delivering speeches on Labour platforms, and it was a remarkable coincidence that in accordance with plans made some weeks earlier he was due to address the annual demonstration of the North Wales Federation of Labour Parties in the Dance Hall, Wrexham, on 29 September 1934 on the subject 'Socialism or Smash'.

He faced an audience still stunned by the calamity at Gresford and, the *Wrexham Leader* reported, 'expressed difficulty in speaking on party politics in face of the appalling disaster which had cast gloom over the whole country';[17] but there was little sign that he felt compunction about using the disaster to point a political moral. Presumably unaware or at least not having much inkling of the full extent of the situation which was to be made public at the forthcoming inquiry, he began with a conventional tribute to 'the heroes who ... in Gresford Pit had given their lives that the community might prosper', and even disclaimed any intention of blaming 'the employers as individuals' or by inference the coal owners as a class 'for the way in which they treated the workers of this country'. That the miners were unfairly treated was undeniable but the reason was that 'however anxious the employers were to give the workers a better standard of life, they had been caught up in a system which refused them that liberty'. Thousands and thousands of people were without coal because they could not afford it; but if the price of coal were reduced to a level at which people could afford it the mine owner would say he would have to 'knock the miners' wages endways', or alternatively that he must close the mine. The system must obviously be changed and the solution was to remove the mine owner from it;[18] then

> the coal could be got, and the miners would go down the mine and the wealth of the country would be increased. The miner would be paid on the same basis as the school teacher and it could be arranged that he would receive his share of the national wealth in that way.

How this programme would dispose of the problems of over-production, declining markets, uneconomic pits and over-manning which were currently at the root of the industry's sickness Cripps probably did not feel called upon to explain, but the speech must have gone down well with the miners in the audience, and it may have been the experience of listening to him which suggested to the local union leaders that here was the man they needed as their advocate in the great showdown which they hoped was about to take place.

The decision to employ Cripps was agreed to by officials of the Miners' Federation, at the request of the North Wales miners, only as a matter of urgency and when it was later reported to the full executive of the Federation, strong disapproval was expressed. The Federation, in consultation with the Secretary for Mines, had recently agreed on the form which the inquiry should take and had nominated its vice president, Joseph Jones, to sit as one of the assessors who would assist the Commissioner, Sir Henry Walker. It had apparently been assumed that following normal precedent senior officials of the Federation would represent the miners, and there was considerable opposition to the idea of turning the job over to an uninstructed outsider, especially to one of the most notoriously expensive members of the Bar. Having very little choice in the circumstances the executive agreed to make itself responsible for counsel's fees but added a warning that this must not form a precedent for future cases. Wounded vanity was soothed by the decision that Cripps and his men would represent only the North Wales Miners' Association; the Miners' Federation, as the senior body, would as usual appoint representatives to speak for the mining community as a whole. In the event the miners were able to have the best of both worlds at no additional cost because, not for the first time where workers were concerned, Cripps gave his services without fee and his juniors took only out-of-pocket expenses.

On the wider political stage Cripps's performance at the Labour Party Conference at Southport, while perhaps less disturbing to the miners than to other delegates, reinforced many doubts about him. Proposing a long series of amendments to the official party programme on behalf of the recently formed and militant Socialist League, he argued that a Labour government must secure a sufficiency of economic power to enable it to go forward with a political programme. It was impossible for the capitalist system to give workers the enlarged payments and rewards which were promised in a programme of social reforms.

> In my view, if we attempt to carry out again the policy of getting as much as we can out of the capitalist system, as we did in 1931, we shall find ourselves in a fresh crisis. We shall find that our economic power will still reside in the hands of the capitalists.[19]

The block votes of the unions disposed of the League's amendments amid 'pleasant chaff', as *The Times* reported, but there was less disposition to take lightly the League's proposals that compensation to the owners of concerns compulsorily acquired should take the form of providing income allowances for a period of years but should not include any provision for capital repayment save in working-class funds for socially useful purposes and individual cases of proven hardship. It was not so much the proposals, unlikely as they were ever to be implemented, which caused consternation, as the impression they might convey of the party from which they emanated. How could it ever go to the country with the reputation for wanting, in the words of one speaker, 'to confiscate one half to two thirds of the value of the property nationalised'? There would be a run on the banks and Labour would alienate most of its own potential supporters. The proposal was defeated by almost two million votes, the biggest majority recorded at the conference; but Cripps was for the first time elected to the party's executive committee in the constituency section and very soon showed how little the rejection of the League's programme had caused him to modify his views.

Speaking at Eastham some days later he contrasted 'the enormous atmosphere of hope for the future which was apparent in every person in Russia' (as observed by his son who had just returned from a visit) with the absence of hope in Britain, 'which was so appalling, and made one doubtful as to the future . . .'.[20] Workers in Britain had no freedom. Anyone who went about the country was constantly coming across examples among all classes, of people who had been victimised for their political opinions. At Bristol, towards the end of October, he warned that when the socialists came to power they must act quickly, 'because men like Walter Runciman were already threatening financial sabotage [and] inciting others to it'.[21] On 3 November, while the Gresford Inquiry was in progress, he told the Oxford University Labour Club that he

> could not imagine the Labour Party coming to power without a first-rate financial crisis . . . Unless they were prepared to challenge, on the very first day of the Labour government, the whole strength of capitalism, in his view it would be perfectly impossible democratically to retain power and start a programme of socialization.[22]

A week later, in Swansea, he forecast, during the first few weeks of a socialist government, 'the most acute political fight that had ever occurred in this country'.[23]

By this time the feeling that he might be something less than 'an unassailable asset to the Party' was gaining ground. The *Daily Herald* considered that he was doing nothing but injury to the cause he wished to serve and playing his opponents' game better than they played it themselves.[24] As for challenging the whole strength of capitalism in the very first days, 'it sounds just silly, and it is just silly'. This was among the more moderate comments. His aunt Beatrice Webb had by this time summed him up as 'oddly immature in intellect and unbalanced in judgment ... ignorant and reckless in his statements and proposals'.[25] To Hugh Dalton he was 'really becoming a dangerous political lunatic', always oversimplifying everything into 'the capitalists' and 'the workers'.[26] Emanuel Shinwell, looking back on the period from a distance of 40 years, dismissed Cripps as suffering from

> a degree of fanaticism and bigotry which weakened any appreciation of practical considerations or the good of all people. Ceaselessly he tried to stir up class strife and he succeeded in bringing himself and the party to which he belonged into contempt.[27]

Walter Citrine was 'perplexed to understand how a man of such legal eminence could utter such incomparable drivel', and astounded at the extreme views expressed in Socialist League publications, which seemed to him to show 'no awareness of the realities of the political world'.[28]

On the other wing of the party these and similar verdicts were seen as, in Michael Foot's words, 'a mean falsification; the people who penned them were discomfitted by [Cripps's] virtues more than his vices'.[29] At that time he was, Foot claims, the most magnetic figure in the party, and 'no one did more, in those dismal years after 1931, to revive the fighting spirit of Labour'.

This was the man who had undertaken to represent the North Wales miners at the inquiry into the Gresford disaster; and while his undoubted motive in accepting the invitation was his desire to do all he could for the miners, he must surely have relished the opportunity it provided for a demonstration, in the clearest possible terms, of the consequences for working men of the capitalist system to whose overthrow he had dedicated himself.

'Cripps ...', Michael Foot has written, 'put the coalowners in the dock at the Gresford Colliery Disaster Inquiry.' That, as will become apparent, is precisely what he did not do. But it is probably true to say that by his performance he did as much as any man to ensure that when the time arrived the coal industry would be the first to come under national ownership.

NOTES

In addition to the biographies listed in the bibliography, the following are among works in which aspects of Cripps's work and personality are discussed: Addison (1994); Jenkins (1974); Marquand (1963); Pimlott (1977); Wyatt (1985). Wyatt also contributed the entry on Cripps in *The Dictionary of National Biography* (Williams and Palmer, 1971, pp. 270–74).

1. See Wyatt (1985), p. 141: 'Stafford's intestines were always in a mess'. The consequence was the strict and fairly frugal diet which he became famous for, and led to Churchill's gibe about 'the morbid doctrine that nothing matters save an equal sharing of miseries'. Wyatt insists that Cripps's reputation for austerity and asceticism was unjustified, and Cripps himself did his best to dispel it. He wrote in *God in our Work* (1949)

> Food, housing, warmth and physical enjoyment are an essential part of our life ... human desires and appetites should rightly be satisfied ... The needs of the body must be served as well as the spirit ... it is certainly no part of the divine plan that we should hurry through the world in discomfort, poverty and disease. (p. 28)

2. Estorick (1949), p. 51.
3. Quoted in Cooke (1957), p. 90.
4. Quoted in Estorick (1949), p. 77.
5. Morrison (1960), p. 150.
6. Private communication; see also Jenkins (1974), p. 105.
7. Cooke (1957), p. 179.
8. *Daily Herald*, 1 October 1934.
9. Quoted in Cooke (1957), p. 153.
10. *Morning Post*, 8 January 1934.
11. In a pamphlet, 'Can Socialism come by Constitutional Methods?' (undated). Several other words and phrases in the present account come from the same source.
12. Article in *The New Clarion* quoted in Cooke (1957), p. 156.
13. *Daily Mail*, 4 October 1933 quoted in Cooke (1957), p. 157.
14. *The Times*, 6 January 1934.
15. *The Times*, 15 January 1934.
16. Dalton included 'a small bunch of the most choice blooms' from Cripps's

pre-war speeches in his own autobiography, *The Fateful Years*, pp. 149–51. In view of the circumstances in which the office of Chancellor of the Exchequer passed from Dalton to Cripps in 1947, Attlee's comment on Dalton is perhaps relevant: 'Perfect ass. His trouble was he *would* talk . . .' quoted in Harris (1982), p. 353.

17. *Wrexham Leader*, 5 October 1934.
18. See Appendix A.
19. *Daily Herald*, 2 October 1934.
20. *The Times*, 16 October 1934.
21. *The Times*, 27 October 1934.
22. *The Times*, 5 November 1934.
23. *The Times*, 12 November 1934.
24. *Daily Herald*, 3 November 1934.
25. Webb (1956), p. 303.
26. Dalton (1957), p. 41.
27. Shinwell (1973), p. 132.
28. Citrine (1964), p. 293.
29. Foot (1962), p. 156.

CHAPTER 8

The Working Mine

The coal industry was front page news so often in the 1920s and 1930s, and especially in 1926, when the whole nation was drawn into its struggles, that even a man so wholly absorbed in his own professional commitments as Cripps could scarcely fail to acquire at least a nodding acquaintance with its problems, but there seems little reason to suppose that up to this time he had interested himself in them particularly. The explosives factory at Queensferry was on the very edge of the North Wales coalfield, a dozen or so miles from Gresford Colliery, and even nearer to some of the Flintshire pits, but his preoccupation with sulphur can have left him little time for studying coal or anything else. His uncle by marriage, Sydney Webb, was an authority on the subject, having been one of the miners' chosen lay representatives on the Sankey Commission of 1919, and was presumably able to provide him with some background information. His own arrival in Parliament occurred too late for him to have heard the debates on the 1930 Coal Bill, and almost from the time he set foot in the House until the change of government 10 months later his energies were devoted to the complicated and demanding Land Tax Bill.

After the election of 1931 the circumstances changed. In the landslide that engulfed Labour only the most massive majorities ensured survival, and they were to be found almost by definition in areas of old-established major industry—South Wales, Lancashire, the West Riding, the North East, Glasgow. The extent of the catastrophe for Labour can be judged by the fact that even mining constituencies were not safe. In Barnsley, the headquarters of the Yorkshire Mine Workers' Association, the sitting Labour member, a checkweighman and treasurer of the Association, was thrown out in favour of a Liberal National timber merchant. This was a somewhat unusual result, and the most notable feature of the new House was that of the 46 members of the Labour Party and six of the Independent Labour Party at least 21 were miners—agents, checkweighmen, union officials—or, like Aneurin Bevan, had left the industry because of ill health. Six of them had been junior ministers in the outgoing government or in the Labour administration of 1924; one had been a whip. By contrast, of the 556 supporters of the National Government, 472 of them Conservatives, only two, according to *The Times* guide, admitted to a direct practical acquaintance with the industry: a mining engineer from Preston and a coal merchant from Sunderland. Eight were directors of colliery companies, and there were numerous directors of public utility companies which depended on coal. One Liberal, Isaac Foot, had briefly been Secretary for Mines in the short-lived National Government which preceded the general election.

In the new House of Commons, therefore, as one of a triumvirate of all-purpose leaders, Cripps would be in constant contact with the mining contingent which made up almost half of the remnant of an army behind him and must have considerably improved his understanding of the coal industry and its problems, which occupied, in the opinion of some observers, a disproportionate amount of parliamentary time. The comprehensive mastery of its technicalities with which he astonished the inquiry and threw the Gresford management into disarray was presumably put together with his customary dedication and skill in the period between his meeting the miners in Southport and the opening of the proceedings in Wrexham.[1] He was certainly well briefed by Cyril Jones, the North Wales miners' solicitor, and probably also by David ('Dai') Grenfell, the Member for Gower, a miners' agent himself, and a future Secretary for Mines in the wartime coalition government, who sat by his side throughout the inquiry.

Among the first things he would learn was that, with the exception of great disasters such as Gresford which temporarily distort the statistical pattern, explosions formed only a very small part of the total number of accidents in the mines. According to Joseph Jones, writing in 1936, lives lost by explosions accounted for little more than five per cent of the total death toll, whereas 90 per cent were caused by falls of rock, accidents on the haulage or in the shaft, and mishaps in a variety of other places, including on the surface. The figures for Lancashire and North Wales in 1933 bear this out: there were two deaths from firedamp, 61 from roof falls, 22 from miscellaneous causes and five on the surface. Mining was one of the most hazardous of occupations. In 1932, of just over 800,000 men employed, 907 met with a fatal accident, a death rate of 1.11

per 1,000. The nearest comparable figure was 0.77 per 1,000, for shipping. In factories of all kinds there were 540 accidents among 4 million workers, a rate of 0.11 per 1,000. In addition, 130,000 men were injured more or less seriously in the mines. There were more killed and injured in the mines every year, Jones asserted in a comparison which at that time still had some emotional significance for his readers, than the casualties of the Gallipoli Expeditionary Force. Most of them were picked off in ones and twos in the incidents, including minor explosions, which were the daily accompaniment of life and work in the pits. In 1932, the Miners' Federation claimed, one man in every five working in the mines was injured. Every working day an average of 450 were injured and five were killed.

Nevertheless it was, not surprisingly, the huge explosion, wiping out so many men almost literally in a flash, which made the most vivid impact on the public imagination and it was probably the comforting belief, nourished by official pronouncements, that such wholesale slaughter was a thing of the past which gave Gresford its power to shock. No comparable disaster had occurred for more than 20 years, and few people living could remember the days when it would have been a very much more common event.

Between 1850 and the nationalisation of the mines in 1947 there were upwards of 20 explosions, in each of which more than a hundred men were killed.[2] The unenviable record for the highest number of deaths is held by Senghenydd, where 439 died in the disaster of 1913. Only three years previously 344 had been killed in the Hulton Pit in Lancashire, a figure surpassed in 1866 at the Oaks Colliery in Yorkshire where the death toll was 361. Two disasters in South Wales, at Abercwm in 1878, and Albion in 1894, accounted for 268 and 278 deaths respectively, leaving Gresford in sixth place in this dishonourable league table. In September 1934 the *Colliery Guardian*, perhaps with a view to mitigating the horror aroused by Gresford, pointed out that the average annual death rate from explosions had dropped from 0.65 per 1,000 employed during the decade 1873–82 to 0.06 for the decade 1923–32. Since 1934 the only disaster of comparable magnitude has occurred at the William Pit in Cumberland where 104 men lost their lives in 1947.

The large-scale explosion was not necessarily, as might be assumed, the consequence of the development of the larger and deeper pits, although inevitably increasing size had some bearing on the number of casualties. It was the scale and frequency of explosions in the smaller pits of the late eighteenth and early nineteenth centuries which, by touching the consciences and arousing the spirit of inquiry in scientists, philanthropists and ultimately politicians, led to the earliest attempts to legislate for safety in mines.

There was no mystery about the agent which gave rise to explosions. Coal gives off gas, known to miners as 'firedamp'.[3] Firedamp consists chiefly of carburetted hydrogen, also commonly known as methane, or marsh gas. When mixed with pure air in the proportion of not less than five per cent and not more than about 14 per cent it is explosive, the most dangerous level being about 10 per cent. Some coal seams produce more firedamp than others, and generally speaking the deeper the mine the greater will be the quantity of firedamp, which may be given off at great pressure. R. L. Galloway, the annalist of the coal industry, tells of a newly-sunk pit in North Wales which he does not identify in which 'the noise made by the gas issuing from ... the coal was so loud as to prevent men hearing each other speak'.[4] Redmayne asserted that the volume of firedamp given off in a large and well-ventilated colliery frequently amounted to more than two million cubic feet in 24 hours.[5]

The best defence against dangerous concentrations of firedamp is good ventilation which, reaching all parts of the mine, not only renews the air which the men breathe but disperses the gas, diluting it in the main current of air and dislodging it from pockets and crannies, particularly in the roof where, being lighter than air, it tends to collect. The deeper the mine, the further the working face from the shaft bottom, the more complex and convoluted the airways and roadways, the more difficult becomes the task of ventilation. Air, drawn through the mine by a fan, will take the shortest route available, bypassing areas into which it is not forced by doors or brattices. If passageways are too narrow, not constantly opened out against the constricting pressures from above and below, the air currents are slowed down. In spaces which are wide, as at the coalface when the loosened coal has been cleared but the roof above the previous day's working has not yet been brought down, the air will again slow down and perhaps fail to flush out any gas that may be lurking in the goaf, or waste.

The various regulations concerning ventilation incorporated in the Coal Mines Act of 1911 were designed to ensure as far as possible that dangerous amounts of gas should not build up unperceived. It was provided that 'an adequate amount of ventilation shall be constantly produced in every mine to dilute and render harmless inflammable and noxious gases ...'; that 'in every mine the quantity of air in the main current and in every split ... shall at least once in every month be measured and entered in a book to be kept for the purpose at the mine'; that the owner, agent or manager should keep in the office at the mine 'a separate plan showing the system of ventilation at the mine, and in particular the general direction of the currents, the points where the quantity of air is measured, and the principal devices for the regulation and distribution of the air'. It was expressly forbidden to 'waft' gas, that is, simply to fan it from one place to another where it might still remain undispersed by the air current.

'An adequate amount of ventilation' was an unspecific phrase, perhaps deliberately left so, since no two mines were alike, but the permissible amount of gas was specified precisely. 'A place shall not be deemed to be in a fit state for working or passing therein if the air contains either less than 19 per cent of oxygen or more than 1 + per cent of carbon monoxide ...'; and again: '... a place shall be deemed dangerous if the percentage of gas in the general body of the air is 2½ or upwards'.

The action to be taken in these circumstances was unambiguously defined: 'If at any time it is found that by reason of the prevalence of inflammable and noxious gases ... any place in the mine is dangerous, every workman shall be withdrawn from the mine or place found dangerous ...'.

A potentially explosive mixture of firedamp and air still requires a source of heat to make it explode, and early legislation concerned itself largely with eliminating the most likely sources, such as matches and smoking materials and the naked lights used by the miners to pierce the total darkness of their working places. Davy's safety lamp worked on the principle that although gases will pass through a piece of gauze, flame will not: if firedamp came into contact with the flame of the lamp it would burn in the form of a very small explosion which could not ignite gas outside the lamp; at the same time the blue 'cap' which formed above the carefully adjusted flame of the lamp was itself a warning of the presence of gas. A number of explosions are credited to damaged safety lamps or to lamps which, having gone out, were opened for relighting at the coalface instead of being taken to a safe place.

Shot firing was a prolific source of mishaps until the practice of using gunpowder was forbidden and a range of 'permitted' explosives was developed, together with stringent rules governing the use of them, especially the very careful testing for gas in the immediate area of the hole which was drilled to take the cartridge. The new explosives proved a blessing in more ways than one. 'The last gunpowder pit I inspected,' one report commented, 'the fumes were so thick and blinding that the man lost his way, and we had some difficulty in finding it again.'

The introduction of electricity into mines was looked at askance by many miners because of the tendency of electrical apparatus to produce sparks which could ignite firedamp. Equipment was specially designed so as to exclude the likelihood as far as was possible, and the regulations provided that

> if at any time in any place in the mine the percentage of inflammable gas in the general body of the air ... is found to exceed one and a quarter per cent, the electrical current shall at once be cut off from all cables and electrical apparatus

and it must remain off until the gas had been cleared.

Electricity did not trouble the Victorian miner, who had yet to be introduced to it, but there was widespread dismay and perplexity when the other measures designed to improve the circulation of air in the mine and reduce the possibility of explosion appeared to be failing. While some experts pinned their hopes on even stricter interpretation and application of the safety regulations, others looked for an as yet unrecognised source of danger. The culprit, they suspected and subsequently proved, was coal dust. It was the presence of this innocuous-looking material in ever-increasing quantities, as mines became larger and production methods were speeded up, which could turn a small localised explosion into a holocaust that could destroy a whole pit and every living thing in it.

Many men contributed to the investigations which led to an understanding of this phenomenon, including Sir William Garforth, a Yorkshire mine owner, William Galloway, Henry Hall, for many years the inspector in charge of the Lancashire and North Wales division, and Sir Richard Redmayne, during whose reign as Chief Inspector of Mines responsibility for research into the subject was taken over by the government and carried on first at Eskmeals on the Cumbrian coast and later at the Safety in Mines Research

Station at Buxton.[6] From here there was issued in 1934, the year of the Gresford disaster, a series of anonymous, lucidly written and strikingly illustrated pamphlets under the title *What Every Mining Man Should Know*, which gave a clear account of the nature of firedamp explosions and of the contribution made to their severity by the presence of coal dust.

Once an explosive mixture had been ignited at any point, the writer explained, the flame would spread in all directions through the explosive gas, gathering strength as it went, and raising a cloud of dust because of the strong wind it made. Coal dust in a pile is difficult to ignite because there is not enough air in it, 'but if it is blown into a cloud so that it mixes with air, then it can be made to explode like gas'. The explosion, begun in the gas by some cause or other, now has another explosive substance to feed on, becoming infinitely more violent, reaching more parts of the mine, setting fire to anything that will burn, and releasing great quantities of carbon monoxide, or afterdamp, which kills almost instantly anything left alive by the explosion.

Here was the explanation of the calamities which had struck so many mines with such grievous loss of life in the last quarter of the nineteenth century. Not all mines produce equal quantities of firedamp—in some coalfields it does not occur at all—but even a moderately 'fiery' mine, in the official phrase, could be turned into a raging furnace by coal dust, which would be manufactured in larger and larger amounts as machines took over from hands the job of prising loose and transporting the coal. Not only did machine cutting produce more dust, which was then blown off the conveyor belts by air currents and spilled at junctions, but with the height-ened pace of working, tubs were banged together more often and more violently, spilling part of their load, and

> the more a coal is crushed by the trampling of men and by the wheels of tubs, the finer does the dust become, and the greater is its explosiveness. The finer dusts are more easily blown into a cloud, the cloud settles more slowly, and the flame of an explosion flashes more quickly through the cloud ...

Fortunately for the survival of the industry a discovery, ranked by some authorities as equal in importance to Davy's work on the safety lamp, provided an antidote. Sir William Garforth showed that a mixture of coal dust and inert stone dust could greatly reduce the force of an explosion and even, in the right proportions, prevent it altogether. Stone dust itself will not burn; if, therefore, a source of heat reaches a mixture of coal and stone dust the stone absorbs some of the heat, reducing the amount available for the coal and preventing it from catching fire and exploding. Different coals, it was discovered, needed different quantities of stone dust to make them safe, and regulations were made, stipulating that enough dust should be spread through the mine to ensure that 'the dust on the floor, roof and sides of roadways shall not contain more than 50 per cent of combustible matter'. As with the air current, regular sampling and analysis was required, and the keeping of records. The regulations were made in 1920 and, the writer of the pamphlet remarked,

> have been willingly obeyed by mine managers, for they are convinced that they are protecting both their men and the pit by spreading the dust ... Since stone dusting came into force, there has been no serious coal dust explosion in any British pit treated with the required amount of stone dust.

Having mastered these elementary principles governing the safe operation of coal mines in general, Sir Stafford Cripps would wish to know how they related to the North Wales coalfield and to Gresford Colliery in particular. He would at once discover that they were most pertinent.

From early times some coalfields had suffered more from firedamp than others, among the worst affected being those in the Flintshire area of North Wales. The opening of pits at Mostyn on the Dee estuary[7] gave rise to difficulties described in a paper by Roger Mostyn, the son of the owner, which was read to the Royal Society in 1677 and printed in the *Philosophical Transactions*.[8] His account is so colourful and provides such a striking picture of the early mining environment that it deserves quotation at length.

The problems began some time in the 1640s. While developing a new pit the miners were troubled by firedamp.

> ... after they had gone a considerable way under the ground, and were scant of wind, the Fire-damp did by little and little begin to breed, and to appear in crevisses [sic] and slits in the Cole ... with a small blewish flame working and moving continually, but not out of its first seal, unless the workmen came and held their Candle to it and then, being weak the blaze of the Candle would drive it, with a sudden fizz, to another Crevess [sic] ...

This was the first time the men had encountered the phenomenon and they 'made a sport of it, and so partly neglected it', until it struck back at them.

> ... upon a morning the first Collier that went down, going forwards with
> his Candle in his hand the damp presently darted out violently at his
> Candle, that it struck the man clear down, singed all his hair and clothes
> and disabled him for working for a while after ...

Heeding this warning the miners treated their adversary more
circumspectly until they had 'wrought the Cole down to the
bottom', after which there were no sightings of firedamp for some
30 years.

It was in 1675 that having discovered a profitable though more
than usually sulphurous 'Roach of Cole' some three-and-a-half
yards thick they began to sink a pit into it about 32 yards down.
The firedamp made many appearances, 'flushing and darting from
side to side of the Pit, and shewing Rainbow-colour-like on the
surface of the water at the bottom', but the movement of air as the
men worked dispersed it and it did no damage. Not so, however, in
an adjacent pit where it reappeared in such quantities that they
could see it 'flashing and shooting from side to side like Sword
blades cross one another, that none durst go down into the pit'.
When tying candles to a pole and holding them over the top of the
shaft did no good—'the Damp would flie up in a long sharp flame
and put out the Candles'—they bound more candles to the hook
that went down on the haulage rope into the pit, but

> up comes the Damp in a full body, blows out the Candles ... burneth a
> great part of the men's hair, beards and clothes and strikes down one of
> them, in the meantime making a noise like the lowing and roaring of a
> Bull, but lowder, and in the end leaving a smoke and smell behind it
> worse than a Carrion.

All work now stopped for three days, Mostyn informed the
Royal Society, giving them the first known description of a pit
explosion:

> ... then the Steward went down and took two men along with him ... he
> was no sooner down but the rest of the Workmen, disdaining to be left
> there in such a time of danger, hasted down with them, and one of them
> more undiscreet than the rest went headlong with his Candle over the Eye
> of the damp-Pit, at which the Damp immediately catched and flew to and
> fro over all the hollows of the work, with a great wind and a continual fire,
> and as it went, keeping up a mighty roaring noise on all sides. The men at
> first appearance of it had most of them fallen on their faces, and hid
> themselves as well as they could in the loose sleck or small Cole, and
> under the shelter of posts; yet nevertheless the Damp ... came up with
> incredible force, the Wind and Fire tore off most of their clothes off their

backs ... the blast falling so sharp on their skin, as if they had been whipped with Rods; some that had least shelter were carried 15 or 16 yards from their first station and beaten against the roof of the Coal [sic], and sides of the posts, and lay afterwards a good while senseless ... As it drew up to the Day-pit, it caught one of the men along with it that was next the Eye, and up it comes with such a terrible crack, not unlike but more shrill than a Canon, that it was heard fifteen miles off along with the Wind, and such a pillar of Smoke as darkened all the sky over head for a good while: The brow of the Hill above the Pit was 18 yards high, and on it grew Trees 14 and 15 yards long, yet the mans Body and other things from the Pit were seen above the tops of the highest Trees at least a hundred yards ...

The date of the calamity is given precisely as 3 February 1675, 'being a Season when all other Damps are scarce felt or heard of'.

If this was the first spectacular disaster to strike the Mostyn pits, as seems probable, it was by no means the last.[9] They continued to be plagued by accidents and in the early nineteenth century at least seven more explosions occurred, two of which accounted for 50 deaths between them.

Mostyn had no monopoly of disaster. There were explosions at various times in Flintshire, at Hope, Hawarden, Bagillt, Eyton (nine or 11 killed, 11 injured), Mold, Holywell and Buckley; in Denbighshire, at Ruabon, several times including three in three years, Brymbo, Minera, and no doubt other places which failed to get into the records.

With the appointment of government inspectors, who began the uphill task of instilling better working methods, there was a slight but steady improvement marred only by one or two explosions of more than usual gravity, the worst of which occurred at Brynmally Colliery in 1889, when 20 men lost their lives, most probably it seemed because some among them had attempted to relight their lamps in the presence of gas. Ten years later the inspector for Lancashire and North Wales was able to announce in his annual report that although firedamp was as frequent as ever, there had not been a fatal explosion of either firedamp or coal dust in this division in 1898, and the past seven years had been a record, with only two lives lost.

The next and, until Gresford, the only other serious accident in North Wales was the explosion at Llay Main in 1924. In 1928 the inspector for the division, who had known it since it was reshaped in pre-war days, was able once again to report a complete absence of explosions. It was, he added, the third occasion since the division was formed, and the seventh year without loss of life (from explosions—there were 150 deaths from other causes in North Wales alone), and reflected credit on those responsible for ventilation and stone dusting of mines.

On the debit side, he commented that more generous application of inert dust was in many cases desirable and that firedamp was frequently found in quantities that necessitated the cessation of work.

These and similar observations made available to Cripps seemed to suggest no serious deficiencies in the management of collieries in the coalfield, but as he mastered the theoretical background to the subject of explosions and the comprehensive provisions of the Coal Mines Act of 1911, still the ultimate authority for the industry, and as he read the preliminary statements of men who were willing or might be prevailed upon to give evidence about working conditions in the Dennis Section of Gresford Colliery, he cannot have regretted his decision to represent the North Wales miners at the forthcoming inquiry. Here in vivid detail was a portrait of one corner of the capitalist system at work, and with his customary assiduity he set himself to master its complexities. When the inquiry opened in Church House, Wrexham, on 25 October he was one of the best-informed and best-equipped men in the room. Peter Lee, the Durham miners' leader who watched him at work throughout the early part of the inquiry, went further: 'Sir Stafford Cripps is the best miner of us all.'

NOTES

1. According to Sir Geoffrey Wilson, the most junior member of Cripps's team, 'Sir Stafford arrived in Wrexham the night before the enquiry [sic] opened without, as far as anybody knew, any detailed knowledge of the technical side of mining'; quoted in Estorick (1949), p. 134; see also Strauss (1943), p. 77. This rather heavily qualified statement carries some suggestion of legend rather than probability, but is supported by Wyatt, who had worked with Cripps, and credited him with 'one of the most acute minds of his generation. He could rapidly comprehend complicated matters so that within a few hours he would understand almost as much of them as the experts' (see p. 73, Notes).

2. Various lists of major explosions exist. The most comprehensive is National

Coal Board (1978), which includes the great majority of incidents from 1850 onwards, classifying them under headings such as 'Explosions—attributed mainly to fire-damp' and so on. The year 1850 was the first for which, following the passing of the Act, formal reports were prepared by inspectors. Another section of the pamphlet lists accidents before 1850, compiled from other, mostly governmental sources. Boyd (1879) includes a 'List of Colliery Explosions entailing the loss of Six lives and upwards from 1850 onwards', pp. 248–50. Duckham and Duckham (1973) have a list of 'the principal mining disasters from 1705 to 1966', pp. 202–09.

3. See note 7 to Chapter 3. The word 'damp' does not, in this context, denote 'moisture', but is derived from the German *Dampf*, which in the plural means 'fumes'.

4. Galloway (1971), Vol. 2, p. 23.

5. Redmayne (1942), p. 159.

6. *Ibid.*, pp. 160–61.

7. *History of the British Coal Industry*, Vol. I, p. 132.

8. A Relation of some strange phenomena, accompanied with mischievous effects in a Cole-work in Flint-shire, sent March 31, 1677, to the Reverend and eminently Learned Dr Bathurst, Dean of Bath and Wells, by an Ingenious Gentleman, Mr Roger Mostyn, of the Inner Temple, who, at the said Doctor's request, obtained it from his Father's Steward, and Overseer of his Cole-works, who was upon the place when the thing was done; the same Mr. Mostyn, being also assured of it from his Father, Sr [sic] Roger Mostyn, Lord of the Mannor [sic], and several others who were Eye-witnesses.

Philosophical Transactions, 25 June 1677, Number 136.

This paper is quoted at some length by Galloway (1971) but in a somewhat garbled version which mars the vigour and colour of the narrative. The whole is well worth reading.

9. See Rogers (1963–73), Vol. 15, p. 135: 'So frequent were the explosions at the Mostyn collieries that the *Chester Chronicle*, by no means a champion of the colliers, accused the owners of "passively leaving their miners to the effects of ignorance and prejudice" ' (*Chester Chronicle*, 1 July 1842).

CHAPTER 9

The Inquiry

The commission appointed to inquire into this Welsh disaster was exclusively English and even more narrowly north-eastern English, consisting of two Yorkshiremen and a Durham-born man who had spent a lifetime in Yorkshire.[1]

The Commissioner was the Chief Inspector of Mines, Sir Henry Walker CBE LLD. Born in 1873 at Saltburn on Sea, he had joined the Inspectorate after studying mining at Newcastle-upon-Tyne, was appointed to the office of Chief Inspector in 1924, the year in which he investigated the accident at Llay Main Colliery, and received his knighthood in 1928.

It was not axiomatic that he should conduct the inquiry and there was some pressure for the appointment of an independent chairman. When the matter was raised in the House shortly after the inquiry had begun the Secretary for Mines replied to a private notice question with an assurance that the constitution of the court had been settled in consultation with, and in accordance with the wishes of, the Miners' Federation of Great Britain. The questioner may have feared that the Commissioner and the department he represented might be prejudiced against the miners, and as time went by the suspicion hardened into a certainty on the miners' side that they were; but for the moment they had to be content with a further assurance from the Minister that the Federation was at liberty to bring forward as witnesses any workmen whose evidence it thought likely to advance the cause of the inquiry.

By the time the hearing was concluded even the Commissioner himself may have wished that he had handed the job over to someone else. Not only did it drag on for the greater part of two years but his conduct of it was frequently under attack, and for reasons which he must have foreseen his position was at times made almost untenable.

No inquiry into the deaths of 265 men is likely to be a routine affair but in spite of the great publicity surrounding the accident and the suggestions in the press of dramatic disclosures to be expected, the authorities seem to have been not wholly aware what they were in for. Church House, Wrexham, the building chosen for the sessions, was barely adequate to accommodate the officials, the witnesses and their representatives, the press and all the local people, chiefly miners, who wanted to listen to the proceedings. It was booked for a bare fortnight, which may have been thought sufficient or perhaps was the longest period available. By the sixteenth day, however, the court was scarcely halfway through Part 1 of an inquiry which had been planned to extend to three parts, and the whole operation was adjourned for ten days and then transferred to the ballroom of a local hotel where facilities for officials and space for the public were even more restricted.

In these cramped conditions, with wretched weather outside— one observer noted the melting snow which slid in melancholy fashion from the roof all through one session—tempers already frayed by a month of waiting, rumour, recrimination and animosity snapped easily. Tension was high and the Commissioner had at least once to threaten to have the room cleared if the jeers and clapping from the public seats continued. A notable incident, epitomising the hostility between the miners and the management, occurred when a deputy, asked if he would be 'surprised to hear' that some men had been forced to crawl along an airway where they should have been able to walk upright, replied acidly, 'I wouldn't be surprised to hear anything, the way many of these men are being paid to give evidence.' Uproar broke out and grew worse when the questioner, representing the miners, suggested that the deputy might want to withdraw the insinuation and received the reply, 'I don't want to withdraw anything.' When order was restored the Commissioner gave instructions for the passage to be deleted from the official record but there was nothing to prevent the press from reporting it in full, and most newspapers carried it verbatim. Moreover the point of expunging it from the record was lost completely when, on the following day, Cripps was allowed to begin the proceedings by explaining that money *had* been paid to witnesses but that it was a travel and subsistence allowance varying from 1s.6d. to 2s.6d. a day for men who had to come long distances and spend a long time at the inquiry.[2]

The deputy's comment was perhaps a *quid pro quo* for the insinuation made repeatedly by the miners' representatives that while the men had been thrown out of work by the accident and left to live on unemployment benefit, the management of the colliery had taken care of the officials by inventing jobs and posts for them as look-out men, land sales representatives and so on as a subterfuge for keeping them on the payroll. After a series of questions had been put along these lines in cross-examination, counsel for the management intervened to assure the Commissioner that nothing underhand was taking place and that it was 'the inevitable practice when a colliery is temporarily stopped and there is a prospect that it will shortly be re-opened'. The wider implication which the Chief Inspector professed not to perceive, was that the newly-created jobs were simply bribes to induce the deputies to give false evidence in favour of the management.

Pressed to say whether or not questions put to the deputies on the subject should or should not be allowed, the Commissioner took refuge behind a statement of policy which goes a long way to explain why the first stages of the inquiry were so wearisomely protracted and why there was later felt to be some truth in the allegation that it had not been an impartial investigation:

> I like everybody to get everything off their chest which they want to get off, but it's a little difficult, and when I come to read the notes I must put on one side all that I think is irrelevant. But I let it go on in the hope that I shall get something out of it when I do read the notes.

Some of the witnesses must have reflected ruefully on the mauling they were subjected to because of the Commissioner's affable wish to see everyone 'get everything off their chest'. Not the least among the offenders were the learned counsel who were able more than once to lead witnesses in a way which, as each took pleasure in demonstrating when accusing the other of a more than usually glaring lapse, would not have been allowed in a court of law.

More serious perhaps than the Commissioner's occasional maladroitness in handling the combatants was the evident ambiguity of his dual role as chairman of a tribunal and as Chief Inspector of Mines in an inquiry into an accident in which the part played by his Inspectorate was a key issue. Wearing one hat he had access to information concerning the state of the mine after the accident which was being made available to only one side in the inquiry, namely the management, but which was crucial to the case being argued by the other. How should he, when wearing the other hat, deal with this information? On one occasion, acknowledging that 'all through these operations I have been engaged at Gresford Colliery in a capacity other than Commissioner', he was adamant that everything he learnt in that capacity could only be discussed at private meetings between himself and counsel; on another occasion he insisted that as Commissioner he had 'no intention of taking any notice' of what he knew as Chief Inspector, but even counsel for the owners felt obliged to point out that this was an impossibility.

> You, in your position as the Inspector, have access to a good deal of information. It would be absurd ... if you were to divide yourself in some way and say 'I must close my eyes and must not look at the report I get ... I must close my eyes to the knowledge I have as Chief Inspector, and must deal with this matter only on the evidence taken in the way dictated by [counsel for the miners]'. Do not let it be thought that the owners acquiesced or agreed in such a course.

His discomfort was raised to its most acute pitch at a later stage of the inquiry when, as Commissioner, he had to listen to an excoriating denunciation by Cripps of the department for which, as Chief Inspector, he was responsible; but that story must be told in its proper place.

The Commissioner's problems were not eased by the fact that the two assessors appointed to assist him with their expert interpretation of the matters raised were, by virtue of their respective offices, unlikely to agree with him or with each other. Joseph Jones CBE JP, the miners' nominee, was general secretary of the Yorkshire Mine Workers' Association, vice president of the Miners' Federation of Great Britain, and author of a book with the bitterly punning title *The Coal Scuttle*. The owners' choice was John Brass, a Durham man who after managing mines in Durham and Yorkshire and holding commissions in the army and the special police during the war had become managing director of Houghton Main Colliery Company, and who, in the words of the *Colliery Year Book*, was 'one of the most prominent figures in the South Yorkshire coal mining industry'. In addition to his membership of a bewildering diversity of committees and boards he was president of the Institute of Mining Engineers and a member of the central committee of the Mining Association of Great Britain, the owners' counterpart to the Miners' Federation. Neither Jones nor Brass made a significant contribution to the conduct of the inquiry; when it was over both disagreed categorically with Walker's conclusions for opposite reasons and wrote reports of their own.

Almost all the parties with a strong interest in the outcome of the investigation appointed representatives to watch events and, if necessary, intervene on their behalf. The colliery managers and the colliery deputies, at both national and local level, nominated the secretaries of their Associations. The owners of the colliery put themselves in the beginning in the hands of a KC, Mr A. T. Miller, who had as his junior Mr Hartley Shawcross, then a young member of the Liverpool circuit. Miller proved to be no match for Cripps and quietly disappeared from the scene towards the end of the second week after a somewhat plaintive protest over Cripps's methods of cross-examination had misfired. Thereafter the full load of responsibility for protecting the owners' interests lay with Shawcross, whose more bellicose style occasionally drew protests from Cripps, himself no novice in the art of aggression. A memorable and widely reported example of Shawcross's technique occurred during his cross-examination of a miner who claimed to have detected gas in his part of the mine some weeks before the accident. Had he, asked Shawcross, reported it to anybody? Yes, the man replied, to one of the deputies, who had died in the explosion.

'Did you report it to anyone who is alive now and can tell us whether or not you did?'

Cripps was on his feet at once. 'Really, this is a most offensive question of my learned friend's ... put purposely in an offensive manner.'

'I don't know if my friend has finished', Shawcross remarked, and put the question in much the same form again.

Although a great improvement on the hapless Miller, he was by no means as well briefed as Cripps. Trying to establish how many men on an average worked on a coalface 40 yards long he was getting evasive and contradictory answers, and when taunted with 'not knowing much about it' agreed candidly 'I don't know *anything* about it.'

He was further at a disadvantage in that he fought single-handed on behalf of the owners, whereas Cripps had two lieutenants who stood in for him when smaller fry were in the chair or when one of his many commitments required his presence elsewhere. The more junior of them, Mr (later Sir) Geoffrey Wilson, played only a minor role; the senior, Arthur Henderson, was frequently in the limelight but proved on the whole a poor substitute for his distinguished leader. The son of 'Uncle Arthur' Henderson, the much loved general secretary of the Labour Party, he had like his father sat as a Member of Parliament until the election of 1931 which had cost both of them their seats. He returned to Parliament in 1935 and after a period of wartime service on the General Staff held office successively as Under-Secretary for War, Financial Secretary to the War Office, Under-Secretary for India and Secretary of State for Air before going to the Lords as a life peer with the title Lord Rowley in 1966, two years before his death. In spite of this impressive record, which failed to secure him a place in Harold Wilson's government in 1964, a colleague recalled him at the Gresford Inquiry as 'a silly little man', a verdict supported by passages of the transcript of evidence which show him easily thrown out of his stride, pettishly aggressive in a pale and misguided imitation of his leader, and inclined, through not having done his homework, to find himself in false positions from which he could only make an ignominious retreat.

The triumvirate of Cripps, Henderson and Wilson and their unofficial aide David Grenfell represented only the men from North Wales. The Miners' Federation of Great Britain sent two men of their own to observe and ask questions. The elder and more picturesque was Peter Lee, known, because of a strong and perhaps carefully cultivated resemblance, as 'Old Shakespeare'. Commemorated today by the new town that bears his name, Peter Lee was in every sense the grand old man of the Durham coalfield. Now in his seventy-first year, he had first gone down the pit at the age of ten, working ten hours a day, and in the next ten years worked at 26 pits before deciding to go back to school to remedy his defective education. In those days he was known as a fighter fond of his ale, but after a brief experience of trade union work and protracted absences in the United States and the gold mines of South Africa, during which he left a wife and four children behind in Britain, he returned to Durham and at the age of 35 became a reformed character, religious, sober, serious, dedicated to the service of the community at large and the Methodist Church and the Durham miners in particular. Virtually unknown outside the county until he was 40, he became a national figure in the 1920s when aspects of his work for social welfare as a leading member of Durham County Council made him temporarily the target for a campaign of press vilification. From 1919 he held office in the Durham Miners' Association, became general secretary in 1928, and in the year preceding Gresford was president of the Miners' Federation. Although much weakened by illness and a quarter of a century of unremitting public service he was still an impressive and for those days unusual sight, as his friend and biographer Jack Lawson recalled him—six feet two in height with long curling hair, great eyes, imperial beard and ample forehead. He took a hand in the inquiry occasionally, questioning witnesses in his slow deliberate fashion, expressing shocked disapproval at the state of affairs being revealed, but was content to let the main burden of the work fall on his colleague Joseph Hall JP, who clearly revelled in it.

Like the Commissioner and one of the assessors, Hall was a Yorkshireman. An uncouth, coarse man, he was financial secretary of the Yorkshire Mine Workers' Association and a colleague of Joseph Jones. He had crossed swords at many an inquiry with Sir Henry Walker who, towards the end of the long haul of Gresford, wrote in exasperation to an acquaintance, 'Hall is a buffoon, neither more nor less!' Cross-examination for him took the form of either abusive bullying of the witness or of attempts to do the Commissioner's work for him by anticipating the outcome of the inquiry. Disputes between the two men were a regular feature of the hearings. 'All right, I don't want any harangue from you,' said Walker, after an outburst from Hall. 'I don't want any either,' Hall retorted: 'It's the first time I've got up this morning.' Arguing with a witness about the practice of two men firing shots on one face at the same time Hall asked, 'You've seen the results that have taken place at Gresford, haven't you?'

'Yes, sir.'

The Commissioner broke in. 'What exactly does that mean?'

'That means this, sir,' Hall responded in typically prolix style, 'that after the evidence that has been proved up to now about shot firing, it's proving this, that if there's a practice made of it throughout the mines of this country, then this country must expect bigger blows as far as explosions are concerned than what they have done in the past. That's what it means.'

'Really you've come to a conclusion as to what caused this explosion.'

'I've not come to any conclusion at all.'

'You say it's "proved" something.'

'I say this, that the object of this inquiry—'

'I know what the object is,' said the Commissioner testily. A few minutes later he was dismissing one of Hall's questions as 'non-sensical'.

Throughout the inquiry Walker was given constant reminders that in venturing as far as Wrexham he was on foreign soil. Witnesses used technical terms that were strange to him—'pyches', meaning tubs of coal, 'banjack', the local name for a compressed air boring machine—and he used terms that were strange to them. Putting questions to a fireman about roof supports he referred to a 'cog'. The representative for the National Association of Colliery Managers suspected that all was not well.

'The Commissioner asked you if you had ever seen a cog put up on top of timber in a big fall; did you understand what was meant by a "cog"?'

'A chock.'

Harris turned to the Commissioner. 'Might I say, sir, that I think we should talk our own language. Terms are being used here that our men don't understand.'

'I agree,' Walker replied, 'but you've had the opportunity to talk your own language, and haven't taken advantage ... "Chock" is my north country word. I came to Wales and got "cog".'

It was more than a semantic nicety. 'He said he'd never seen a cog set,' Harris pointed out, 'and now he says he *has* seen a chock set.'

A good deal of time was wasted on trivial misunderstandings of this kind, and a great deal more on sorting out a confusion of nomenclature which several times brought the hearing to a halt. A large map purporting to show the detailed layout of the Dennis Section of the colliery on the day of the accident dominated the room throughout the inquiry and was constantly referred to by questioners and witnesses. But there are no name-plates on the roads of a coal mine, which are usually known by numbers, and if the system of numbering, as at Gresford, is not closely controlled the result can be chaotic. The Dennis Section had been pushed forward, outward and downward for 12 years with a cheerful disregard for consistency in the naming of its parts, and the efforts of the participants in the inquiry to locate anything on the plan sometimes read more like the script of a farce than an investigation into the deaths of 265 men. The assertion of one of Cripps's biographers that he arrived in Wrexham the day before the inquiry opened and that 'by the time he reached the Court he carried in his mind a mental map of every nook and cranny in Gresford Colliery' is a tribute to her admiration for his powers; he himself may have begun by thinking that he did but before long his despairing conclusion, echoed by the Commissioner, was 'At present, as far as my mind is concerned, it's a complete chaos where these roads were.'

The confusion began in the first hour or so.

MR CHARLTON:	How is this district described on the plan—No 4 East?
THE COMMISSIONER:	No 4 East is described as—what—61s district, or No 4 North Bottom End? I don't know which is No 4 North.
MR CHARLTON:	Which is No 4 North: is it 20s or 61s?
THE WITNESS:	The whole district, yes.

Numbers were allocated according to a logic that defied analysis: '23s face' was in 109s district, but '24s face' was in 95s; '24s road' was not the same as '24s airway'; '14s face' was also known as '14s side of 109s'; '37s place' was in a different part of the mine from '37s heading'.

Q	Had you any men in the return airway—the return from 37s?
A	From 147s.
Q	From 37s conveyor face?
A	I haven't 37s.
THE COMMISSIONER:	109s wasn't it?
THE WITNESS:	You mean 23s, yes.

No wonder the Commissioner observed plaintively 'I don't know what you do at this colliery with all these numbers.' On another occasion he remarked that he'd had enough and was going home early. Later still an attempt to establish exactly what had happened to a very complex airway following a series of rock falls in 14s district led to a complete deadlock, whereupon he suspended the proceedings for the day and announced that he proposed to call a special meeting of the men who had worked in the area so that they could argue the matter out and arrive at an agreed statement without wasting everyone else's time.

In addition to these hazards there was a language problem which went far deeper than pit jargon—as deep perhaps as those centuries-old conflicts which had carried the national boundary hereabouts to and fro across Offa's Dyke, complicating the linguistic pattern each time they passed.

Sir Geoffrey Wilson recalled his surprise on discovering how many of the men at the inquiry wished to give their evidence in Welsh. It is impossible to discover what the number was because the transcript records all the proceedings in English.

At the time of the Gresford disaster the Wrexham area seems to have been in a state of linguistic confusion. According to the 1931 census the boundary dividing Welsh from English ran one-and-a-half miles to the west of Wrexham but a writer in 1930 noted that, although situated right on the Welsh border, in the midst of alien influences, Wrexham had remained largely a Welsh town containing one of the best Welsh publishing firms.[3] How much Welsh was spoken in the town was a matter of guesswork but according to one man who was in a position to know, at Hafod Colliery, a short distance away to the south-west and manned almost entirely by men from the village of Rhosllanerchrugog, the minutes of lodge meetings in the 1920s were kept in Welsh. Most Welsh-speakers were probably bilingual but there is evidence in some mildly acrimonious correspondence preserved in the Public Record Office which suggests that some of them were not.

The first mention occurs in a letter sent by A. J. Cook on behalf of the Miners' Federation to the Secretary for Mines, Colonel Lane-Fox, on 17 January 1926.

> My Executive Committee instructs me to write to you with reference to the appointment of Mines Inspectors and Assistant Inspectors who are unable to speak or understand the Welsh language. My Committee thinks these qualifications are essential in a district where a large number of workmen are monoglot Welshmen, such as in North Wales and parts of South Wales; such men very often in reply to questions put answer 'yes' when they should answer 'no', and vice versa.
>
> My Committee would be glad if you could see your way clear to give an assurance that a knowledge of the Welsh language shall be an essential qualification when making appointments in these districts.

A quick check in North Wales showed that the senior inspector, the junior inspector and one of the sub-inspectors spoke and understood Welsh; over the other sub-inspector there was a query. In South Wales, according to an irritable note in the handwriting of a senior civil servant in the Mines Department, the position was almost the reverse of the one implied by Cook. 'Some of the Inspectors in South Wales are so steeped in Welsh that they can hardly express themselves in English. The tail should not be allowed to wag the dog—it is ridiculous.'

The Minister's obligations were set out clearly in the Coal Mines Act 1911, Section 97(1): '... in the appointment of Inspectors of Mines in Wales and Monmouthshire, among candidates otherwise equally qualified, persons having a knowledge of the Welsh language shall be preferred'.

A suitably mollifying reply drawing attention to the words of the Act was drafted for despatch to Cook.

> In making appointments to the Inspectorate in Wales and Monmouthshire regard has always been paid to this provision and as a result nearly all (most of) the Inspectors there speak or understand the Welsh language. Colonel Lane-Fox fully appreciates the importance of the point raised by your Federation, and will continue scrupulously to observe the duty laid upon him by the statute. But he regrets that he cannot go so far as to give the undertaking you ask for in your letter, as this would amount to overruling the intention of an Act of Parliament.

There the matter was allowed to rest for the time being but there were further protests in 1930 and again in 1933, when the new junior inspector with special responsibility for North Wales turned out to be a Mr P. G. Dominy from Scotland. By this time only the two inspectors for metalliferous mines and quarries, neither of whom had any responsibility for coal mines, spoke Welsh. The Mines Department remained unrepentant. 'So far as I am concerned,' a senior official wrote to a colleague, 'and as I told the late Mr Tom Richards (Member for Wrexham), I think the miners would benefit if all the Inspectors in Wales—North and South—were English or Scotch. The Welsh are far too clannish.'

How many men in the Dennis Section of Gresford spoke only Welsh, how many spoke and understood English only with difficulty, how many spoke and understood it perfectly but wouldn't, what tensions this bilingual situation gave rise to, and whether it would have made the slightest difference if Mr Dominy had spoken Welsh like a native, are questions to which there are now no answers. For witnesses who had no English a bilingual speaker was asked to stand by throughout the inquiry and interpret as required. A number of men availed themselves of his services, and the result shows perhaps in the occasional awkwardness or ambiguity in the transcript of evidence. Many witnesses probably felt and behaved like William Thomas Richards who, on being asked by Henderson whether he would rather give evidence in English or

Welsh, replied with quiet dignity, 'I am a Welshman, but I will have to try to do my best in English.'

NOTES

1. Although often referred to as a 'Royal Commission', this was a Court of Inquiry set up by the Board of Trade under the Coal Mines Act 1911, and the Mining Industry Act 1920, to carry out a 'formal investigation ... into the causes and circumstances of the explosion in the Gresford Mine ...'. The first meeting of the court took place on 24 October 1934 and the 38th and final session was held on 18 July 1936.

2. 1911 Act 83 (i) (d): 'Persons attending as witnesses before the court shall be allowed such expenses as would be allowed to witnesses attending a court of record.'

3. Davies, W. W. (1930).

CHAPTER 10

The Management

At the start of the inquiry the Commissioner faced a dilemma, and he opened the proceedings by explaining what he intended to do about it. Because of the fire and the sealing off of the pit it was impossible to carry out any exploration underground, and for obvious reasons none of the men who had been anywhere near the scene of the explosion was present to give evidence. It would therefore be impossible to make much progress with the investigation into the cause of the explosion. In these circumstances the course which the inquiry could best follow for the time being would be to take evidence as to the condition of the mine and the operations connected with its working prior to the explosion; to take evidence of the occurrence of the explosion and the events following it; and to take such evidence as to the cause as was at present available. Having completed the first and second parts they might have to consider whether the inquiry should stand adjourned until such time as further evidence as to the cause was available.

It was an unsatisfactory situation, not least from the point of view of the miners, who had every reason for wishing to see responsibility for the disaster placed firmly where they believed it should lie, but there was clearly no feasible alternative and in the absence of objections the first witness was called. The general order of batting was to be that the Mines Department would present the witnesses whom it believed the Commissioner should hear, then the miners would present their witnesses and finally the owners theirs. When the examination of each witness had been concluded representatives of the other parties to the inquiry might put questions to him in accordance with a pecking order which began with the learned counsel and ended with spokesmen for the various professional associations.

Witnesses called by the Mines Department were examined by Charlton, the divisional inspector for Lancashire and North Wales, whose transfer from Swansea had aroused opposition on the grounds of his inability to speak Welsh. On the basis of his

99

performance at the inquiry, especially when giving evidence himself as he was later called on to do, he seems to have been inclined to garrulity and a good opinion of himself, and it is not clear whether he foresaw the disastrous course which the inquiry would take for the Inspectorate as a whole and his staff in particular. Their role will be examined in greater detail later but in general it may be assumed that, as the head at that time of one of the busiest divisions in the country, Charlton would have had no cause to pay special attention to one pit in North Wales in the light of the reports he received about it from his subordinates. No defects were apparent in the system, no risks were being taken, no arrangements observed which aroused anxiety or called for comment, apart perhaps from a puzzling omission to drive a short length of road which would have provided 29s with its own ventilation rather than a diminished supply of air which had already been hauled round three other districts in the Dennis Section.

There was nothing here to suggest that William Bonsall had been anything other than a competent and conscientious manager, but as Charlton rose to put questions designed to elicit information already in his hands he knew that Cripps was in possession of the same information, and even with no previous opportunity to watch him in action he must have had an inkling of the use which a shrewd counsel would make of it.

Bonsall's state of mind as he faced his interrogation is not difficult to imagine. After the initial numbing shock of the disaster, a month of living within sight of the silent, stricken mine, and the experience of being the target for the insults, threats and hatred of a whole community, apprehension verging on panic had reduced him, he later claimed, to 'an awful mental state' in which 'I scarcely knew what I was saying at times'. Clearly he was expecting a rough ride and must have known how vulnerable he was to attack, but in spite of the picture built up with cold contempt by Cripps and calculated malice by Hall, of a ruthless, cynical, slave-driving villain, the impression he leaves is of a weak man, driven beyond his capabilities, losing control of events, and ultimately paying the penalty partly of his own incompetence and partly of the intractable circumstances in which he was obliged to operate.

Like many managers—90 per cent according to an estimate made in 1936—he had risen from the ranks. He had worked for nine years as a filler, holer and contractor, four years as a haulage hand, three as a deputy, three as an overman, and two as an under-manager, most of the time in Derbyshire. He came to Gresford as under-manager in 1914 and succeeded to the top job when the manager, Groves, retired through ill health in 1917. In the old days, when a man could rise to this level simply by virtue of seniority or the favour of the owner, with no training or educational require-ment, there had been repeated complaints of 'want of competency' on the part of managers, but even so the proposal to subject them to some kind of test had been resisted on the ground that 'it interfered with the right of masters to employ whomsoever they considered competent to manage their property'. It was an Act passed in 1872 which made it compulsory for managers to hold a certificate and the later Act of 1911 which imposed the same obligation on firemen or deputies; and in the opinion of W. D. Stewart, writing in 1935, the results had not been beneficial to the rank and file miners. The intention of the Acts had been to promote safety, but by allowing the owners to use officials for the purpose of supervising production they created a dual responsibility and a clash of interests in which, with his eye mainly on his own position, the official might succumb to the temptation to give production priority over safety. Moreover when deputies, many of them young men, were given duties in connection with safety the manager, although still bearing full responsibility in law, was forced to share and even surrender some of it in practice.

The Royal Commission on Safety in Mines, set up in 1935 largely as a result of Gresford, stressed what it described as 'the fiction, embodied in Section 2(1) of the Act [of 1911] that the manager always has "the control, management and direction of the mine"', and referred to the difficulty of proof by the owner or agent that, in accordance with Section 102(1)(b), he had made all the financial and other provisions necessary to enable the manager to carry out his duties.

> The manager may have been told 'you are to do everything the Act requires, and I shall make all the necessary provisions for you to do so', but may have been under some heavy pressure from the owner to keep down costs of production, and ... may have crossed the border between proper and unlawful economy.

It was commonly said in Wrexham that Gresford was controlled not by the manager but by the owners, especially Henry Dyke Dennis, described by one who had dealings with him as 'a very powerful man'. It was alleged that when a deputation from Hafod Colliery, by no means a timorous band of men, needed to see him they would take a minister of religion with them.

For most of his period of service as manager of Gresford, Bonsall had at his side Sydney Cockin, the agent who had super-vised the sinking of the colliery in 1909 and was a trained mining engineer. Throughout his time Gresford had a good safety record, and as an educated man he may have had less difficulty than the largely self-made Bonsall in standing up to the imperious Dyke Dennis. An official well acquainted with him recalled that

> Up to the time when Mr Cockin, agent, retired about two years ago Mr Bonsall spent a fair amount of time in the pit; I believe it was his practice to go underground more or less every day, or at least several days a week. He certainly did much more underground work than many colliery managers.

When Cockin retired he was not replaced by a man of his own standing and technical competence. The role of agent was assumed by J. A. Harrop, the company secretary. Bonsall had now not only lost his expert support and adviser but was wholly at the mercy of the commercial and profit-conscious influences in the company. The consequences were spelt out in detail and in the fierce glare of publicity before the tribunal in Wrexham. In the words of a later manager of Gresford, 'in two years the pit was raped', and the man in the middle, with no access to the board of directors, and sharply conscious that in the critical state of the industry spare managers were as plentiful as spare miners, was the not too efficient or forceful Bonsall.

As a man he seems to have lacked most of the qualities of leadership. Recollections of him range from 'a gentleman', from a miner who was only 16 at the time of the accident and probably in awe of him, to 'thin, very curt, not friendly to the workers—didn't see much of him'. A middle-of-the-road opinion dismissed him as 'not a bad chap, but driven by the owners'. According to his own account, which was accepted by the Commissioner, the reason why the men in the Dennis Section had seen little of him in the months before the explosion was that he had been busy superintending the installation of new machinery in another part of the mine. The rank and file miners seemed to show little animosity towards him—they reserved that for targets nearer their own level. It was the forensic virtuosity of Stafford Cripps, and to a somewhat smaller extent the crude malice of Joe Hall, which set him in the pillory as the principal architect of the horror of Gresford.

The early stages of his examination were pure frustration for everyone. He seemed incapable of grasping what was said to him or giving a coherent answer to a question or even reading the plan of his own pit which was put in front of him so that he could identify significant features. Tempers were for the most part controlled and eventually he settled down to provide, in reply to Charlton's not too hostile questions, a reasonably straightforward account of what appeared to be the normal operation of the mine. But even here there were sombre patches, unavoidable indications of lax and illicit practices for which he was clearly bound to be called to account in due course, and although Charlton allowed him, perhaps unconsciously, opportunities to put the best face on things he was already visibly under stress when on the second day he was handed over to Cripps for cross-examination.

A member of Cripps's chambers has left an interesting impression of him in action.

> Cripps was very free of mannerisms in court. His manner was cool and collected and meticulously polite. His voice, which was well modulated, was capable of keeping the same pitch for days on end ... His notes were invariably indexed with cross references ... All this gave an impression of formidable confidence, which was only slightly affected in moments of stress by the careful rolling up and unravelling of the tab of his silk gown.[1]

Another admirer claimed that 'it was impossible to make him lose his patience or even to induce an edge of irritation into his voice', from which it is clear that she had not been present at the Gresford Inquiry or even read the transcript of the proceedings. It seems also to have been far from easy for him to indulge in humour. In all the long days of examination and cross-examination at Wrexham the few jokes stand out like nails in the sole of a shoe. Discussing with Charlton whether there were any mice in the pit he commented, 'I hear somebody suggested the mice had had their fur rubbed off going through the airways!', and immediately apologised: 'I'm afraid that was rather wicked of me, Mr. Charlton.' A little later, having listened to a catalogue of mishaps which Charlton complained had prevented him from carrying out some duty or other, Cripps remarked: 'What some people call ODTAA?'

'I beg your pardon?'

'One Damned Thing After Another.'

'Quite so.'

Now and then he would try a little heavy-handed sarcasm. 'We may as well get our vocabulary right. I'm only a poor Englishman. I didn't know that "occasionally" and "many times" meant the same thing. But to you it does?'

'Yes.'

'Very well. We'll remember that.'

With one unimpressionable miner the technique failed.

'I don't know what the term "charter master" means. I'm very ignorant in these things.'

'I know you are. I've heard you.'

These were among the very rare light moments in an otherwise aggressive, frequently acid performance which was for the most part markedly out of keeping with the image of the imperturbable, scrupulously courteous Cripps of the pen portraits, the advocate, as portrayed by another of his biographers, to whom the cold impersonality required of the Common Law barrister was distasteful and even at times distressing, because 'where a pitiless examination of witnesses, frightened or lying, was required ... he could not separate his legal technique from a generosity of heart towards human beings in difficulties'.[2]

Facing some of the chief witnesses at Wrexham in a battle concerning their conduct, Cripps had little difficulty in subduing his generosity of heart, which had been reserved wholly for the other side. The offensive began at the moment when he rose for the first time to cross-examine Bonsall, and his performance, which seemed to stun not only the witness but most of the management side, set the level of acrimony at which the rest of the inquiry was conducted. Since it raised every issue which became a subject for controversy and was the basis for his condemnation of private ownership of the coal mines, it is worth examining in some detail.

He began with a history of the mine and within little more than a minute had elicited information which put many other events in perspective. Of the principal districts in the Dennis Section no less than four—20s, 61s, 109s and 14s—were 'dying', that is, reaching the point of exhaustion, as their eventual replacement 95s was being opened; 29s, although not mentioned, had presumably a long-term future. The total output of the mine had gone up with the return of full-time working, largely, Bonsall agreed, because of an increase in the quota it was allowed to produce under the 1930 Act. Cripps suggested there had been a deliberate policy of 'speeding up'. Bonsall preferred to put it down to 'better organisation'.

Q Let us see. Have you put in mechanical devices?
A We have.
Q Is the purpose of that to get more coal in a shorter time?
A It's to do away with labour as far as possible; the arduous labour, too.
Q Is it in order to get more coal in a shorter time?
A All mechanical devices are for that, of course.
Q And as a result of that, the whole speed of getting coal throughout, the conveying system and everything else in the mine is quickened up?
A The appliances are so much better.
Q Yes, but it's all speeded up; that's the object of the whole arrangement isn't it?
A The object is to get a bigger tonnage from a smaller area.
Q Exactly, and in order to do that you've got to cut the coal quicker, move it quicker, and get it away quicker, and get it to the pithead quicker?
A That is so.

Having secured this concession, the first of many, Cripps moved on to the question of working conditions in Gresford. It was, he suggested, a 'hot mine'. Bonsall, pointing out that it was half a mile deep in places, would only go as far as 'naturally warm . . . about 70 degrees'.

Q That's just a pleasant, not very warm summer's day?
A That would vary, of course, in different parts.
Q So that the temperature at the bottom of this mine was that of a cool summer's day?
A It would be about 70, I should think.
Q I suggest to you that that is a perfectly fantastic answer.
A A certain part of the year the temperature would be about 70.
Q In what part of the year was the temperature 70 degrees?
A It would vary. It would depend on the temperature of the surface.
Q At what temperature of the surface would the temperature at the bottom of the mine be 70?
A The increase in temperature is about one degree for every 60 feet.
Q Just answer the question. Kindly tell me the temperature at the surface to which you refer when you say the temperature at the bottom of the mine would be 70 degrees.
A I say that the increase in temperature would be about one degree—
Q Just answer the question Mr Bonsall, if you don't mind.
A I couldn't say the exact temperature at the surface.

At Cripps's suggestion they assumed a surface temperature of 60 degrees, picked a point at the end of a road 2,400 feet down, did a calculation and arrived at a figure of 100 degrees, which Bonsall dismissed as ridiculous. He admitted to having found it 'warm' in 14s and settled for a figure of 80 degrees.

He fared no better when they moved on to the supervision of the pit, especially during the night shift, which was when the explosion had occurred. He couldn't remember when he'd last been down at night. There wasn't normally an under-manager (i.e. a manager underground) on duty at night in the Dennis Section, only an overman who had charge of the whole pit and would have had to travel a very large distance to get round all of it.

Q What are the hours of the undermanager?

A I'm afraid they're rather long. He goes on with the morning shift and he comes up late, about two or three o'clock in the afternoon.

Q So that between that time and the evening shift there's neither an overman nor an assistant manager on this part of the pit?

A Well, the overman did go in that part.

Q You know, you told us yesterday that the afternoon shift overman didn't have anything to do with this part of the mine.

A He hasn't been going in this part for some time.

Q So that there wasn't very much supervision as regards the firemen carrying out their duties in the afternoon shift and the night shift in this part of the pit?

A The firemen were quite competent.

Q I didn't ask whether they were competent or not. I asked whether there was any supervision to see that they did their duties. The answer is, there wasn't any?

A The answer is they were quite competent.

Q You were relying entirely upon the competence of the firemen without supervision.

And so to the whole vexed question of ventilation, probed by Cripps at relentless and devastating length. The book containing the firemen's records of measurements of air in the pit, which the Act specified should be taken at least once a month at certain points, contained no entries after June 1934. Why not? The person who took the measurements, Bonsall replied, hadn't entered them in the book. But wasn't the manager required to countersign them?

A They weren't given to me.

Q I didn't ask whether they were given to you. I asked you why you didn't see that they were there. You're managing the mine, not Mr Cuffin.

A That was an omission on my part.

Q And you realise that that's a breach of the Act?

A I realise that that was an omission on my part.

Q And do you realise whether that omission was a breach of the Act?

A I can't go any further than that.

Q Mr Bonsall, do you know what your duties are as a mine manager?

A I do.

Q Was it one of your duties to see that this book was filled up after a reading once a month?

A It was my duty to countersign—

Q I didn't ask you that. I said was it your duty to see this book was filled up once every month after the readings had been taken?

A It was my duty to sign the register.

Q Are you incapable of answering the question I put to you?

A I'm not incapable.

Q Very well, if you can't answer it I'll leave it and pass it by.

They turned to the plan of the mine and Cripps showed, with a bewildering command of the complex statistics provided for him, that the volume of air which flowed past certain specified points measured in cubic feet per minute had dropped alarmingly over a period of years, in one case by more than half. The reason, he suggested, and Bonsall could only agree, was 'a general obstruction of ventilation'. There was nothing else that could account for it.

The background to a long and complicated exchange which followed, and largely destroyed Bonsall's credibility as a man competent to manage a mine, was the question which had puzzled the former sub-inspector for North Wales. Why had the management allowed the district known as 29s to be ventilated by air which had already been circulated round three other districts, 109s, 95s and 14s? Why hadn't they driven intake and return airways directly to 29s, so making it an independent district? Why try to force air round a long and labyrinthine set of passages, especially when its natural tendency would be to take the shortest available route back to the surface?

The objective to which Cripps was working was the contention, which he proposed to advance later in the inquiry, that the most probable location of the explosion was 14s district, which was so badly ventilated that part of it at least was seldom free from gas; and that the reason for the bad ventilation was the poor condition of many of the airways in the Dennis Section, which obstructed the flow of air and encouraged it to bypass 14s altogether and take a short cut through 29s. A 'vast quantity', in Cripps's phrase—18,000 cubic feet was the figure arrived at—was lost somewhere along the way, and before it could reach the most distant part of the mine it had to pass, or try to pass, some not very airtight doors which led into 29s. Cripps invited Bonsall to agree that it didn't pass them but went through them. Bonsall refused.

> Q Have you ever before studied this problem and tried to account for it?
> A In my opinion we didn't get that actual loss.
> Q Mr Bonsall, can you answer a question. Have you ever studied this question of this loss of air before, and tried to get an explanation?
> A Yes, we were studying it all the time.
> Q What conclusions have you arrived at? Come along, Mr Bonsall.
> A I've come to this conclusion, that I'm quite positive that that quantity of air couldn't go through those doors.
> Q Very well, it couldn't go through 29s. Now where could it go?
> A I can never understand where it was going.
> Q Then you didn't take any steps to prevent it, I take it?
> A We attended to the ventilation appliances all that's possible.
> Q But you didn't take any steps . . . to try and prevent that leakage?
> A It was always a mystery to me where it went.
> Q I know that, and what I want to get clear is that, as it was a mystery to you, you didn't do anything to stop it?
> A We did everything possible to stop it.
> Q As you didn't know where it was going, nothing was possible to stop it? Is that right? And it was still going on up to the day of the explosion, wasn't it, so far as you know? That's right, isn't it?
> A Leakages would be going on.

Cripps announced that he had come to the end of what he wanted to ask about ventilation, and was all for starting on another topic but the Commissioner thought they had better adjourn until Monday. After two days in the witness chair, Bonsall was said to be in a state of near collapse.

When they resumed after the weekend Cripps began with 'a word about overtime'.

> Q Was it common practice in your mine on Friday and Sunday to work overtime?
> A Yes, we brought men in on Friday night that had been working on Friday.
> Q That was a common practice?
> A Yes.
> Q Of course you knew that was a breach of the 1908 Act?[3]
> A Well, many of the men liked it, and they asked for it.
> Q I didn't ask whether they liked it. I asked you whether you knew it was a breach of the 1908 Act?
> A Yes.

Leaving the question of overtime in abeyance for the time being, Cripps returned to the subject of the books in which the firemen recorded air measurements. Each book provided for a top copy of the fireman's report, to be kept in the mine office, and a carbon copy which would be torn out. For 20s district in August 1934 only the duplicates were available; the book containing the top copies had been allowed to go down the mine.

Q That of course is a clear breach of the Regulations?
A Well, not on my part.
Q You are the manager. The mine isn't managed in accordance with the Act unless these records are kept properly at the office.
A Every report has been made by the firemen.
Q I'm not asking you whether a report has been made or not.
A And I've no doubt at all that report is in the upcast pit bottom.
Q I don't care whether it's in the upcast pit bottom or not. What I'm asking is, why were these reports not kept at the office of the mine, or copies of them, in accordance with the provisions of the Act?
A Apparently the boy let it go down the mine.
Q But didn't you, as manager of the mine, take care to see that this regulation was complied with? Do you let the mine be run by boys?
A How can I look after every boy in the mine?
Q I'm not asking you to look after every boy. I'm asking you to look after every record which the Act says shall be kept in your office.
A I can't keep every record.
Q I didn't ask if you could keep them. I said could you look after them.
A The reports have been made, and I haven't the slightest doubt that that's gone down into the pit bottom.
Q That's the only excuse you have, is it?
A It's not an excuse.

Probably no subject dealt with at the inquiry took up more time than shot firing, partly because of the obvious possibility that it was a shot fired in the presence of gas that caused the explosion and partly because it lay at the heart of the charge with which Cripps was determined to destroy the management—that they had neglected safety, not simply, as Bonsall's other evidence might have implied, through incompetence, laziness or thoughtlessness, but in the calculated pursuit of maximum production. The men at the centre of the controversy were not only the shot firers but also the deputies, or firemen, who in addition to their primary duty of attending to the safety of their districts were authorised to fire shots. All the surviving officials from the Dennis Section were due to face interrogation at a later stage but clearly Bonsall as manager was responsible for their activities.

The crux of the argument, which gave rise to interminable assertion, counter-assertion and arithmetic, was how long it took to fire a shot, carrying out all the prescribed procedures, and how many shots could safely be fired in the course of a shift. In a report on an explosion at a pit in Scotland in 1932 Sir Henry Walker had quoted estimates ranging from 5¼ minutes to 11 minutes and concluded that as conditions varied from mine to mine, and from seam to seam in the same mine, it was not possible to lay down the time required by a shot firer to carry out the various provisions of the Explosives in Coal Mines Order prior to firing a shot.[4] The best that could be done, he suggested, was to carry out a test and add to the time taken a reasonable margin for contingencies.

Cripps read out these observations and then tossed the problem to Bonsall: what was a reasonable time for firing a shot? Bonsall would rather not say: it was up to the individual fireman.

> Q You put it on the fireman, do you? I suggest it's the duty of the manager to see whether the shots are fired properly?
> A You don't suggest that I should take hold of 2,000 men and see that they do their work?
> Q I don't, but there are certain aspects of danger in a mine.
> A You seem to suggest the manager should do everything. I think it's ridiculous some of the questions you're asking me.
> Q If you try to keep your temper and be a little patient we shall get along.
> A I think I've been patient long enough.
> Q If you start being rude we may take a very much longer time.
> A I've told you three or four times I've never tested the time of these shots.
> Q I suggest you should have done.

The records, which Cripps worked through with his usual unrelenting attention to detail, showed that in parts of the Dennis Section firemen had been firing as many as 63 shots in an eight-hour shift with an average in the region of 40. Moreover, these were men who had many other and more important duties to perform: yet the men officially appointed to do nothing except fire shots usually managed only far smaller totals, perhaps 28 or 30 per shift. Wasn't there, Cripps asked, something wrong there?

> A No, I don't admit there's anything wrong.
> Q How do you explain it?

A Perhaps the fireman can explain that. I don't know why he should fire more shots like that.

Q It's quite obvious, isn't it, that no man could fire that quantity of shots and take due precautions?

A I'm not prepared to say that. I don't think our firemen would fire them unless they carried out their statutory duty.

Q That really is an idle remark, Mr Bonsall.

A I think you'd better ask them. I wasn't there.

Q But it's your job to see the returns from the men?

A It's not my job to see the shot firing reports every day.

Q You accept no responsibility for the fact that men were put on to fire more shots than they were capable of firing, with due regard for safety?

A I've never put a man on to fire more shots than they were capable of.

Q Well, I needn't go through all these shot firers?

A No, you've just taken the exceptional.

Q Naturally, because it's the exceptional occurrence that creates the explosion in the mine.

A regulation to which Cripps had already drawn Bonsall's attention stipulated that no shot should be fired in a haulage road—that is, a road along which tubs of coal were drawn—without special permission in writing from the manager or under-manager and unless all the workmen had been withdrawn from the seam in which it was to be fired and from all the seams communicating with it.[5] The regulation, like so many others, had to say the least not been scrupulously observed in the Dennis Section. In pressing this point home Cripps provoked the outburst which had long been threatening.

Q I asked whether you knew firing those shots without withdrawing those men was a breach of the Regulations?

A I know it's perfectly safe and we did fire.

Q Just try to answer the question. Did you—

A I don't intend to answer any more.

Q I'll give you one more opportunity, and the world will know if you answer the question. Are you ready to answer the question?

A I'm not.

Q I think people can draw their own conclusions.

A Yes, and I hope they will do.

Sensing that the situation was getting out of hand the Commissioner intervened to try what a little courtesy would do.

Q Mr Bonsall, will you answer *me* a question? Have you ever considered Clause 7(c) of the Coal Mines Orders with reference to firing shots at this place?

A Yes.
Q And they still fired there?
A They did fire there, yes.

Shortly after this, having provoked Bonsall into a last protesta-
tion that 'every fireman had very strict instructions to report every
possible trace of gas and we had no large quantity of gas at all', and
that they were 'continually taking steps to improve the ventilation',
Cripps let him go. The Commissioner, aware that the emotional
atmosphere in the room had become seriously overheated,
adjourned the session early.

It was only a temporary respite for Bonsall for on the following
day he had to face Joe Hall who, lacking the authority and polish of
Cripps, had nevertheless the advantage of being a miner. Where
Cripps the virtuoso had conducted an exhaustive and at times
bewildering dissection of Bonsall's sins of omission and commission, Hall ranged in a far more clumsy but equally hostile fashion
over issues of general interest to the mining community. During a
rambling and detailed scrutiny of the cycle of operations in the
Dennis Section he came inevitably to the subject of shot firing and
was, like Cripps, baulked by Bonsall's reluctance to be drawn. Even
with the help of a tactful intervention by the Commissioner—'You
must have some idea, Mr Bonsall, how long it takes to fire a shot . . .
just try to do yourself justice'—Hall made little progress and sat
down shortly afterwards. The representatives of the North Wales
Deputies' Association and the Association of Colliery Managers
decided not to enter the contest and it was left to Mr Miller KC,
counsel for the owners, to retrieve what he could from the ruins.
His first question, despite his profession of concern for Bonsall,
showed with cruel clarity the lonely position which the manager
occupied.

Q Mr Bonsall, I'm afraid you must be getting tired after all this long
examination. I'll make my questions to you as short as possible. I
would like you to consider first of all the suggestion put to you that
you were working here under rather undue pressure to produce
output. Is there any foundation for that?
A No.
Q I'm glad to have your denial . . . I pass to another matter. As manager
of the mine have your relations been cordial with the company and the
directors?[6]
A Yes.

Q And in the matter of finances, moneys required by you for upkeep and maintenance, has there ever been any stint?
A None whatever.
Q It was, of course, for you to consider as manager what appliances or safety precautions were desirable or necessary?
A Yes.
Q Have you always found that you could get what you wanted in the way of money to carry out your wishes in those respects?
A Yes, I have.

Some figures prepared by the accountant's department to give, as Miller put it, 'some precision' to Bonsall's assurances showed that expenditure in 1934 was larger than in previous years, that money spent in the Dennis Section had risen in proportion to the outlay in other areas, and that the proportion spent on stores had similarly increased. But in general, beyond persuading Bonsall to agree, largely against his own interests, that he had been neither driven hard not kept short by the directors, there was little Miller could do except give him the opportunity to deny Cripps's many damaging inferences and imputations. Bonsall had always given priority to safety: whether he had kept all the firemen's records or whether he hadn't, he had 'got the matter in mind' throughout his control of the mine. As to ventilation, they had new airways always under construction, even though some of them hadn't made progress for some time; in any case the ventilation as a whole was 'quite sufficient: it was good'.

And so, inexorably, to shot firing. Here as elsewhere Miller was plainly handicapped by being far less well briefed than Cripps was to deal with the technical aspects of the subject and was being helped, not very adequately, by 'some of the gentlemen advising me' as he went along. At last he read out a notice which Bonsall had sent to 'all underground officials' on 12 December 1932:

> You will have seen from the daily press that another explosion has occurred. I want to further impress upon you the necessity of rigidly carrying out the Rules and Regulations with regard to shot firing. Proceedings will be taken against any official who is found firing in the presence of gas, however slight. Remember that it is almost impossible to have an explosion if you carry out the Regulations with regard to shot firing.
> (Signed) William Bonsall. Manager.

But an explosion *had* occurred at Gresford: was there not therefore at least a strong presumption that the regulations with regard to shot firing had *not* been carried out? As a riposte to the damage wrought by Cripps, the introduction of this document was inept, and as an example of Miller's tactics may have contributed to the decision taken some days later that he should withdraw from the proceedings.

When Miller had done his ineffectual best for him Bonsall was at last released from this part of his ordeal, having answered or evaded close on 4,000 questions in 20 hours of testimony. On the following morning it was the turn of the under-manager, Andrew Williams.

There was widespread sympathy for Williams. Employed at the nearby colliery at Hafod for 24 years, he had later spent nine years in comparative exile as agent and manager of a colliery in Carmarthenshire before returning to North Wales in January 1934 as under-manager at Gresford in charge of the Dennis Section. It was generally assumed—indeed the Commissioner said as much in his Report—that on taking a close look at his territory he had diagnosed its dangerous condition and set to work to put it right, but neither time nor the owners were on his side. The faults in the Dennis Section could not be rectified in nine months in the face of a beleaguered, cost-conscious board of directors, and before he could make much progress the pit blew up. A quietly-spoken man regularly working a 12-hour day, he had, as Miller persuaded him to admit, personal reasons for wanting a safely run pit.

> Q You said you had three sons working in this mine?
> A Well, I had 860 men and boys worked down there. They all belonged to somebody.
> Q I know. I'm venturing to ask you a little personal matter.
> A Well, I had three sons.
> Q What ages were they?
> A 26, 22 and 16 ... one was working on 14s face ... one was on haulage ... one with the rope-splicers.
> Q And they knew if there was any risk you were running it. Were you conscious of running any risk, other than that which is inevitable in coal-mining, in the condition of this mine?
> A I wouldn't run any risk.

None of this protected him from Cripps, who dealt with him no less harshly than he had dealt with Bonsall but found him a tougher proposition, by no means so woolly-minded, and prepared if need be to swap punches with him. At times, even so, Cripps's footwork was too dazzling for this inexperienced opponent and for the referee.

Q Apart from the examination of the process of a particular shot being fired, which you may watch ... the only way which you can check as to the safe time being used is by seeing the number of shots being fired? That's right, isn't it?

A We don't see this record ... every day, but I do see the men, the shotsmen and firemen, and I would expect them to tell me if they had too much to do or had to neglect their duty in any way.

Q You'd expect the shot firer to come along to you and say in the morning, 'Look here, Mr Williams, I didn't take proper precautions yesterday. I risked the lives of all the men in the pit, and I propose to go on doing it tomorrow.' Is that what you expect him to do?

A No, I wouldn't expect him to do that.

It was not what Williams had said and not what he meant but the Commissioner, who would almost certainly not have allowed Joe Hall to get away with such a gross distortion, accepted it from Cripps without demur.

The cross-examination of Williams took the inquiry over much the same ground as it had already been required to traverse in the company of Bonsall and with as little in the way of conclusive results.

Having sustained the major attack on the management's opening pair for the better part of a week, Cripps took himself off temporarily, leaving his lieutenants in charge, and it was during his absence that a predictable storm broke. The final provocation came in the course of an exchange between Hall and Williams.

MR HALL:	Now if severe punishment was meted out for such catastrophes as this do you really think that more care and attention—
THE COMMISSIONER:	Who is the severe punishment going to be handed out to?
MR HALL:	To the persons responsible for the safety of the mine.
MR MILLER:	I would like to say, sir, if I might interpose, you are engaged on an inquiry. A good deal of the questioning that has been going on here suggests an attack, and this last question in particular I regard as extremely improper and not suitable to the nature of the proceedings.
MR HENDERSON:	I hope your suggestions don't refer to Sir Stafford Cripps's questions.
MR MILLER:	I certainly referred to Sir Stafford Cripps's questions as they developed into the nature

MR HENDERSON: of an attack, and I see no reason to qualify
                  what I've said.
                  I ask my friend to repeat his remarks when
                  Sir Stafford is here.
MR MILLER: Certainly: you may report it to him.

The next morning Cripps was in his place claiming, somewhat disingenuously, not to understand what Miller's objections were and inviting him to elaborate them. Miller obliged. His clients were present, ostensibly, to assist the Commissioner in an inquiry as to the cause of an explosion, but they had been 'subjected to hours and hours of questions' concerning breaches of regulations 'which ... are only remotely connected with anything we are here to investigate'. But of course nothing was further from his thoughts than to criticise his learned friend's conduct.

Once again Cripps demonstrated his superior ring craft, throwing on to the Commissioner the responsibility for keeping him in order. Every question he had put had been directed to discovering the truth about the condition of the mine. 'If you think we're not here to put every conceivable question you think material, no doubt you will say so, and we shall conduct ourselves accordingly.'

On receiving this clear invitation to say something the Commissioner let it be known that he took the learned counsels' observations as a reflection on himself. He didn't like it and went on to expound his policy of letting everybody 'get everything out that they feel ought to come out'. There were questions, no doubt, with little or no bearing on the subject, 'but I let them pass for the time being. Whether we shall take any notice of them later remains to be seen.'

A day or two later Miller, having come off very much the worse in the encounter which he had sought or perhaps been pushed into, withdrew from the inquiry—whether at his own request or that of those who had briefed him is not clear.

As for Cripps's performance, there is little doubt that despite his disclaimers, what he intended and what he brilliantly achieved was an attack, and there can be little quarrel with Sir Geoffrey Wilson's conclusion 40 years after the event that the inquiry, in which he participated, was not an impartial one.[7]

Bonsall was merely a substitute, and a particularly vulnerable one, for the real target, the owners not only of Gresford but of all the coal mines of Britain. That he was an incompetent manager is beyond dispute; that he deliberately put production before safety is open to question; that his breaches of the Regulations caused or contributed to the explosion was explicitly denied by the prosecution in subsequent legal proceedings (see p. 203 below).

Perhaps the most remarkable sentence in the Commissioner's 170-page report on Gresford was 'I have an uneasy feeling that Mr. Bonsall was over-ridden.'[8] If Walker had such a fear why did he do nothing to allay it? A Member of Parliament, himself a coal-owner, remarked,

> We couldn't have had an admission of that kind if a man trained in the law had conducted the Inquiry. Either that question would have been probed to the bottom, as in my opinion it should have been, or else that uneasy feeling ... should not have been expressed.

Another Member put it more bluntly:

> The Inquiry fell short of completeness in that it didn't ... consider the relations between the management of the mine and the directors. The directors have in law as well as in common sense a practical as well as a financial responsibility, and I doubt whether any inquiry can be regarded as complete which doesn't deal fully with that point.[9]

The Commissioner included in his report a recommendation that large collieries should not be worked without some able mining engineer in authority and superior to the manager. 'The person appointed ... needs to be of strong character and able if necessary to resist those in control of the commercial side of the concern.' The Royal Commission on Safety in Mines proposed that the law on mines should be brought into line with the Factories Act with a provision that would enable 'proceedings to be taken against any director, secretary or other officer of the company if it could be proved that he had consented to, connived at, or by neglect facilitated the commission of an offence'.

All this was too late to be of assistance to the unfortunate Bonsall, who came to grief, with the deaths of 265 men possibly on his conscience, through a combination of his own shortcomings, the crude and inexorable commercial logic of the industry he worked in and the remorseless destructive powers of a brilliant and politically motivated advocate.

NOTES

1. Quoted in Estorick (1949), p. 62.
2. Cooke (1957), p. 82.
3. See p. 29 and note 2 to Chapter 4 above.
4. See p. 124 below.
5. See Commissioner's question below.
6. See Appendix D.
7. Private communication.
8. For the Commissioner's reasons see his report, pp. 112–13.
9. See Appendix D.

CHAPTER 11

The Firemen

The opening stages of the inquiry had been in the nature of single combat between ill-matched pairs of opponents. When the senior management retired from the arena to bind up their wounds the conflict became more general, a mêlée involving counsel, officials, miners and spokesmen for all parties.

One of the most significant facts to emerge from the evidence of Bonsall and Williams was that at the time of the accident, and indeed during most night shifts, the pit was for practical purposes being run by the officials, that is, the overman and the firemen in charge of the various districts. (Terminology in this area was as bewilderingly capricious as elsewhere in the mine. The 'overman' was inferior to the 'under-manager' but during his shift had charge of the whole pit.) As Bonsall had conceded in reply to Cripps, there was a period before the night shift came on when the Dennis Section was without even an overman; and when the night shift overman did come on he could scarcely have time to travel once round the whole area during his spell of duty. Supervision of the pit was therefore largely in the hands of the firemen; it was to them that the Commission must look for a detailed picture of the state of the pit on the fateful night, and it was their ambiguous role in the hierarchy of management which virtually ensured that the picture would be as obscure and misleading as they could make it.

The fireman's function had its origin in early experiences with firedamp of the kind described by Roger Mostyn in his paper to the Royal Society.[1] After the mishap to the collier whom it disabled, Mostyn explained:

> some other small warnings it gave them, insomuch that they resolved to employ a man of purpose, that was more resolute than the rest, to go down a while before them every Morning to chase it from place to place, and so to weaken it. His usual manner was to put on the worst raggs [sic] he had, and to wet them well with water, and as soon as he came within the danger of it, then he fell grovelling down on his belly and went so forward, holding in one hand a long wand or pole, at the end whereof he tied Candles burning, and reached them by degrees towards it, then the

119

> Damp would flie at them, and if it miss'd of putting them out, it would quench it self with a blast, and leave an ill-sented [sic] smoke behind it.

Similar methods were used in other coalfields in England and Wales, until pits became too large and deep for such primitive methods and the emphasis shifted to ways of dispersing the firedamp through better ventilation. The 'fireman' continued to exist, retaining his responsibility for ensuring the safety of his fellow workers and extending it as time went by to cover more and more aspects of their working conditions, until under the Coal Mines Regulation Act of 1872 his role was formally recognised and his duties were defined.

> A competent person ... who shall be appointed for the purpose shall, at least once in every twenty-four hours, examine the state of the external parts of the machinery, and the state of the headgear, working places, levels, planes, ropes, chains and other works of the mine which are in actual use, and once at least in every week shall examine the state of the shafts by which persons ascend or descend ... and shall make a true report of such examination, and such report shall be recorded in a book to be kept at the mine for the purpose ...

So although the manager was in the last resort still responsible for the safe working of the pit, the fireman was his right-hand man where safety was concerned. However, as 'deputy overman' he gradually took over, or was saddled with, other duties regarding the general operation of the pit: he became the 'NCO' of the mine and in doing so inevitably came under pressure to identify himself less with the men, whose safety he was to ensure, and more with the management, on whose behalf he accepted responsibility for coal production and the profitability of the part of the pit that he was in charge of. The result, common throughout most of the coalfields of Britain, was the situation bitterly described by the general secretary of the North Wales Miners' Association in 1910.

> I am sorry to say that the bulk of the present day Firemen ... are so much afraid of losing their jobs and have so much to do; one competing against another for the greatest amount of coal sent out—and in the rush and fear of their superior officers on the question of cost, the safety of life and limb is very often forgotten ... I do not criticize Firemen who are aware and conscious of their responsibility, and will do their duties of deputy-overman without fear of anyone, whether they get coal out or not, but I do wish to criticize them in authority for employing a man as fireman because he can get plenty of coal out, and is a good bully, and can frighten men and boys by his abusive language.

At the time when these words were written a Royal Commission had been studying the problem as part of the preparation for a complete overhaul of the law relating to mining which was shortly to be undertaken by Parliament. The Act of 1911 attempted to end the conflict of loyalties by requiring the fireman to pass an examination before he could be appointed and by limiting him to prescribed duties in the sphere of safety, except that he might also, in the words of a later Royal Commission, 'be employed on additional duties measuring the work done by persons in his district or firing shots in his district . . .'. The drawback to this provision was that while it was adequate for those mines in which coal was got by hand by individual miners who had the time and the skill to attend to the safety of their own workplace, it was not appropriate to the mechanised pit, where teams of men worked at high pressure keeping up with machines which in themselves created a new range of hazards calling for more intensive supervision. Appointing officials to oversee these activities, with responsibilities for production as distinct from safety, merely gave rise to further tensions because of the exceptionally close relationship in a coal mine between output and safe working.

'If the fireman reports gas in his section beyond a certain percentage', W. D. H. Stewart pointed out in 1937:

> it means by law the withdrawal of the men, and therefore the loss of output, and he may in consequence run the risk of incurring the displeasure of the manager, who it is important to remember is himself in most cases today only a subordinate official. On the other hand, if the fireman does not report the presence of gas when it is present, and he has to fire shots in his section, it may easily cause a violent explosion.

Closely linked with this was the question of the number of shots which might safely be fired in the course of a shift. The law required the men to be withdrawn from the face while shots were being fired. In more leisurely times this caused little disruption. In the intensive round-the-clock operation of a mechanised pit, with the emphasis on output at all costs, strict observance of the regulations could have produced the absurdity of a coalface from which the men were never able to clear coal because they were always taking cover from the shots which were being fired to bring down the coal. It is therefore no matter for surprise that the longest and bitterest engagements at the Gresford Inquiry were fought over the issues of the amount of gas alleged to have been present in the

Dennis Section and the readiness of deputies to fire shots there at all times and in all circumstances.

There was no doubt as to the fireman's place in the scheme of things at Gresford, as Bonsall was persuaded to agree in reply to questions from Cripps about the fireman's duties.

> Q ... I suppose he has got to see that the men continue working; I mean, supervise them in that way?
>
> A He has to look after his district.
>
> Q He is responsible for the output from the district?
>
> A Well, no, he's not responsible. We have 'doggies' and haulage hands for that.
>
> Q Are the doggies in control of supervising the coal cutters and so on?
>
> A ... The doggies don't go on the coal face.
>
> Q So that the fireman is responsible for the output from the coal face?
>
> A Well, he's responsible for the safety.
>
> Q But whom do you communicate with if, say in 14s, you find that the output is not what it ought to be?
>
> A The undermanager.
>
> Q And whom does he communicate with?
>
> A I suppose the doggies and the fireman.
>
> Q *And* the fireman?
>
> A The doggies and the fireman.

As might have been expected the firemen repudiated any suggestion that they were under pressure from the management. Joe Hall, on behalf of the miners, failed to breach the defences of the self-confident 29-year-old fireman Davies from the afternoon shift in 29s.

> Q ... In addition to the worries of shot firing you have to undertake as fireman, there's the worry of coal production, isn't there?
>
> A Well, I don't worry about it. If the coal comes out, it's all right; if it doesn't you can't help it.
>
> Q In addition to the worries of fireman and shot firing there's the worry of transport. Do you worry about that?
>
> A No, I have doggies for that.
>
> Q You have the worry of safety in the roads relative to combustion, coal dust accumulation, haven't you?
>
> A Yes, to a certain extent I have.
>
> Q You have all these worries, and you continue to work at the speed you've been working at?
>
> A Yes.
>
> Q And you feel no effect physically through it?
>
> A None whatever. I get plenty [of] good food.
>
> Q Do you believe that a fireman ought to execute the duties of a shot firer as well?

A Well, yes.

Q Well, I'm more than surprised at your answer, but I've got to take it. A fireman is certainly connected with the productive side of his District?

A Yes, he is.

Q And of course, production is connected with costs, isn't it?

A Yes.

Q And if your cost is in any way over and above what the colliery company thinks it ought to be, then of course you're pulled over the rails for it, aren't you?

A No, I haven't been yet.

Q No, but you have the fear of it ultimately if the production isn't kept up?

A No, I haven't the fear.

This was an ill-conceived and unprofitable line of attack: no man is going to allow himself to be trapped into a public admission that he is not up to the job he is paid to do even if he has private doubts on the subject, as these men clearly had not.

Although the use of pneumatic picks for bringing the coal down once it had been undercut was said to be gaining ground in Britain in the 1930s, shot firing remained the most favoured method. In 1934 over 53 million shots were fired (not all of them in coal), with the aid of 25 million pounds of explosive consisting chiefly of nitro-glycerine and ammonium nitrate. Firing the shots was a specialised trade, and one of the apparent anomalies of the industry was the permission granted over the years to firemen, who already had their own area of responsibility, to move in on the territory of the shot firer. In Gresford, in spite of their heavy load of other duties, some firemen managed to detonate more explosive than the regular shot firers.

The holes for the shots, about four feet deep, were bored into the coal by one of the other workmen ready for the shot firer when he came on duty. Besides his explosive equipment he carried two special tools, a scraper made of copper, with a flattened end for clearing out the hole and feeling for breaks, and a stemmer made of wood with perhaps a copper end, for pushing home the charge and the plug of clay which followed it. As the author of *What Every Mining Man Should Know* explained, 'the rapidity of many chemical processes, such as the burning of gunpowder, can be increased if they take place under high pressure', and the reason for stemming the shot hole was therefore 'to increase the power of the explosive and to keep the gasses [sic] that are formed by the burning of the explosive confined until they have built up sufficient pressure to burst open the shot hole and break down the coal or rock'. The high explosive used 'can detonate with extreme rapidity ... the flame travels through it at the rate of more than a mile a second, so that a cartridge six inches long would detonate in about one twelve-thousandth part of a second'. Moreover, 'the temperature of the flames ... is extremely high, and they can ignite firedamp readily'. For this reason 'permitted' explosives had been developed in which a high explosive had been mixed with 'cooling salts' to reduce the temperature of the flame. 'Permitted explosives are not flameless ... they are still capable of causing the ignition of firedamp, though they will not do so if fired with care.'

Needless to say, Parliament had tried to ensure that an operation potentially so lethal, especially when performed in the confined space of a coal mine, should be undertaken only with the maximum of safeguards which were set out in the 'Explosives in Coal Mines Order' 1913. Among other provisions the Order specified that:

> 2. b) ... only clay or other non-inflammable substances shall be used for stemming, and shall be provided by the owner, agent or manager.
>
> e) The person firing the shot shall ... see that all persons in the vicinity have taken proper shelter ... He shall himself take proper shelter.
>
> g) The person ... shall, after the shot has been fired, make a careful examination of the face and see that it is safe in all respects.

The point of examining *after* firing (in addition to a thorough examination beforehand) was that the explosion could release gas which might be ignited by a subsequent explosion.

> h) [The firer] shall himself couple up the cable to the fuse or detonating wires, and shall do so before coupling up the cable, [which must be] not less than 20 yards in length, to the firing apparatus.

Further clauses specified that no shot should be fired unless the shot firer

> has examined with a locked safety lamp ... the place where the shot is to be fired and all contiguous places within a radius of 20 yards ... and has found them clear of gas ... [and] has examined floor, roof and sides ... within a radius of 5 yards ... and has taken steps to render any dust harmless.

Two or more shots must not be fired simultaneously and the examination routine must be followed for every shot. In the hope, presumably, of removing the most obvious temptation to aim at a high rate of output, the Order stipulated that '... no person shall be ... appointed [as a shot firer] if his wages depend on the amount of mineral to be gotten'.

Clearly there was no more responsible job in a mine than the setting off of these controlled explosions, and as far back as 1871 the inspector of mines for Lancashire and North Wales had remarked,

> It is very difficult to believe that a fireman who is paid regular wages would be foolish enough to fire a shot without making a careful inspection of the place, or to ignite the fuse if gas could be seen, knowing that his own life, in the event of an explosion, would be in danger.

Nevertheless, the tally of explosions mounted year by year and continued to do so in spite of the legislation of 1913, largely for the reason suggested by Sir Henry Walker in the first annual report he wrote, in 1925, after his appointment as Chief Inspector. 'It is difficult ... to devise by Regulations and Orders means to overcome human failings, and I think progress lies in the better training and education of the persons on whom the responsible duty of shot firing is cast.'

In common with their colleagues in every division the inspectors in North Wales appeared to have done their best to bring home to those firing shots the gravity of their responsibilities. In his report for 1933 Charlton wrote:

> On a few occasions I have had to complain of the excessive number of shots fired ... The conditions vary so greatly that it is impossible to lay down a limited maximum, but managements who require men to fire large numbers of shots ought to satisfy themselves that all the requirements of the Explosives in Coal Mines Order can be properly performed. Shots should be fired in deliberation, not hastily.

The Commissioner's verdict at the end of his exhaustive inquiry into the situation in Gresford was that:

> ... on frequent occasions and in some districts regularly, some of the deputies and shot firers ... fired more shots per shift than they could possibly have fired with proper care and proper attention to the requirements of the Explosives in Coal Mines Order ... In the conditions prevailing in the Dennis Section 40 shots was a reasonable shift's work for a shot firer, and no deputy should have been allowed to fire any shots except on special occasions. In general I think it is desirable that deputies should not be called upon to fire any shots at all. Their duties should be supervisory only ... it must not be forgotten that falls of ground account for about 50 per cent of all reportable accidents in mines; it is far more

important that the deputies should devote their energies and experience
to seeing that the roofs and sides of roads and workings are properly
supported than that their time should be taken up with the firing of
shots.[2]

There were in the week of the explosion 14 firemen employed in
the Dennis Section, one for each shift in each of five districts except
for the night shift, when one fireman had charge of two districts, 20s
and 61s, which had not yet been mechanised, relied far less on the
use of explosives, and in general needed less supervision. Of the
four deputies on duty on the night of 21/22 September one, David
Jones from 29s, came out of the pit alive; the other three died in the
explosion. All 11 surviving firemen gave evidence to the inquiry and
to a man refused to concede that their districts fell in any way short
of perfection.

Although a great deal of time was devoted to conditions in 109s
and 95s, the district on which attention came to be concentrated was
14s, which had long been notorious both in the pit and in the
immediate neighbourhood. There was not, never has been, and
never will be, any direct evidence showing 14s to have been the
scene of an explosion, but the great weight of opinion among the
miners, especially those with practical experience of the district,
was that the Dennis Section of Gresford Colliery was destroyed by
some mishap—a badly-fired shot, a spark from a faulty cable—
igniting the gas which, they insisted, was a constant and menacing
feature of their lives in 14s.

The district had a short but chequered history. Opened in the
first place as part of 109s, it had been stopped in June 1932 and
restarted as an independent district in December 1933. As with
most coalfaces the seam did not run horizontally but sloped from
right (the 'top end' or 'rise end') to left (the 'bottom end'). Air came
in at the bottom end, passed up the face and left by way of the
return airway at the top end. This airway had been made through
the goaf, or waste, left behind as the face was pushed forward at the
rate of some seven yards a week.

Throughout 1934, 14s face broadened out until it became one of
the most productive parts of the mine with an output of 1,617 tons
per week, in spite of a series of major setbacks, all of which occurred
at the top end of the face, where the return airway ran alongside a
fault. In April a small fall of rock temporarily blocked the airway. In
May a much larger fall blocked it completely, causing it to be

abandoned and replaced by three other roads which were brought back into service after a long period of neglect and followed an extraordinarily devious route back to the main return. This brought the air at one point to within four yards of the intake airway from which it was separated only by two doors, with the obvious possibility that the incoming air, already depleted by a long journey round the other districts, would simply slip through the doors into the return, by-passing 14s face altogether. The three old roads which constituted this makeshift airway were in a bad state, much narrower and lower than when they had last been in use. Some time in June, men were put to renovate them and had completed the task by 15 September. By that time another fall had occurred at the top end of the face, and yet another section of old road had been brought back into service as a return airway. Because of the confusion created by these and other expedients there was always a possibility that a witness, dating some event in terms of 'the accident', would be taken as referring to the explosion when what he really meant was the rock fall of 1 September, and vice versa.

An airway spatchcocked together out of three old roads and meandering round the district like a convoluted stretch of the River Dee was plainly inadequate for an intensively-worked machine face like 14s, and the general view was that Andrew Williams, the new under-manager who had arrived at the beginning of the year, had recognised both the inadequacy of the arrangement and the simplest remedy.[3] A short length of new road, between 50 and 100 yards long, would cut out one of the longest and most sharply-angled bends, including the dangerous approach to the intake airway. Work was put in hand in July to drive it through from both ends but by 22 September the two sections had not joined up; work on it ceased in August. The workmen were continually being taken away to get coal on the face; moreover, 14s was rapidly approaching exhaustion and the directors, including the cost-conscious Mr Harrop, may have needed much convincing of the need to spend any more money on it, especially as 95s district, which had a far longer and more profitable future, was sorely in need of its own new airway. The management may have consciously taken a calculated risk with the safety of 14s; more probably they simply improvised from one day to the next, like men in a leaky ship, with Bonsall, the man on the bridge, too harassed to deal with the realities of the situation, Williams rushing from place to place struggling to plug the holes before one of them let in enough water to sink them all, and the deputies concentrating on getting the last ounce of performance out of the engines with the aid of an overworked, mutinous and disunited crew.

The complaints from the men came under three general heads: that it was intolerably hot in 14s; that there was always gas about in the district, but especially at the top end of the face; and that the deputies persisted in firing shots without taking the prescribed precautions.

The heat was caused partly by the depth of the district and partly by the inadequate ventilation, which failed to provide a refreshing flow of air past the men. The poor ventilation also contributed to the accumulation of gas at the top end of the face where a powerful flow was needed to force it through a right-angled turn and downhill to the return airway. In the absence of that strong flow the mixture of gas and air became sluggish at the top end, sometimes hardly moving. Gas lingered in cavities in the roof and in the loosely packed waste left behind as the face moved forward. As the day went on and the concentration built up, gas would spread further and further down the face. The deputy, or the shot firer, needing a gas-free area in which to fire a shot in the coal, and unable to rely on the ventilation to provide it, resorted to artificial means. The regulations expressly forbade him to 'waft' or brush gas away because it could simply drift back again or into some other place where it might prove equally dangerous. But nothing was said about 'blowing', and on the face was the 'banjack', or compressed air machine. This was provided for boring shot holes but could be borrowed and its jet of air directed on to a pocket of gas, blowing it away and creating at least temporarily a free area in which the shots could be fired. Opponents of the practice equated it with the proscribed 'wafting'; others (including Shawcross, in his final submission to the tribunal) claimed that it was different and even beneficial because the stream of air both diluted the gas and helped it along into the return airway. However that might be, it is certain that without the banjack, shot firing in 14s and other districts would have been much reduced in scale, to the detriment of output and to the increased peace of mind of some, but by no means all, of the workers concerned.

The deputy in charge of 14s on the night of the disaster, Robert Jones, was one of the victims, and the burden of the attack on the district therefore fell on his colleagues on the other two shifts, John Harold Thomas and Harold Amos.

Thomas, whose brother was fireman of the corresponding shift in 29s, emerges as one of the least likable men in the pit. It was his allegation that the miners were being bribed to give evidence which had to be struck out of the record; he and his family had to put up with much vilification because of the impression created, though belatedly denied by the authorities, that it was his panic-stricken bungling of the manager's message which had sent the three rescue workers to their unnecessary deaths. The Commissioner's report declined to accept his evidence on matters of importance as truthful, and at least one emotional partisan would have liked to see him prosecuted for perjury.

Unperturbed by the revelations which had preceded his own appearance in the witness chair, Thomas offered his own view of the general condition of Gresford on the day of the accident.

> The state of the mine, on the last shift, I consider ... better than ... the last three weeks. The airways had been completed and the conditions were far better. I considered the state of the pit ... as good and better I should think than 90 per cent of the collieries in the country.

He agreed that 14s face had been 'very hot' at times, chiefly because the earlier falls of rock had temporarily interfered with the ventilation, but that had since been cured; and he strenuously denied that the men working there had ever complained about the presence of gas.

As he must have been aware, there were rows of men waiting in the room for an opportunity to contradict him. There was, for example, William Davies, who had worked on repairs to the emergency airway. After describing how in places it had collapsed from its original height of about six feet to about four feet—'the roof was broken, the bottom swollen, the sides crushed and the timber broken'—he was asked about a conversation he'd overheard between his mate Richards and the fireman Thomas.

> A We came on on the morning shift and I heard my mate report to the fireman when he came on at about half-past eleven ... Richards said there was gas present that morning.
> Q Where from?
> A I took it it came from the old road.
> Q Had you smelt it yourself?
> A Yes.

Q Was it very strong?
A I don't think I'd have been here now if I'd popped my head much
   further in.
Q When you complained to Thomas ... did he make any reply?
A He said that he'd had a shift working there on the Saturday.

Ralph James Rogers had worked on the night shift in 14s from
February until 13 September when, providentially for him, he met
with an accident which kept him off work.

Q What was the temperature condition of that face? Was it hot or cold?
A It was very hot. There wasn't a breath of air.
Q Could you feel any draught of air along the face at all?
A None at all.
Q Did you ever notice any gas on that face?
A Yes sir ... Our lamps were continually going out about 20 or 30 yards
   from the top end.
Q When did you last experience a lamp going out there?
A On the night I met with my accident: my own lamp went out.
Q Who was the fireman there?
A Robert Jones.
Q Do you remember shortly before the accident some men refusing to go
   up the face?
A Yes.
Q Did the fireman say anything about it?
A Robert Jones said to them that Harold Thomas had told him that if his
   men could work there, our men could work there.
Q Did the men go up?
A Yes. They had an electric lamp off the chargehand, to go up and finish
   working.

William Melling had at various times worked on all three shifts
on 14s face.

Q Have you ever actually complained to your fireman about gas?
A Yes.
Q Which fireman was it?
A Harold Thomas, and Harold Amos, too.
Q When did you complain to Harold Thomas?
A Well, one morning when he fetched me up there to get a piece of coal
   with a pick. I told him there was some stuff there when I was knocking
   a bit of coal down. 'Yes,' he said, 'but it isn't as bad as it has been.'
Q Did he make any test?
A No, he didn't make any test that day.

Leonard Price had worked in 14s, he told Henderson, since
February of that year and had complained to the fireman about gas
at the top end of the face.

I told Ted Williams that there was gas there, and that it would put my lamp out, and I wouldn't work in it ... He just hummed and hawed for a minute, and he said 'Get in where you can and get what you can ...'. I got as far as I could. Where my lamp won't burn I won't work.

Among the most forthright critics of the firemen was Thomas Gibson. Wasn't it his duty, Shawcross asked him, to himself if not to anybody else, to test for gas when he went into the face?

A   If we tested for gas and told the fireman there was gas there, he'd soon give us his answer. He'd tell us that *he'd* tell *us* when there was gas there.

Q   And if he said that, that would satisfy you?

A   We knew there was gas there.

Q   Did you call him a liar?

A   I didn't need to call him a liar. He knew he was a liar.

There was probably in much of this an element of paying off old scores and Shawcross, on behalf of the management, had little difficulty in ridiculing some of the wilder spirits, such as the man who spoke of gas so bad that it had put lamps out for 60 yards down the face, and his mate who, having mentioned an occasion when the banjack was used to blow away some gas, responded to Shawcross's request for more details.

Q   ... the gas was coming out of the hole, was it?

A   No, it was all up the face, from the floor to the roof.

Q   All the time you were there?

A   Practically all the time I was there, yes.

Q   I suppose your lamp went out a lot?

A   Yes, my lamp did go out a lot.

Q   Work was going on in this place, of course, where the gas was thick from top to bottom?

A   Yes, it was carried on.

How it was carried on, Shawcross commented in his closing submission, the witness had not been able to explain. 'It would have been most useful if he had. It would have conveyed much knowledge to the science of the mining engineer.'

Cripps had devoted much time to building up through the evidence of several witnesses an impression of conditions at the top end of the face on the afternoon shift before the explosion. If all the statements were collated it seemed that four or five men spread out along 30 or so yards of coalface had been working for considerable periods by the light of one safety lamp turned down as low as it would go (the others having all gone out because of gas).

It was a telling picture but it had one drawback from the point of view of Cripps's thesis concerning the 'drive for output'. Shawcross reminded the Commission,

> You remember, this was the face ... which was turning over, according to my learned friend, with such extreme and excessive rapidity. This was the face where lamps were continually going out, for a large proportion of its length men working in darkness, casting coal for long distances in complete absence of any light at all ...

If this evidence was accepted, Shawcross commented, conditions there were such that no work could be done at all.

The Commissioner had also listened patiently in accordance with his declared intention while the men 'got everything off their chests' and had drawn his own conclusions.

> The evidence of the deputies and shot firers themselves seems to me on analysis to warrant the conclusion that at times, and not infrequently, the ventilation of 14s face was inadequate and that in consequence gas, which was not reported by the deputies, accumulated more particularly at the top end ...

As for witnesses called on behalf of the North Wales Miners' Association, the Commissioner was frankly sceptical.

> Having seen and heard these men I felt at the time, and feel still, that some of them exaggerated unconsciously and some knowingly; that some drew little distinction between heat and gas, and believe that as the top end was certainly hot it must certainly be full of gas; and that all of them, except one, based their evidence on general impressions and had not made any specific test by means of their flame safety lamps which would have enabled them to determine as a fact the size and composition of any body of gas which might have been present.[4]

The exception, William Duckworth, had given a detailed and convincing account of his procedure for testing for gas.

> I reckon a collier's duties start when he draws his lamp from the lamp room, and he would turn his lamp as low as he could ... When I proceeded to the top end that's how I would have my lamp, as low as I could, and I would go in gradually, a yard at a time, and test, and if I thought I could still go ahead I would go until I could go no further. Then if there was too much I would get the banjack and use that.

Duckworth had been transferred at his own request from 29s to 14s, and had been working there on the afternoon before the accident.

Q Would you agree ... that Thomas and Amos and Jones were conscientious men doing their work with regard to safety properly?
A Well, I've seen Mr Amos on that top end refusing to fire.
Q That sounds as if he was doing his job. What do you say about Thomas and Jones? Were they conscientious men?
A Well, Harold Thomas never did much shot firing.
Q But as a fireman he was a conscientious man doing his job? You got on with him all right?
A I always got on with him all right. As far as I could see he was doing his job. If he wasn't, it wasn't up to me to dictate.

Other men had formed different impressions of the deputies and their fitness for their jobs. Alfred Tomlinson, who claimed to have found gas at the top end of 14s every time he went up there, complained on different occasions to both morning and afternoon firemen, and once had a serious altercation with Harold Amos after some roof had fallen and left a cavity.

A I put my head up in there and I had a dose of it. There was three holes in this piece of coal. So when he came to fire I said, 'Harold, I wouldn't fire here if I were you.' He dabbed his hand across my mouth and told me to shut up. I asked him to do it again, and he wouldn't do it. We nearly came to blows over it. So he told me to go home. I cursed him a bit, and I said, 'I'll be waiting on the bank for you.' Then he called one of my mates up, and he said, 'Have you heard what this fellow said?', and he said, 'Yes, and he's right' ... So when I picked up my tools he said, 'You'd better come back and stay.'
Q Did you stay?
A Yes, I stayed.

Amos, when invited to comment on the story, of course denied it. Similar allegations were made against Harold Thomas. A collier described a conversation which he claimed had taken place between Thomas and a shot firer called Williams.

Ernest Parry and me were working together when Harold Thomas came down and met Williams just by where we were working, and Thomas said, 'You refused to fire at the top end.' Williams said, 'Yes it wasn't fit.' Thomas said, 'I cleared it in five minutes and I fired it.' Williams said, 'I don't mind, I've done what I ought to do.' So Harold said, 'This face isn't big enough for us two. One of us will have to go from here.'

Thomas had his own very different version of what had occurred.

Q Do you remember a case when Mr Williams [said] to you, 'I can't fire because of gas'?
A Very likely he has done.
Q Did you reply, 'If you can't clear it you're no use here'?

A I didn't, sir. I said to him, 'Leave it and I'll clear it'.
Q Were the shots actually fired by you about fifteen minutes later?
A They was fired about two hours later.

Williams appeared before the Commission and largely through inadvertence let some very inconvenient cats out of the bag. He gave his occupation as 'fireman', claiming to have equal authority on the face with Thomas, a division of responsibility not commonly met with. As far as the Commission was concerned the ambiguity over his status was never resolved, but he clearly had a high opinion of himself and very little sense of humour. Miners had a reputation for hitting on witty and sometimes cruelly appropriate nicknames for workmates and officials and it was not difficult to see why, to his extreme annoyance and indignation, Williams was known throughout the pit as 'Bladder'. During his examination by Charlton some interesting clues to his relationship with the men emerged. He claimed, during his 15 years in Gresford, to have fired shots in almost every part of the pit.

Q And what was your practice with regard to charging the holes: did you always charge several before you fired any of them?
A Previous to going to 14s I never fired but one, rammed one and charged one, [but] when I went to 14s the men humbugged you to that effect, till you have to do more to keep them going.
   (LAUGHTER FROM THE AUDIENCE)
   There they are, they can answer the truth.
Q After you went to 14s you found that to get through the work you had to do, you charged more than one?
A Yes, I had to.
Q Up to how many would you charge?
A Up to 5 or 6.
Q Did you make an inspection before firing every shot?
A Yes, I did.
Q There were several occasions, weren't there, when you wouldn't fire shots in 14s?
A Yes.
Q Because there was too much gas about?
A There's always too much if there's any. There was gas there, and I won't fire where there's gas.
Q On several occasions you had little discussions or altercations with Mr Thomas about firing shots, didn't you?
A Oh yes, and with the men on the face remember. It was their fault as the bother occurs in that place, a lot of it. They come down and want you to fire, and they've been up there and making examinations, and they know no more about the lamp than this book, or not so much.

Q That's not their job is it?

A I don't know. When I worked on the coal I always used to make examinations before I fetched the fireman to fire. I'd be ashamed to fetch a fireman the way some of them do it.

They passed on to techniques of safe shot firing and the problem of getting the men to withdraw to a safe distance from the shot to be fired.

Q You always took certain precautions that you got plenty of distance away from it?

A That's right. That's the trouble with the men, is getting them away, but they had to go with me. Ask them. They're here. They have to go.

Q Of course, you're hardly saying that with surety, are you?

A I am, and there's not one that can deny it, either. They'd shout, 'He's come: one-at-a-time.' 'Never mind, get out of it', and 'All out of it'. It isn't all our fault you see. We've been drummed by these men a lot, to do what we've been doing.

It might have been Williams's inability to see a joke which made him misinterpret some innocent leg-pulling from the men. But the Commissioner, putting questions to a miner, had already been given corroboration of the allegation. They had got on to the subject of the firing of shots during the night shift when Robert Jones, the deputy who had been killed in the explosion, was in charge.

Q What happened after the firing of one shot?

A With Robert Jones, he'd only ram one hole at a time. We'd go back and ram the other hole. He'd fire that.

Q Seth Davis was the fireman at one time on nights in your district . . . Can you tell me what his practice was?

A He used to ram five or six holes at a time and then fire them one after each other.

Q Did he ever make any examination?

A No. The chaps used to go out to couple up. He'd stop by his battery.

This placed events in a different light. In his closing submission Cripps found in this situation the perfect proof of his central thesis, representing Williams as a man who in 14s had been corrupted by the management's 'drive for output' into abandoning his safe methods of working while at the same time the men's need for money became the excuse for their own pressure on the deputies to increase output from the face. The Commissioner, in a passage in his report which received far less attention than Cripps's denunciation of the management, distributed his disapproval less partially.

> My conclusion on the evidence ... is that shot firing in 14s district was
> carried on with little regard for the requirements laid down in the
> Explosives in Coal Mines Order, and that the workmen were just as keen
> to get the shots fired speedily as those who were firing the shots were
> under the necessity of firing them quickly—if they were to get through
> their shift's work ...
>
> According to their evidence, there were many workmen who not only
> saw the deputies and shot firers breaking the law, but also assisted them in
> their offences. In such circumstances it was not likely that they would
> draw the attention of the Inspectors to these malpractices.
>
> Whilst officials who do not obey the regulations have no excuse,
> workmen who aid and abet these officials cannot be held to be free from
> blame. They first take part in law-breaking and then, after an accident,
> turn round and blame those with whom they have acted in collusion.[5]

The note of tartness in the defensive reference to the Inspectorate was hardly surprising. Besides having to endure adverse
comment on his own performance in his dual role at the inquiry,
Walker had been compelled to listen, for the most part in silence, to
a sustained and ferocious assault on his department and his subordinates for the negligence and ineptitude which, Cripps asserted,
had contributed to the disaster. Some of the conduct in question
was inexcusable on any grounds but some of the attack was based on
at best a misconception and at worst a misrepresentation of the
position. It is difficult to accept that one of the leading advocates of
the day, who was allegedly capable of memorising 'every nook and
cranny' of the Dennis Section before going into the inquiry, took no
pains to acquaint himself with the powers available to an inspector
and the philosophy on which government supervision of the industry was based.

NOTES

1. See note 8 to Chapter 8.
2. Report of inquiry, p. 74.
3. *Ibid.*, p. 38.

> The measures taken to provide an alternative district return airway after
> the first was lost in May, 1934, were, in my opinion, dilatory and
> unsatisfactory, and it was not proper to continue to work 14s face until
> a connection direct to the main return airway had been made. At the time

of the explosion and for several months previously, the general layout of the ventilation was bad.

And again: 'Work on 14s face should have been stopped altogether until a return aircourse, far removed from the intake, was made' (*ibid.*, p. 63).

4. *Ibid.*, p. 51.
5. *Ibid.*, p. 72.

CHAPTER 12

The Inspectorate

The Mines Inspectorate was one of the earliest products of the dilemma with which the emerging social conscience of the nineteenth century was forced to grapple: how to mitigate the worst sufferings of the industrial worker without restricting the freedom of the entrepreneur to pursue his private and legitimate aim of making money. In the light of the starkly illustrated report of the Children's Employment Commission, on the long hours and at times almost bestial conditions in which even tiny children (and grown women) were required to work underground, there could be no serious opposition to the widespread demand that these abuses should cease. Proposals for the necessary legislation appeared in the form of a Bill promoted by Lord Ashley, which provided that, after 1 March 1843, it would be unlawful to employ women and girls underground in any capacity and to employ boys underground below the age of ten; boys of less than ten were not to be bound apprentice and no apprenticeship should last for more than eight years. The penalties for infringement of any of these conditions were fixed at not less than £5 and not more than £10. The legislation, according to Boyd, the historian of the Inspectorate,'was characterized as a useless and mischievous prying into the affairs of private individuals'; Lord Londonderry described it as a measure which 'might be regarded as the commencement of a series of grievances which would be got up for the purpose of working on that hypocritical humanity which reigned so much'; but it became law in spite of him.

In a timorous attempt to secure compliance with the Act, Parliament empowered the Secretary of State to appoint 'proper persons to inspect mines and collieries'. The first and only inspector appointed was a clergyman, Seymour Tremenheere,[1] whose beat was the 2,000 or so coal mines of Great Britain, or rather the surface area of the mines, for it had been concluded, possibly in his own interests, that he had better not venture underground. His appointment was predictably unpopular with the colliery owners, and Lord

Londonderry had let it be known that he would say to an inspector, 'You may go down the pit how you can, and when you are down you may remain there.' Lord Ashley himself had considered under-ground inspection impossible, 'and indeed if it were possible it would not be safe ... I for one should be loth to go down a shaft for the purpose of doing some act that was likely to be distasteful to the colliers down below'. Among the acts likely to have displeased the colliers would have been to inquire too closely into the ages of the boys working alongside them, who were usually their own sons, brought down the pit at the earliest moment when they could earn a few pence towards their keep.[2]

Tremenheere carried out his solitary task for eight years. His role was little more than that of welfare officer and his powers, effectively, were limited to persuasion, the giving of advice and the investigation of grievances. During the whole time, according to a contemporary, he probably never went down a mine and with the owners he could never afford to drop his guard. He wrote in later years,

> It may be imagined that I found these great and wealthy owners of mines, collieries and ironworks and the Agents and Managers ... in a not very comfortable state of mind ... They were, for the most part (for there were some admirable exceptions) exceedingly rough and uncultivated (though many of them were rich) and I found I had need of all the 'conciliatory manners' with which Lord Lansdowne had credited me to keep them in a moderate temper.

As in other problem areas, such as education and public health, the Victorian reformers soon learned that by taking one step they had set out on a road on which there was no turning back. Removing women and small children from the mines made their lives a little easier and saved them from being killed by explosions but did nothing for their menfolk, who continued to be slaughtered in appalling numbers. Prosecutions of offending employers had little effect. Innovations in mining technique were resisted or ignored because they would cost money or, it was alleged, would fail to work. The only answer was some kind of independent supervision of the pits, and the miners themselves brought forward a petition in 1847 praying that 'inspectors should be appointed to visit all mines and that some of these inspectors should be men acquainted with colliery work'. According to Boyd writing in the 1870s, 'the colliers gave expression to their idea, so erroneously entertained, but persistently advocated for many years, that the responsibility of management should be borne by the Government inspector'. A measure introduced into Parliament as a consequence of the petition was opposed by the Home Secretary on precisely these grounds: 'that it was extremely desirable that no portion of the responsibility which justly attached to the owner should be transferred to Government or Parliament'. Nevertheless, Parliament found itself being pushed reluctantly but inexorably towards the solution it had formerly held back from. There must be inspection beyond the limits imposed on Tremenheere. The inspector, *pace* Lord Londonderry, must be allowed to go down the mine; he should also be able to recommend the adoption of the appropriate system of ventilation for the conditions he found there.

In the opinion of some he should have the power to insist on the implementation of his recommendations but to this there was the apparently insuperable objection that it implied, once again, the right of government to intervene in the affairs of private citizens by prescribing not merely, as in the past, whom they were and were not to employ but how they were to apply their own capital, skill and enterprise. Inspectors, it was generally agreed, must be allowed only to go down the mine, look around and examine the working plans; and their duties should be confined, in the words of a Select Committee of the House of Lords, to 'recording and reporting, making suggestions and communicating information to managers and owners'. A Bill to this effect was at length brought before Parliament and passed without much difficulty in August 1850 as 'An Act for Inspection of Coal Mines in Great Britain'. The inspectors, of whom there were to be four at a salary of £400 per annum, were given power to go into all parts of the mine to inquire into 'all Matters and Things connected with or relating to the safety of Persons employed'. If a dangerous situation, having been drawn to the manager's attention, was not attended to within a reasonable time the inspector was empowered to report the matter to the Secretary of State, but the inspectors were categorically instructed that it was 'no part of [their] duty to enforce any particular mode of ventilation or working'.

Disraeli described the Act as 'a piece of hasty and ill-considered legislation',[3] but he was perhaps merely fulfilling the duty of the opposition to oppose. Lord Brougham unexpectedly considered it an 'unjustifiable interference' not with private property but with 'the rights of labour'.

When the country was divided into four for the purpose of implementing the Act North Wales became part of a district which also included Lancashire, Cheshire, Staffordshire, Shropshire and Worcestershire, and the man to whom this extensive territory was assigned was a 31-year-old Tynesider, Joseph Dickinson. A Fellow of the Geological Society of London, he had taught at an Experimental Mining School in Cornwall, supervised the Dowlais ironworks and collieries in South Wales, studied for four years at the Museum of Practical Geology, and at the time of his appointment was an agent at an iron, coal and lead mine works in Scotland. He served as inspector, with Manchester as his base, for 41 years, becoming one of the leading authorities on mining matters, advising the government on mining legislation and sitting on the Commission which in 1871 reassured the country that its coal supplies would not be exhausted for at least 267 years.

Dickinson was described in later life as 'a man of old-fashioned, gentle courtesy, quiet self-possession [and] characteristic modesty', at first sight hardly the qualities which would enable him to stand up to the 'rough and uncultivated' men who ran collieries. But these attributes probably stood him in better stead than a more aggressive, authoritarian approach would have done because, as the *Mining Journal* contemptuously pointed out in 1853, 'Inspectors do not have the power to enforce the simplest and most reasonable rules', and Dickinson himself, in the same year, provided a pathetic glimpse of the realities of life in the mid-nineteenth-century coalfields. He wrote in his annual report,

> In one instance (Bent Colliery, Oldham), the circumstances under which the colliery is carried on are so exceedingly dangerous that beyond urging upon the proprietor the necessity of suspending operations until the ventilation can be arranged, *I have not dared to hazard any suggestion.* (author's italics)

Within two years of the inauguration of the Inspectorate it was evident that the size of the task and the workload laid upon the inspectors had been underestimated. With 1,200 collieries to be inspected each man would have to visit 300 mines a year, and, somewhat grudgingly, two further appointments were made. The inadequacies of the system continued to be shown up at every turn and in 1855, when the Inspection Act was renewed for a further five years, the number of inspectors was doubled, their salaries were increased, and so were their duties, which now included the promulgation of General and Special Rules designed to promote safer working in the pits.

As a result of the reorganisation Dickinson's North West Division, which now included the whole of Lancashire, Cheshire and North Wales with a total of 879 pits, was split: he retained East Lancashire and Cheshire and a new man, Peter Higson, took over West Lancashire, centred on the Wigan and St Helens districts, and North Wales. Higson had been a colliery manager and was a tougher and, to judge by his prose style, a more flamboyant character than Dickinson with a taste for the occasional purple patch to enliven his reports.

> We hope from time to time the tide of destruction is beginning to ebb, when suddenly and perhaps in the middle of a dead calm, the quiet serenity of some rural district is disturbed by some fearful casualty, the angel of death has passed over it, and the wailing of widows with their helpless offspring in their arms tells us, in unmistakable language, the work of destruction has been terrible and complete. Anxious spectators group round the scene and in consternation and amazement ask the cause and inquire if nothing can be done to prevent such fearful recurrences. (1860)

In Higson's district there were 190 collieries consisting of '430 working pits, of which 99 are pits for ventilation only'. Many of them were deep, output from them was increasing, and even with the smaller area to oversee the inspector's workload was heavy. In the three years since his appointment, he recorded in February 1859, he had paid 660 visits in his own district and 13 in others; he had attended a great many inquests and devoted 36 days to prosecutions, besides dealing with the correspondence, 'which is tedious and voluminous, and sufficient to employ a clerk'. He, like his colleagues, was therefore not best pleased by the attacks which were continually launched against the Inspectorate by miners, some of them from his own division. At the National Conference in 1863 it was alleged that in 13 years some pits in North Wales had never seen the inspector, and that in those which he did visit he 'never went further than the bottom of the pit'; there were demands for the appointment of practical miners to act as sub-inspectors and even for 60 additional inspectors in North Wales.

At the root of much of the argument was what constituted inspection, what it could hope to achieve, and what might be the unintended consequences of too much rather than too little of it.

'Some maintain', Higson asserted, and there seems little doubt that he was one of them,

> that [constant and periodical supervision] would cause managers and underlookers to feel relieved in some degree of responsibility ... if Inspectors' visits were made more frequently, those of management would naturally become fewer ... I am not prepared to deny that something more is wanted, but I think that requirement should be supplied by the owners of mines. I have been astonished at their not rendering Government inspection unnecessary.[4]

Unfortunately, on his own showing there were too many pits where owners were unable or unwilling to shoulder their responsibilities. The only solution was more inspection, little though he liked the idea. 'With so many painful casualties before me, which if an inspector had been expected might not have occurred, I am of opinion that if more inspection be considered necessary and desirable, each inspector should have a few assistants ...'. They should be young men, he added, because 'there are mines through which a man advanced in years would not be able to travel'.

The government had been slowly coming round to the same point of view and in its comprehensive Mines Regulation Act of 1872 (described by a conference of mine managers as a measure for 'inflicting severe penalties on managers and owners, and greatly increasing the price of coal'[5]) it provided for the appointment of 12 assistant inspectors and, under a separate Act, for two inspectors of metalliferous mines. The strength of the Inspectorate had thus grown in 20 years from four to 26, for whom in due course a set of 'Instructions as to Inspection Duties' was issued. It was henceforth the duty of the inspector to visit a mine on invitation, or on complaint, or where he had reason to believe that it was not being conducted safely or in accordance with the law, or wherever he thought he might be of service; and in a largely vain attempt to anticipate the complaint which has bedevilled inspection in all walks of life at all times the inspector was instructed to visit the mine 'without notice'. And these, according to the Royal Commission on Safety in Mines, were 'substantially the guiding principles' on which the work of the Inspectorate was still organised when the Commission reported in 1937, three years after Gresford.

Higson's 20 years' service coincided with a period of rapid growth and comparative prosperity in the coalfields. His successor Henry Hall inherited West Lancashire and North Wales at a time when the industry was faced with the paradox that increasing and more stringent inspection was accompanied only by more frequent and often more devastating explosions. In the circumstances it was natural that the miners should include among the targets of their wrath the inspectors, whom they accused of failing them. Alexander Macdonald,[6] who had played a large part in the campaign for the Act of 1872, launched a bitter attack following the great disaster at Blantyre which cost 207 lives. The inspectors in his view were not worth their keep. They were paid £800 per annum and £400 travelling expenses, when a stout Highlander or Irish policeman could have done the job just as well for £2 a week. The inspectors for their part stressed the limitations under which, in spite of the Act, they were still required to operate, and the size of their task. With only one assistant they had perhaps hundreds of pits scattered over a wide area to visit; and, as Hall protested, 'an extensive colliery cannot be inspected in an hour or a day like a workshop, and the conditions are constantly changing'.

The government recognised some of these difficulties and increased the number of inspectors yet again, but at the same time increased the scope of their duties so that their workload was as burdensome as ever. By the turn of the century Hall, with three assistants, was responsible for coal mines and metalliferous mines in West Lancashire, parts of Cheshire, the whole of Flintshire and Denbighshire, Montgomeryshire, Caernarvonshire and Anglesey, a total of 817 works. In 1902 they carried out between them more than 1,600 inspections of mines and quarries above and below ground, dealt with 603 separate accidents, attended 100 inquests, maintained correspondence with more than 800 establishments, kept up to date long lists of works and managers, drew up and promulgated special rules, deposited plans of mines and 'worked at other matters too numerous to mention'—all in the days before the company car and the telephone. For many years the inspectors conducted all their official business from their own homes (in Hall's case Liverpool), and it was not until 1889 that the government provided an annual grant of £25 for clerical assistance with the 'tedious and voluminous correspondence' of which Higson had complained.

The question which this kind of timetable raised was what constituted 'a thorough inspection of a mine'? A clause in the Mines Bill which was before the House in 1904 stated, 'In every district an inspector shall make a complete examination of every mine and *every part thereof* at least once every six months.' But as Hall pointed out, at the only colliery in his area where the men had recently exercised their right under the Act of 1872 to carry out their own inspection, 'the time occupied by the two examiners amounted to 20 days of eight hours: the firm in question has two pits'. Inevitably in practice the rules were modified, especially in coal mines, where the investigation of serious accidents, which occurred daily, took up much of the time which in theory should have been spent on systematic inspection. All mines, Hall claimed, were inspected both underground and on the surface, although it was true that 'inspection by sample' was all that could sometimes be attained;

> but an inspector is seldom at a loss when looking over plans to know to which part of a mine his steps should be directed. To start and examine each working place would be a simple waste of time and money; such work must be done by the colliery officials.

Hall retired in 1910, collecting a well-earned knighthood and in 1928 the Gold Medal of the Institute of Mining Engineers; like Dickinson he lived on into his nineties, dying in 1937. In the succeeding 24 years the division, the greater part of which had known only two incumbents in 55 years, passed through a number of hands and underwent several changes of boundary which need not be traced in detail. In the month of the Gresford disaster it was known as the North Western Division and consisted of Lancashire, Cheshire, North Staffordshire and the six northern counties of Wales. The inspector for the division was William John Charlton, who had been promoted a year or two earlier from South Wales. Under him were two senior inspectors of whom only one, Thomas Boydell, was concerned with Gresford; his territory was the whole of the North West Division and his responsibilities extended to metalliferous mines and quarries. In North Wales the staff consisted of one junior inspector, who was mainly concerned with coal mines. There were numerous other staff whose duties interlocked and sometimes overlapped.

Until March 1933 the junior inspector in North Wales, responsible for Gresford among other collieries, was John Taylor Shaw. His evidence to the inquiry was that he had paid a number of visits to the mine about which he was questioned by Shawcross in some detail. He had found nothing out of the ordinary with regard to gas in the Dennis Section and agreed that the firemen were performing their duties fully and conscientiously, and that the management were always ready to comply with any requirement or suggestion that he advocated.

Shaw was transferred to another area in March 1933 and was succeeded by Percy George Dominy, whose contribution to the inquiry was surpassed only by that of Bonsall for its remarkable revelations and their reception by Cripps.

The examination-in-chief of all the inspectors was conducted by their own superior, the divisional inspector, and one wonders what were Charlton's feelings as he prepared to reveal in public to *his* superior, Sir Henry Walker, the manner in which he had allowed a subordinate to conduct the affairs of the Inspectorate in the matter of Gresford Colliery. Whether Dominy knew what was in store for him is not clear but he had sat in the room throughout the inquiry watching Cripps at work, and must have felt at least a twinge of apprehension as he approached the witness chair.

Charlton did his best for Dominy, confining himself as far as he dared to eliciting a plain recital of the facts of Dominy's stewardship and resisting the temptation which he yielded to with other witnesses to comment on or probe any irregularities which came to light. The main outline of what he established was that Dominy had been a junior inspector for 13 years and since being transferred to North Wales had visited Gresford 24 times. He hadn't always gone down the pit and when he did go it wasn't always to the Dennis Section. He had only once found gas in Gresford, in 109s district, in September 1933. In December of that year, after going through the records in the manager's office, he had pointed out to Bonsall that 'as many as 69 shots were being fired on occasions by shot firers, and 45 by firemen'. He had told Bonsall that he thought 40 shots for a shot firer and 20 for a fireman were quite sufficient: Bonsall had agreed and promised to 'start another shot firer at once'.

His last visit had been made on 10 September 1934. His report was read out, a harmless statement of the way coal was being got in 29s district. 'No firedamp was observed and no contraventions were noted. The coal cutter had no fence. Mr Bonsall, manager, promised to provide one. Both means of egress travelled. Lamps have no ignition pins. 6 pairs of gloves in use.'

There was a moment of light relief when in reply to a question about the clothing he wore when he went into the Dennis Section he replied, 'Flannel trousers, singlet, overalls, and an overcoat as far as the 29s turn.' Hurriedly trying to quell the laughter from the audience of miners, Charlton led him to agree that he left his overcoat at the turn and went on in his overalls. He had found 14s face 'pretty warm'? No, not when he was there. But that was last March wasn't it, when 14s face hadn't advanced so far from the main road? He agreed.

He had never discussed with Mr Bonsall in detail the fact that 29s district was being ventilated largely by air which had already passed round other districts. He had thought that the situation with regard to dust in the Dennis Section was very good because in the main roads he could see the roads were plainly being thoroughly dusted and in the auxiliary roads he did not see any coal dust.

Charlton could do no more for him and turned him over to Cripps, who dealt first with those visits to Gresford which had not included a descent of the pit. Under persistent questioning he agreed that during his visits to the colliery he had never noticed that essential records were not being kept and that although he could tell from the books that measurements of air, required by the regulations, were not being taken he had neither raised the matter with the manager, nor taken any samples himself, nor attempted to discover why the ventilation wasn't operating as it was intended to.

This set the pattern for a systematic and ruthless annihilation of the junior inspector. Apparently an easy-going, rather muddle-headed young man, he constantly found his vague answers turned against him and his shortcomings exposed.

On his last visit to Gresford, 12 days before the accident, there had been some question of gas being found by a fireman.

A On that day I met the fireman at the top end of the face. I had seen no gas up to that time and I said to him, 'Have you seen any gas here?', and he said, 'Yes, we had a little this morning in this top end here.' I said, 'Well, let's come and have another look', and we both inspected again, and I said, 'There's no gas now', and he agreed with me.

Q Did you see when you went up whether he'd entered that record of gas in his report?

A No, I don't suppose he'd have made his report by that time.

Q In those circumstances is it your view that he ought or ought not to have entered that?

A I don't think he should have entered it.

Q Is it your view that if a fireman discovers gas in a pit, and subsequently he finds that it's not there, he shouldn't enter his discovery?

A He should enter it on a separate report, yes, not on his statutory inspection.

Q What separate book is there for him to make that report in?

A There isn't one ...

Q Why didn't you mention the incident in your report?

A Because there was no gas there when I saw it.

Q If it's of importance for the fireman to enter the fact that gas has been present, isn't it equally important for the inspector to mention it?

A Yes.

Q Did you ever go to those places where you saw that gas was constantly being reported by the firemen, to see what it was, or whether it was there, or wasn't there?

A In 81s place, no ... It was explained to me that it was a small quantity in a cavity.

Q Really! Who explained it?

A The manager.

Q Do you mean to say you satisfy yourself with an explanation from the manager? I wonder you trouble to go down the pit at all.

A There are a few honest men in the world.

Q I'm not suggesting there aren't honest people, but do you think it's the job of His Majesty's Inspector to go to the surface and ask the manager what he thinks of the pit?

A I go down too.[7]

It was Dominy's first attempt at a riposte and it did nothing to help his cause. They came to the question of the firemen's reports that were missing because, having been taken down the pit, in contravention of the rules, they were presumed to have been destroyed in the explosion (some of them were subsequently recovered).[8]

Q You realise that ... at all times there must be either the original or a duplicate in the office of the mine?

A Yes.

Q That wasn't done?

A That wasn't done as far as I could see. If the explosion hadn't taken place and the books been lost you'd either have had the duplicates—

Q But, Mr Dominy, the explosion did take place, you see, unfortunately. Why didn't you, when you went there, see that that instruction of the Act was obeyed?

A Because I didn't think for a moment that an explosion would take place.

Dominy admitted that he had never seen shots being fired in the Dennis Section but claimed to be satisfied that after December 1933 no shot firer was exceeding 40 per shift and no fireman 20. Cripps read out the records for July 1934: 54, 55, 52, 57, 60, and so on. Dominy agreed that these figures were not satisfactory, and that he hadn't in fact looked at any records of shot firing since his surface inspection in February 1934.

It was Dominy who on official instructions had carried out an investigation into overtime in the area and failed to uncover the irregularities at Gresford.

> Q Did you make any inquiries to ascertain whether there was anything in addition to what was shown by the books by way of overtime?
> A No ... I merely took the record from the register.
> Q Surely a simple question to Mr Bonsall, 'Do you work overtime in this pit?' would have brought the answer, 'Of course we do, every Friday night and every Sunday night'?
> A It possibly would.
> Q ... Really the fact is that you looked through these books, and apparently you didn't care a pin whether they complied with the Regulations or not.
> A If the records were good I thought they were all right.
> Q But you never noticed anything wrong?
> A There wasn't anything.
> Q Well, you never noticed it anyway?
> A There wasn't anything wrong as far as I saw.

After much more of the same Cripps pronounced his own verdict.

> Q I suggest to you that so far as your supervision of this pit was concerned while you were there it was a farce.
> A That is wrong, sir.

Cripps had finished with Dominy but Peter Lee, making a rare contribution on behalf of the Miners' Federation, had not. Taking each district in turn he forced Dominy to admit that in spite of his contention that he knew the mine well he had never travelled some of the main haulage roads and had never seen most of the return airways although, as he conceded, allowing one day to each district he could have acquired a good general knowledge of the whole in about two weeks. 'Now,' said Peter Lee, 'don't you think it would give the workmen greater confidence if they'd seen you more in the mine?'

> A But my time is spread over other mines as well as this one, Mr Lee ... I have 20 large pits to look after and I have 20 working days in the month. That's one to each pit. That's not counting small pits and metal mines and quarries.

Q Can you tell me that you haven't had time to give a fortnight to this big mine?

A That could have been done, yes; I could have done it and neglected other ones.

Q You don't mean seriously to tell me that you have more work than you can do efficiently?

A No, but if I'm at Gresford for a fortnight I can't be anywhere else for a fortnight.

Peter Lee was not satisfied: could Dominy give him any reason why in 18 months he had not acquired a general knowledge of Gresford and the other pits in his charge? Dominy could not and was finally allowed to stand down.

The embarrassing ordeal of the Inspectorate was not yet over. It was all very well to have a junior inspector's inadequacies ruthlessly exposed but what had his superiors been doing all this time? The senior inspector, Thomas Boydell, was questioned in formal terms by the divisional inspector, Charlton, and more searchingly by Stafford Cripps. The main point at issue soon became one which had been familiar since the days of Higson, Hall and their contemporaries: how much work an inspector had to do and how well he could do it in the time available.

The answer, which took much probing to arrive at, was that there was far too much work and far too little time to do it in. Boydell spent four days a week inspecting pits and only one day a week in North Wales. He had never made an inspection of Gresford, for want of time and opportunity; but he *had* written a favourable report on conditions in the mine. Cripps read it aloud and suggested that there was no information on which it could have been based.

A That's almost like telling me I've written something which is a lie.

Q You've written something, if you wish me to express my opinion on it, which was wholly unjustifiable on the material which you had at your disposal.

A I haven't written that without I've had some information to that effect.

Q Well, I want that information.

A Well, I don't know where it is. I've not written that without having had some information.

Q I'm not prepared to accept that, Mr Boydell.

A It doesn't matter to me whether you do or not. I say that is so.

There remained one further level at which the investigation of the Inspectorate's role must be pursued, and since the divisional inspector could hardly examine himself Cripps took on the task.

Charlton was a voluble man who gave the impression of being unabashed by the disclosures of the preceding days, and Cripps treated him with greater deference than his subordinates had been shown, so that it took a little time for battle to be usefully joined. The inquiry heard that there were 286 mines in the division, about half of them large ones, and that Charlton had last inspected Gresford in 1915 during a previous spell of duty in the area. 'That', remarked Cripps drily, 'would not be of much assistance now.' It was also made clear that the divisional inspector was entirely dependent on his staff to draw his attention to anything amiss in a mine. But when an inspector expressed concern in a report at the small amount of air arriving at the coalface at Gresford compared with the amount being delivered from the surface, Charlton had not sent for a plan of the mine to see what was happening; he didn't have in his office plans of all the mines and even if he'd had them he couldn't have 'digested' them. It was the same with the forms on which readings of air samples and so on were recorded. They came to him and were sent straight on to the Mines Department for the statistics to be recorded; they were not used for control purposes, as the Act of Parliament had intended.

> Q I see you say in another report of yours, that of 1932: 'The chief preventive measure against the danger of explosions is good ventilation ... Too often it is only when pressing difficulties arise that investigation is made, and defects in the general layout are revealed.' You might almost have written that about Gresford, mightn't you?
> A Yes, that's true.

Under examination Charlton could only discuss the matters on which he was questioned, but unlike others who came under attack he had the privilege in the final stages of the inquiry of addressing the tribunal. He naturally took the opportunity to make a spirited defence of the Inspectorate in general and himself and his staff in particular. In essence he accused Cripps of painting a false picture of the powers of the Inspectorate and contrasted the inspector's position with that of the management and the workmen.

> I find nowhere in the Coal Mines Act any provisions giving overriding powers of control of a mine to an inspector. On the contrary, his powers are very strictly limited. The number of mines which one manager may control is strictly limited by law. The size of a fireman's district is limited.

> The manager must exercise daily supervision. The fireman must inspect twice in the course of his shift. An inspector may, under favourable circumstances, manage to visit a mine twice in the course of a month. Yet, says Counsel for the North Wales miners, the inspectors are equally responsible for the alleged conditions of the mine ...
>
> Sir Stafford Cripps and those he represents put forward alleged waste of air, alleged small size of returns, as the result of the negligence of myself and my staff. I find nothing in the Statute governing these matters. In respect of them I have no powers at all.

When these remarks were made in the spring of 1936 the Royal Commission on Safety in Coal Mines had been taking evidence concerning 'the proper limits and objectives of Government inspection of mines', and had been hearing from the permanent under-secretary for the Mines Department the conclusions which an earlier commission had come to. Charlton quoted from the relevant passage.

> It is apparent that if the contention is accepted that all the underground workings of every mine must be thoroughly examined even once a year it will require a very much larger staff of inspectors—probably three or four times larger—than is at present employed ... Apart from considerations of the public expenditure which would be involved in the appointment of such an army of inspectors we do not think such a course could be justified. If it were admitted that to inspect a colliery the inspector must visit every 'nook and cranny' of each mine ... the question arises whether he could even then express an exact opinion as to the conditions of the mine, which are changing from day to day, and whether he ought not to be there more frequently, or even constantly. Such a system would involve an inspector in performing the duties which should naturally fall on the officials of the colliery, and it appears to us alien to the objectives of Government inspection.

That was still the official view, the permanent under-secretary told the Royal Commission. 'Any different view of the matter which contemplated an enlargement of the responsibilities of the inspectors and the administration would need to have regard to their powers as well as their duties.'

Power, Charlton pointed out more than once, was what the inspector was denied as things stood. 'He can advise—he cannot order.' Moreover, to be effective he needed cooperation, and this also he was often refused, and not only by managements. In the matter of excessive overtime at Gresford, for example: 'Overtime could have been stopped—brought to my knowledge by any workman, by the Secretary of Gresford Branch, or by the miners' agent for North Wales.' But no complaints were received and the breach of the law was connived at by everybody.

> It is a hard saying that an inspector must discover breaches of the law when management and workmen alike combine in keeping it [sic] from his knowledge ... One thing is clear, that if the Government Inspection service is to supervise and enforce in detail the vast extent of safety law without help from, and even in the face of hindrance by, those whom the law is designed to protect, then indeed its task will be a formidable one and radically different in character and extent from their present duty.

Any suggestion that men who had endured the conditions of the Dennis Section might bear some share of responsibility for what had happened there was bitterly resented; Cripps, protesting at 'this attempt ... to try to throw blame on them', described it as 'most discreditable'. There was no denying, however, that some of them had knowingly broken the law, others had, in Charlton's phrase, 'connived at' breaches of the safety regulations and many had without effective protest continued to go down a pit day after day well aware of the exceptional risks they were running. Tom Ellis, later the Member of Parliament for Wrexham, then a boy living in Rhosllanerchrugog, heard a Gresford man say, 'One of these days we'll be blown sky high'; he died in the explosion. A man from 95s, asked by Shawcross if he had expected conditions there to give rise to an explosion, replied, 'It could have happened before now.' What then had been the attitude of the workmen to the question of their own safety and survival?

NOTES

1. Before becoming the inspector of mines, Tremenheere had been the first inspector of schools (1839–43) and an Assistant Poor Law Commissioner.

2. The classic account of boys' work underground is provided by the reports of the Children's Employment Commission (Mines) 1842. The Commissioner for North Wales found evidence of a few cases of children as young as six 'if the seam of coal be thin, as for instance from 2 to 3 feet'. Seven was 'by no means an uncommon age in the Ruabon district' (in other coalfields it was often as low as five). Boyd, a former inspector, recorded that 'the men themselves ... considered the almost prohibitory restriction on the labour of boys as a great hardship'. As the age limit was raised by degrees to 10 and then 12, inspectors in North Wales

expressed guarded disapproval. In 1870 Higson, a former mine manager, asserted that it would be

> an act of injustice to prohibit boys working underground under the age of 12 years ... To keep young persons from work till they are 12 years of age will, I fear, create an objection to labour which through life they may never be able to overcome ... At that age many will never be able to work in mines 14 or 16 inches thick.

As late as 1900 Hall, commenting on 'the feeling abroad that 12 years is rather early to send boys to work below ground', ventured to disagree.

> I don't think they take much harm and they always seem very merry, though some of them are very little chaps. It may make a great difference to a workman's family where there are six or seven young children, when the eldest begins to earn even the rent of the cottage.

3. Quoted in Woodward, *The Age of Reform*, p. 156.
4. Reports 1865, 1866, 1870.
5. Boyd (1879), p. 195.
6. Almost every possible variant of this man's surname occurs, sometimes in two different forms on the same page. This appears to be the most favoured version.
7. For the legislation relevant to this passage see the 1911 Act, Part II 64 (3):

> A full and accurate report, specifying whether or not, and where, if any, noxious or inflammatory gas was found ... shall be recorded without delay in a book to be kept at the mine for the purpose, and accessible to the workmen ... and signed by ... the person who made the inspection.

8. 1911 Act, Part I 24 (1): 'All such books as are required by this Act to be kept at a mine ... shall be in the prescribed form, and the books, or a correct copy thereof, shall be kept at the office of the mine...'.

CHAPTER 13

The Miners

One of the distinctions regularly and ruefully claimed by inspectors of mines for the North Wales area in the late nineteenth and early twentieth centuries was the worst record for fatal accidents in British coalfields. By 1882 the loss of life had become so alarming that Henry Hall's assistant was sent to live in Chester rather than Liverpool, 'to enable him to devote more of his time to the North Wales collieries'. Thereafter the situation showed some improvement, partly as a result of more stringent safety regulations, but North Wales continued to be a problem child.

Successive inspectors were puzzled to find a cause and apportion blame for this unfortunate pre-eminence. In the primitive days of the 1850s Joseph Dickinson noted that there were in North Wales 'some very rough samples of mining', and with that capacity for understatement which his gentle nature prompted he added that the comparative absence of accidents 'seems more attributable to the greater care with which the workmen of that part regard their lives than to any superiority of provision for their safety'. An inspector in a neighbouring division was more forthright: 'The majority of accidents are attributable to the recklessness and neglect of the proprietors and managers of mines.'

Dickinson's successor Higson stressed the need for better education among miners, especially those in positions of responsibility, but as the years went by the emphasis in his reports shifted from concern over the standards of management to something like exasperation with the indifference and fatalistic attitude of the individual miner in the matter of safety. Mining was always attended with danger but the miner himself seemed to think least about it.

> He sees or hears of explosions destroying hundreds at a time: of falls of roof upon his fellow workmen or assistants; of inburst water inundating a mine ... and still he pursues his daily calling, and relies for all necessary protection on those who are in charge of the works. On finding anything wrong in his place of work he may perhaps mention it to the underlooker or fireman ... but he seldom makes such communications to the owner or

155

principal agent, and never to the Inspector of Mines. I have received a
few letters during the year from miners' agents ... but I cannot now recall
a single instance of having received information from a workman,
although I am pretty generally known throughout the country and those
who have not my address can easily obtain it.[1]

Seventy years later, in the inquiry room at Wrexham, he would
have found little cause to amend that paragraph.

Hall, who came to the division shortly after the passing of the
Act of 1872, conceded that the mines there were deeper and more
difficult to work than those of Lancashire, 'but these causes are not
sufficient to account for the wide difference in result'. He was
inclined on further reflection to put the great loss of life among
single individuals down to 'managers neglecting to enforce discipline [according to] the special rules'. In 1892, in a probably
unconscious echo of Engels's conclusion that 'In the whole British
Empire there is no occupation in which a man may meet his end in
so many diverse ways as in this one',[2] Hall supported his report of
23 deaths in North Wales alone with the observation that 'the
character of the accidents have [sic] been very various, and men
have met their deaths by burning, drowning, suffocation, and every
kind of mangling of body and limbs by falls of roof and entangle-
ment of machinery'.

Twenty years on, and five years before Gresford, the inspector
for the division was still reporting the accident rate in North Wales
as 'high compared to some other divisions'.[3] As an extenuating
circumstance he noted that 'the natural conditions of the division
are more difficult than in any other parts of the country ... the coal
measures are much faulted [and] seams lie near together at high
inclination'; on the other hand, 'many accidents are the result of
victims "taking a chance", and any effort directed to discouraging
workmen from taking needless risks is commendable'. The consequences of the industrial and political upheaval of the past decade,
accelerating the general decline of the coalfield, were underlined by
his comment that 'the economic working of collieries in some
instances must have approached very near the time when safe
working was about to be sacrificed in order to keep pits from
being closed down'. In spite of this his annual report recorded his
pleasure on being able to point to an entire absence of accidents due
to explosions of firedamp, although there had been a total of 30
deaths during the preceding 15 years.

It would be unfair and unwise to judge every generation of North Wales miners by the same inflexible standard but there are certain characteristics of the coalfield which persisted over sufficiently long periods to give rise to a suspicion that they may have played some part in shaping attitudes to safety at Gresford in the early 1930s.

The least relevant perhaps, but certainly one of the more extraordinary, was the hostility which persisted throughout most of the nineteenth century to the use of the safety lamp with, as its corollary, indifference to the danger presented by naked lights.[4] In the 1860s the North Wales men were known to go on strike rather than use safety lamps, and in 1876 Hall reported that the feeling against them, both among managers and men, was so strong that he felt it was almost hopeless to suggest introducing them. Many managers for their part clung to the ancient method of ventilating pits by means of a furnace placed at the bottom of the upcast shaft, on the principle that hot air, rising up the shaft, would draw fresh air behind it through the pit.[5] As it also drew the firedamp, which had often to pass through the flames on its way out, an explosion was always on the cards and sometimes occurred; but, as Higson commented, 'many colliery managers cannot be taught except by disastrous personal experience'.

Most firedamp explosions were small-scale affairs resulting in only one or two deaths. A significant exception was the explosion at Brynmally Colliery, near Wrexham, in 1889, which was not only the worst recorded in North Wales until Gresford but also introduces a theme which perhaps has relevance to the situation in Gresford itself.

In this accident 20 men were killed because, as Hall explained,[6] the rules governing the use of safety lamps—in this case the relighting of lamps which had gone out—were flouted.

> Lamp stations for re-lighting were established in the mine, but certain persons appear to have taken it upon themselves to open lamps at points nearer to the face of the workings. Both Mr Thomas and myself were of the opinion that this state of things was largely due to the fact that the contractors or butties were selected by the management as the persons to control the opening and re-lighting of safety lamps. The livelihood of the butties depends upon those whom they employ getting the coal as rapidly as possible, and sometimes apparently when their 'hands' lost their lights from any cause they were tempted to avoid the delay which would be caused by taking the lamps out to the proper stations to be relighted.

This is our first meeting with the 'butties'[7] who figure so largely in the history of the North Wales coalfield, more usually under their local name of 'charter masters' or occasionally 'chalter masters'. Accounts of the origin of the butty system vary. According to one historian of the coal industry it was a phenomenon which flourished primarily in the Midlands and had largely been abandoned by the middle of the nineteenth century, except in South Staffordshire and East Worcestershire where it lingered on well into the twentieth. A similar system seems to have been in operation in South Wales, introduced there perhaps by men from the Midlands who had been imported to help develop the local pits. It certainly flourished in North Wales down to quite recent times, but was apparently little known in Lancashire, where the inspector for the joint area recorded, in connection with some rules introduced in 1855, that 'provision as to Charter Masters is confined almost exclusively to North Wales'.

In his earliest manifestation the butty or charter master was in essence a middle-man. The colliery owner sank the shafts and provided the wherewithal to raise the coal. An agent supervised technical development, marketing and legal and financial matters, and the butty undertook to get the coal out at an agreed price per ton. He was to all intents and purposes the boss underground. He took on his own labour, paid the wages and provided the necessary tools and equipment for the job, for which he sometimes charged the workmen. In return for having these burdens taken from their shoulders, owners and managers gave the charter masters virtually a free hand in the running of the pit, with the result that, in the words of one authority, 'these men dreaded inspection by the owner almost as much as the owner by the Government'. They were hated by their own labour force, not only in their role as employer but because their profitable operation of the pits enabled them to branch out into other activities, notably the ownership of shops and public houses which the colliers and their wives were expected and often compelled to patronise.

Tremenheere, the first inspector of mines, paid a visit to North Wales in 1851 to investigate the truck system. His report gave interesting evidence of the scale on which the charter masters operated:

> Thomas Barrow. I am a charter-master to Mr H Darby at the Bye Pit, Brymbo. We are nine contractors (butties) in partnership and we employ 180 men and boys. This is the principal pit in North Wales.

> Th. Jones. I am a charter-master at the Engine Pit. We are four partners employing 40 men and boys. I have been a charter-master eight years.

By the second half of the century the truck system was no longer a problem but the charter masters were still a force in the pits. The inspectors held them responsible for much of the neglect of safety which occurred below ground. There were cases, Hall reported, of charter masters being appointed as the 'competent persons' to fire shots.[8] 'A more inappropriate choice could not be made, as these persons are more directly interested in the quantity of mineral gotten than any others, and therefore more likely to run risk.' In 1899, recording that the death rate in North Wales was nearly twice as bad as the average for the rest of the kingdom (one per 376 persons employed, compared with one per 602), he stated emphatically:

> I believe this ... is due principally to the 'butty' system of working which prevails ... proper discipline is seldom maintained, the charter master or butty being deputed to look after the safety of the workmen employed by him, and although he is under the supervision of the officials acting under the certificated manager, it is naturally assumed that he must to a great extent be responsible for the safety of those he directly employs.

Ten years later, reporting for North Wales once again the worst record in the United Kingdom for accidents (although no death or injury from explosion) he laid the blame squarely on the charter masters, 'who stand between management and the general body of the miners, and prevent that close contact which tends to discipline and enforcement of better methods and precautions'.

Why the charter master system held its own in North Wales long after it had succumbed elsewhere is difficult to understand but there is clear evidence that it had still some life in it at the time of the Gresford disaster and that it had left some sour memories behind it. One retired collier, who had worked in Gresford and lost a brother in the explosion, explained that there might be perhaps 13 men working on one face with one charter master in charge—'the bigger the bully the better for the management'. On Friday or Saturday, whichever was pay-day, all the money earned on the face was paid out to this man who then distributed it. 'He paid you according to how much he liked the look of your face.' He had to pay the minimum rate but 'if you weren't well in with him you didn't get any more than the minimum; if you scratched him well you might get a couple of shillings a day above the minimum.' If the face had had a good week 'he stood to pick up three or four times as much as the man who'd worked as hard as himself'. How did the charter master get appointed? 'Perhaps he went to the same club as the manager, and bought him enough whiskies.'

Another former miner, later to become a senior colliery official, recalled his earliest brush with the system. The money to be divided up was placed in a tin, the total available being known only to the charter master. You waited your turn to be summoned to his presence and at all times kept your eyes averted from the tin. On this occasion, having been led to expect something substantially above the standard rate, the young man had arranged to take his girl friend to Llandudno but the coin which was dropped into his hand proved to be a sixpence. In a rage he flung it to the ground and turned away, only to be reproved and advised to apologise by the colliery manager, who had seen the incident.

Confirmation that the system was still in existence in 1934 is provided by the minutes of the executive committee of the North Wales Miners' Association. In April 1934, on the initiative of Bersham Lodge, the meeting 'emphatically refuse[d] to countenance the re-establishment of the Charter system in the mines of North Wales'. A year later, seven months after the Gresford disaster, Bersham returned to the attack with the proposition which was carried unanimously, 'that this Association calls on all lodges where the Charter system is in operation to take immediate steps to have same abolished'.

There were only brief references to charter masters at the inquiry. Confronting an obstinate and perhaps elderly collier, described as 'a chargehand', whom he had clearly decided to handle with some tact, Cripps asked, 'Will you tell me what a charter master is?'

'I suppose he's a charter master', was the obtuse reply, 'and I suppose he has all the rule of the place where he's working.'

'That doesn't tell me what he does.'

'I work on the face as much as any of the men that has ever worked for me, and I dare say more.'

'Are you what other men who have given evidence have called a chargehand?'

'I give orders to them.'

Another witness, asked to explain the difference between a

collier and a filler, gave the revealing reply, '... the colliers were contractors but the fillers weren't. They were simply getting a day wage from the men.'

'From the contractors?'

'Yes.'

The colliers, as contractors, paid a day wage to the fillers. A third witness, also described as a chargehand, clearly fulfilled some of the functions of a charter master. He was paid extra money to be 'in charge of the face'; he carried the men's complaints and his own about the men to the management. According to the under-manager, 'he asked me to remove two or three of the sets [of men], that they were not doing their duty'. He was not a deputy but he was 'solely in charge of the output so far as the 14s set was concerned', and 'practically speaking responsible for the output on that face'.

How widespread the charter master system was at this time it is now difficult to establish, but its survival in Gresford must have played some part in stifling criticism in a deteriorating situation. If you had to take on not only the management and the officials but also a virtually self-appointed tyrant from your own ranks at whose whim you could be paid less than you felt you had earned and even be summarily dismissed from the face, the pressures to keep silent would be strong. The management had no need of deputies to keep the men in line when 'the chalter master could get rid of the trouble-makers'.

The necessity for avoiding a reputation as a trouble-maker may help to explain another feature of the coalfield which was much commented on down the years, and at the Gresford Inquiry, although it was by no means confined to North Wales.

In the 1860s, when the miners were demanding that the newly created inspection system should be made more effective, part of the government's response was to lob the ball back into their court. Under Rule 30 of the Coal Mines Regulation Act of 1872 it was provided that:

> The persons employed in a mine may from time to time appoint two of their number to inspect the mine at their own cost, and the persons so appointed shall be allowed, once in every month, accompanied, if the owner, agent or manager of the mine thinks fit, by himself or one or more officers of the mine, to go to every part of the mine, and to inspect the shafts, levels, planes, working places, return airways, ventilation

> apparatus, old workings and machinery, and shall be afforded by the
> owner, agent and manager, and all persons in the mine, every facility for
> the purpose of such inspection, and shall make a true report of the result
> of such inspection, and such report shall be recorded in a book to be kept
> at the mine for the purpose, and shall be signed by the persons who made
> the same.

The men of North Wales showed little interest in the power
granted them. By 1879, as far as Hall knew, they had not made use
of it once.

> They naturally say that under present arrangements they would receive
> no payment for doing this work, and so long as this is so their view seems
> reasonable, for it is quite impossible to deny that this work is in the
> manager's province and ought to be done either by himself or by persons
> employed by him; he may employ the workmen if he thinks fit.

No records of workmen's inspections appear to have been kept
in the early days and the next reference to them in the West
Lancashire and North Wales division is another nil return in
1912. In 1914, however, there were somewhat unexpectedly 149
inspections at 18 mines. Most of them were in the St Helens area of
Lancashire but three were in North Wales, and concerning one of
them there is detailed information. It took place at Gresford, then a
recently opened but rapidly expanding pit; the inspectors, chosen
by ballot, were Edward Williams and W. H. Williams, and their
report, handsomely and probably expensively printed on good
quality paper, dated 12 November 1914, and addressed 'To the
Committee of the Workmen at Gresford Colliery, and the Council
of the North Wales Miners' Association', survived in the archives of
the National Union of Mineworkers in Wrexham.

The inspection by the two men was spread over six days—in
itself a comment on the performance demanded of the official
Inspectorate by Cripps and others—and their report, which runs
to six pages, conveys something of the self-confidence of the miner
in those heady days of the supposed supremacy of the coal industry.

They began in the Main East District where the first return
airway they travelled was 'in very good condition'. However:

> In Driving 52 we found a cap of gas (about 2%) in the general ventilation,
> and we drew the under-manager's attention to same, and he ordered the
> men to re-arrange the ventilation pipes ... and he ordered the men not to
> go in the heading again until the fireman examined the place; we then
> proceeded to 48 Driving, where we found over 2½% of gas in the general
> atmosphere, and the men were withdrawn and the place fenced off ...

> The men in 34 were busy boring a shot hole, but the under-manager stopped them and told them it could not be fired.

They submitted a long sequence of working places to a very thorough going-over, finding gas in some, ventilation variable, all the roads in a safe condition but the manholes far from satisfactory on various counts. 'We drew the under-manager's attention to them all.' They also found that the regulation concerning the spacing of tubs was not being complied with.

The next day was spent in an equally searching examination of the South East District, in the course of which they found among other imperfections that one air course was 'very small, and the air roaring as passing through it. Four men were immediately sent to enlarge this place.'

So they worked their way through the whole mine, giving credit where it was due but stating plainly the respects in which in their view the law was not being complied with. By the end they had done a very skilful and thorough job to their own satisfaction and no doubt to that of the men they represented but not, it is hardly surprising to be told, to that of the management. 'We have decided to inform you of some unpleasantness between us and some of the officials during this inspection.'

The disputed areas were the South and South East Districts where the inspectors maintained that obstructions had 'annihilated' the ventilation, producing an accumulation of gas.

> But the manager repudiated our legitimate rights to report accordingly, and that the cap of gas was not as we reported, and also that he would contest the ballot by which we were appointed inspectors. No doubt both sides said more than was wise, but we told the manager we should write to the Home Office for a definition regarding this point he raised before we should acquiesce, and that we were prepared to visit the places again with Mr Cockin, the Agent, to verify the cap of gas; and as to the ballot, he could do whatever he liked, as there was no irregularity that we knew of.

The appeal to the Home Office produced an unequivocal reply: 'You were entitled to state in the report of the inspection made under Section 16 the condition of the places you mention.' The inspector for the district also gave the men his support: 'I am quite convinced that your examinations of Gresford Colliery is [sic] doing good work, although it may not always please the officials, as you assist to keep them doing things to keep the Colliery in safe working order.'

It was a famous victory and the two miners closed their report with a declaration which must have seemed to augur well for the future of the coalfield and of Gresford Colliery:

> We have been charged with having some spite against the under-manager and firemen, and that is the reason for our reporting every little thing. This is too frivolous to attempt an explanation here ... and we shall consider it nothing less than an excuse for any laxity that may have existed to create such a changed state of affairs in connection with the safety of the mine.

The strength and confidence implied by these words proved to be an illusion. By 1926, the year of the General Strike, workmen's inspections, according to the divisional inspector, were once again 'rapidly becoming a dead letter'. At Gresford, which had set such a stirring example in 1914, Bonsall could recall none between 1921 and 1934.

The *Daily Worker*, for all its stridently expressed sympathy with the victims of the explosion and their dependants, felt that there was no satisfactory answer to the question why no inspections had been carried out during those years, and there was much head-shaking at the inquiry, together with expressions of regret reiterated in the Commissioner's report, at the failure of the Gresford men to avail themselves of the opportunity provided by the law to point out at their own expense to Harrop, Bonsall, Williams and their various deputies the imperfections of the Dennis Section.

Although the decision whether or not to carry out their own inspections was left to the miners, there were a number of areas in which the law laid on them specific obligations in the interests of their own safety, and it was here that Shawcross and others uncovered what appeared to be some unhelpful attitudes on the part of the men.

The Coal Mines Act of 1911 and the supplementary regulations and orders made it clear that the responsibility for the safety of the mine did not lie solely with the management and the officials:

> 67(4) If a workman discovers the presence of inflammable gas in his working place he shall immediately withdraw therefrom and inform the fireman, examiner or deputy.
>
> (5) Every workman engaged at the face, or in stonework ... shall carefully examine his working place before commencing work and before recommencing work after the firing of a shot ...
>
> (17) Every workman working at the face shall to the best of his power ...

leave his working place at the end of his shift in such condition as to allow of work being safely resumed therein.

It was the intention of those who drafted the Act that no workman should remain unaware of what was expected of him.

88(1) For the purpose of making known the provisions of this Act and the regulations of the mine to all persons employed in or about a mine

    (a) The owner, agent or manager shall cause a copy of the regulations with the name and address of the inspector of the division ... to be posted up in some conspicuous place at or near the mine, where they may be conveniently read or seen by the persons employed ...

    (b) ... shall supply gratis to each person employed ... at the commencement of his employment ... a book containing so much of the regulations ... as the [Minister] may prescribe ...

Provision was also made for the workman to satisfy himself that those who were made responsible for his safety were doing their job properly:

17(1) It shall be the duty of every person on whom responsible duties are imposed with respect to safety or to the conditions ... at a mine ... to make ... full and accurate reports of the matters falling within the scope of his duties.

  (2) Copies of the reports required ... relating to inspections ... shall be posted up at the pit head not later than ten o'clock in the morning on the day following the day on which the reports were made, and remain posted until ten o'clock in the morning on the following day.

The good intentions of those who had framed these provisions were apparently wasted, at least as far as Gresford was concerned. Cripps sought to lay the blame on the management.

Q Did you think it was the duty of the firemen in this pit to look after the safety regulations?

A Yes.

Q Have you ever been told that it was your duty to look after the safety regulations in this pit?

A No, sir.

Q Have the management or the firemen ever instructed you as to what the regulations are?

A No, sir.

Q Were you given, when you were engaged in this pit, any book containing the regulations for the mine?

A No.

Q Have you ever been asked to attend any lecture or talk or anything where they might be explained to you by the management?

A No, sir.
Q Has any step ever been taken to your knowledge in any way to ask for the co-operation of yourself or any other miner in this pit?
A No.

This brief exchange was an attempt to restore the balance following a long series of damaging and angrily received cross-examinations by Shawcross, suggesting that the miners had shown less interest than might have been expected in the question of their own safety and the protection which the Act sought to provide for them. The response from man after man revealed the degree of apathy, non-cooperation and sense of helplessness that prevailed throughout the mine.

Q Have you ever seen the firemen's reports posted at the pithead?
A No, sir.
Q You've never seen them?
A Well, when a man's going to his work he hasn't much time to look around at the top of the colliery. He's anxious to get down to his work.

★   ★   ★   ★   ★

Q Having made the complaint [to the fireman] did it occur to you to look at his report to see whether he was making any report about gas?
A When you've had a shift on 14s, and you come out, you don't want to stop to bother to look at anything.

★   ★   ★   ★   ★

Q Having reported [the presence of gas] to Amos did it occur to you to notice whether Amos had himself reported it to the management?
A No, I don't know.
Q Were you not curious to find out whether it had been put in the report?
A That was no business of mine, to see the reports.

★   ★   ★   ★   ★

Q Did you know there was such a thing as an inspector of mines?
A Oh, yes.
Q Did you take any steps to bring this matter to his notice?
A I've never seen him.
Q Did you take any steps to bring the matter to his notice?
A I didn't know his address.

★   ★   ★   ★   ★

Q Did it ever occur to you that the matter was so serious that you ought to communicate with the inspector of mines?
A Well, look here, I thought it was, but I'm telling you this: I was taking the same chance as the firemen was taking, and I had to take the same

chance as them. If they were afraid to say that, I think I was afraid to say it.

Q You were prepared to risk not only your own safety but the safety of your mates?

A I had to.

* * * * *

Q Your work down on 14s face was of such a character that your idea was getting coal out?

A Yes, that's all I went there for.

Q And you left the inspection for gas and other things to the person that was responsible for the inspection?

A Nothing to do with me.

* * * * *

Q When you got to your working place, did you make any examination, and test [for gas] then?

A No, that's nothing to do with me, is it? After you pass the lamp station you're in the fireman's hands.

Q Didn't you know that under the regulations you're supposed to carefully examine your working place before commencing work?

A ... Not for gas. The place is supposed to be fit for us when we go past the fireman's station.

* * * * *

Q I suppose you thought this gas, spreading down like that, was a very serious thing?

A I did, very serious, and I was glad to get out of it.

Q You knew a lot of other men would be coming into it, unless they were warned?

A And I'm sorry for them, too.

Q I believe that. Did it occur to you, noticing this gas which you thought was a very dangerous thing, and which you were glad to get out of, that you ought to warn somebody about it?

A Well, I did warn the cutter. I said, 'God help you, Tom, you've got a hell of a place to go to tonight', and he's down there now.

Q If you'd told somebody in authority he might not be down there now?

A I don't know.

Q When you knew the conditions that Friday night were becoming so serious that you were glad to get out of it, you took no steps to prevent the men going in?

A Well, the management knowed about it. The management knowed about it.

* * * * *

Q As a practical miner why haven't you mentioned this danger to someone if you realised it was dangerous?

A It was there to be seen. I did what I was told to do.
Q But you know the section of the Act which says you are responsible as much as the fireman?
A I did what I was told to do.

＊ ＊ ＊ ＊ ＊

Q Have you considered the conditions dangerous for some time?
A I never did care about the place since I started there.
Q Did it ever occur to you that it would be right to see some steps taken about the conditions?
A We could never say a word about it.
Q Did it ever occur to you ... to write to the inspector?
A I thought about it many a time.
Q Why didn't you do it?
A I didn't want to bother with it, I suppose.

Among those from 14s district who admitted to something more than apathy in the face of danger, two main reasons were put forward for failing to take action. The first was that it was, or would have been, a waste of time.

Q Didn't you think it was rather important that the management should know there was gas down there?
A When I complained to the fireman he told me to shut my mouth and do what I was told, or else get out, so I thought I'd said enough then.
Q Did you complain to any of the others?
A No ... As far as I can see it's no use complaining.

＊ ＊ ＊ ＊ ＊

Q You wouldn't have any timidity in speaking to the fireman over the head of the chargeman, would you?
A I have done, many a time, and got into a row over it. I've opened my mouth a lot, but it's no use.
Q Have you walked a hundred yards with anyone this last four or five months and not talked over this condition of things?
A We've always been talking about it.
Q But you haven't discussed any steps to be taken to stop that kind of thing?
A It was no use. We'd failed, and that was enough, wasn't it?

＊ ＊ ＊ ＊ ＊

Q You were constantly going into this place which was, according to your evidence, extremely dangerous?
A Yes.
Q You were taking no steps whatever to bring this danger to the notice of the management?
A I took the first steps with Harold Amos, the fireman, and when it didn't go any further with him I never bothered after.

Q You expected the management to take action if it was reported?
A They'd have laughed at you.

★ ★ ★ ★ ★

Q Did you men discuss this matter that particular night when you saw this gas coming down?
A Yes, me and my mate Edward Matthews was talking about it during snapping time. There was more gas this top end, and we said together that it was coming down the face.
Q Did you decide to do anything by way of speaking to someone else?
A If you talked to a fireman it was like talking to a prop.
Q Did you never realise that you had a responsibility as a mining man?
A Well, mining is a different thing today to what it used to be. You dursn't open your mouth, and the best plan you can do is to shut your mouth.
Q Aren't you aware by shutting your mouth you're contributing to a state—
A Yes, I partly know all about that, but you've got to look at it many ways.

'You dursn't open your mouth.' Man after man asserted that in the current state of the industry it would have been more than his job was worth to attempt to make any sort of stand. Victimisation was the almost universal dread.

Q Has it ever occurred to you to stop at the pit top rather than go down, if that was the condition there?
A No, we had to go down.
Q Why did you have to go down?
A That is our living.
Q Even at the expense of what might occur?
A Well, we had to risk it, didn't we?

★ ★ ★ ★ ★

Q Did you find [the fireman] a conscientious man?
A To a certain extent ... He should have fetched us away from there.
Q You realized the conditions were bad, and you stayed because you weren't fetched away.
A Certainly. If we came out on our own we would be sacked.
Q I can understand your anxiety about your job, but did you really place your job before the safety, not of yourself, but of your mates?
A We were all there weren't we?

The suggestion of solidarity in the face of common misfortune contrasted sharply with the picture presented almost casually to Charlton by another collier.

A ... I take a very proud interest in my colliery.
Q You do, and in the safety of the men employed there?

A   In the colliery, you know, it's the survival of the fittest, every man for himself, isn't it?

Charlton didn't think it was but left it there. Under pressure from Hall the man conceded that the philosophy was perhaps personal to himself and assured Hall that he had intended nothing detrimental to the Miners' Federation, for which he had always had great respect, but he had underlined, perhaps unconsciously but with brutal bluntness, the crucial weakness of Gresford. It had virtually cut itself off from the trade union movement and the community of purpose that it represented. Of the 262 men who died in the explosion only 82 were union members. In the colliery as a whole, faith in the union was non-existent, even among those who retained a token membership.

A   ... There was only one time when I was in the Union and we made a protest against a fine for dirty coal to the Union, and they said they could do nothing.
Q   And after that you thought it was no good approaching your Union about the dangerous conditions in which you were working?
A   I never gave it a thought.

★ ★ ★ ★ ★

Q   You're a member of your Union?
A   That's right.
Q   You knew the Union had meetings from time to time?
A   I never attended any, if there were.
Q   And you took no steps to get the matter reported to them?
A   No, it was our place to report to the fireman.

★ ★ ★ ★ ★

Q   Are you a member of the Union?
A   Yes.
Q   Did you not think the Union could protect you from losing your job?
A   No.

★ ★ ★ ★ ★

Q   Do you know Harry Lloyd?
A   Yes.
Q   Do you know Frank Powell?
A   Yes.
Q   Do you know Edward Jones ... the agent of the miners?
A   Yes, I know the miners' agent.
Q   You know those men are representing the workmen in everything appertaining to their interests at the colliery?

A Yes.
Q If this thing was the danger that you stated ... why haven't you mentioned the matter to one of those men?
A Well, my bread and butter depends on the colliery.
Q That is your reason?
A It's my fear of victimisation.
Q From the colliery company?
A From the colliery company, by making a complaint as to the conditions.

There is no doubt that the union counted for very little at Gresford at this time and was treated by the management with contempt and hostility, but no example was given at the inquiry, perhaps because none was asked for, of a man being sacked in the kind of circumstances which were alleged to be feared; and the answers given by one or two men suggested that the true obstacle may have been an unwillingness even to put the matter to the test.

Q Did you think your job was more important than the safety of other men working down there with you?
A I don't say anything about the safety of the other men, but I say I was looking after my own job for my family's sake.
Q Are you a member of the Union?
A Yes.
Q You knew there was an agent?
A Yes.
Q Did you take any steps to report it to him?
A No, sir.
Q Did you think you would be victimised if you did that?
A No, sir.

Another young man who had come to North Wales after working in mines in Lancashire, Shropshire, Yorkshire and Kent went to the heart of the matter.

Q Are you a union member?
A Yes.
Q Do you think it would have been a good thing if you'd made some complaint to the Union so that they could take the matter up?
A I know it would have been if I'd been in Yorkshire.

It was generally agreed, and the Commissioner made a point of stressing in his report, that Gresford was unfortunate in being without a strong union membership at this time, however little the management might have welcomed one; but it was no part of the inquiry's function to try to discover the reason. A plea along the lines of the harshness of the times would require some qualification.

The misfortunes of the mining industry had hit every coalfield hard, some even harder than others. Yet in some of the worst-hit areas the union was still a force to be reckoned with. In South Wales in the year of Gresford, resolute action by the miners brought them victory in a dispute over the minimum wage, and at one pit the men, in defiance of the owner and of the Coal Mines Act, stayed below ground for nine days in a successful defence of their right to join the South Wales Miners' Federation rather than the 'non-political' company union. Even in the darkest and most desperate days, thousands of almost destitute unemployed in the Rhondda valley somehow found a penny a week as a nominal subscription to the union which allowed them to remain in benefit.[9] Was North Wales as a whole less union-minded? Had it weathered the storm less well? Or was Gresford untypical even in its own coalfield?

NOTES

1. Higson's report, 1862.

2. Engels, *Die Lage der arbeitenden Klasse in England*, first published in Leipzig, 1845. The first English edition, entitled *The Condition of the Working Class in England in 1844*, was published in New York in 1887 and in London in 1892. This edition was reprinted in 1969 by Panther Books, with the words 'in 1844' omitted to retain Engels's title, and a note explaining that 'The English text published here is the work of the Institute of Marxism-Leninism, Moscow, and was verified by the Institute against the text of the Second German Edition.' It is interesting to compare this translation of the passage quoted on p. 156 above with the same sentence as it appears in the translation published by Henderson and Chaloner (Oxford, 1958): 'In no industry in the United Kingdom are there so many fatal accidents as in mining.' The original German text is as follows: 'Im ganzen britischen Reich gibt es keine Arbeit, bei der man auf so vielerlei Weise ums Leben kommen kann, wie gerade diese. Die Kohlengrube ist der Schauplatz einer Menge der schreckenerregendsten Unfälle . . .' ('The coal-mine is the scene of a multitude of the most terrifying calamities . . .').

3. A. D. Nicholson, report for 1929.

4. See Appendix B.

5. Griffin (1977) records that 'The last ventilation furnace, at Walsall Wood, Staffordshire, did not go out of use until 1950' (p. 112).

6. Report, 1890.

7. See Appendix C.

8. Report, 1879.

9. Griffiths (1969), p. 35.

CHAPTER 14

The Union

The early history of trade unionism in the North Wales coalfield follows, broadly speaking, the national pattern, with some features which were more strongly marked than elsewhere and were still in evidence at the time of the accident at Gresford.[1]

Action to improve the lot of the miner began to be organised around 1830, in response to similar activity in Lancashire. Local strikes, and preparations for larger ones, led to an incident known as the Cinder Hill Riots, when the colliers of the Ruabon area, reinforced later by a massive contingent from Flint where the strike movement had started, secured improved wages from the coal owners, the closing of the British Iron Company's Tommy Shop, and the banishment of the Company's hated agent. But in spite of this and one or two similar shows of strength, interest in organisation seems to have petered out shortly afterwards, and the next concerted movement fared little better. The Miners' Association of Great Britain, formed in the Yorkshire coalfield in 1841 and reputed to have at one time had 100,000 members, sent representatives variously described as 'lecturers' and 'missionary organisers' into all the coalfields of Britain. The response from North Wales was unenthusiastic, even though the depression in the iron trade had brought many collieries to a standstill. A delegate to the union's National Conference held in Wakefield in 1843 described the miners of North Wales as being worse used by their 'slave drivers' than human beings anywhere; some of them it was alleged had 'never received a coin for their labours for the last two years'. After a year's work the lecturers had recruited less than 1,000 members, and the union in North Wales failed to survive the collapse which overtook the parent body following the severe slump in the coal trade towards the end of the 1840s.

For the next two or three decades attempts to revive unionism in the coalfield were weakened and obstructed by local versions of the jealousies and open conflicts which retarded progress at the national level, and above all by a malady which continued to plague North

173

Wales right down to the time of Gresford—a reluctance to face the cost of good organisation and to recognise the indissoluble connection between militant action and financial resources. In the 1860s a miners' leader with a long experience of the problem laid down the fundamental principle: 'Cash is the cementing element in general combinations.' Small strikes make little impression; large ones fail without the money to back them. The lesson was hammered home repeatedly during the next 50 years but too often fell on unreceptive ears. As a disgruntled official complained after an unsuccessful strike, they 'might as well try to draw a collier's tooth out as induce him to pay threepence towards the Union'.

By the mid-1880s trade unionism in North Wales was to all intents and purposes dead but the drawbacks of disunity were becoming too obvious to be ignored. Lancashire was known to be making common cause with Yorkshire over a pay claim for which the economic outlook was propitious. North Wales asked to be associated with it and other Midland counties joined in. Soon a powerful new body, the Miners' Federation of Great Britain, was in being, representing all the coalfields which were not hampered by adherence to a 'sliding scale' based on coal prices as the regulator of wages, or had not rejected militancy as an appropriate philosophy. The predilection of North Wales for rocking the boat manifested itself when there were local objections to a nationally planned strike but the area was pulled back into line in time, and when another of the Federation's ardently pursued objectives, the eight-hour shift, was under discussion the North Wales men were overwhelmingly in favour. A call in 1893 for concerted action against a proposed cut of 25 per cent in wages found them similarly prepared to throw in their lot with the majority of the Federation. Throughout the lock-out which followed they stood firm and apparently united and gained their reward when the owners capitulated. The Miners' Federation of Great Britain had triumphantly passed its first severe ordeal and North Wales might be considered entitled to a share of the credit. But appearances were as ever deceptive, and support for the stand taken by the Federation by no means reflected support for the Federation in North Wales. Of the total work force of about 12,500 the union men represented little more than a quarter, and the ostensibly united front suggested by the votes of delegates at national conferences masked the usual internal strife at local level. Membership in the coalfield declined to less than 2,000, helped downwards by the discovery of peculation on the part of the agent, who resigned, leaving the important post vacant.

There now appeared, or re-appeared, on the scene a man who by his ability and force of character succeeded in halting the collapse and bringing about a transformation. Edward Hughes, a Flintshire man who had spent a brief period of exile in Durham when his early enthusiasm for trade unionism made him unpopular with the local colliery owners, returned to his native county in 1887, found work at Point of Ayr Colliery, and by 1892 was financial secretary to the Denbighshire and Flintshire Miners' Association. Within a few months he was forced to resign because, paradoxically, of his strong opposition to the Miners' Federation policy at a time when the North Wales miners were in accord with it. In 1897, with the fortunes of the local organisation at their nadir, the members found that they could not do without him and made him their general and financial secretary and later their agent. From this time until his death in 1925 he was the dominant figure in trade unionism and on the civic stage in North Wales.

Among Hughes's first tasks had been to put the Association's finances on a firmer basis with increased contributions from members. He gained his point but was seldom able to go for long without having to fight the same battle all over again, and with it the battle to retain membership. From the low point of 1897 the numerical strength of the Association rose in five years to over 9,000 and its reserves to more than £4,000. The depression of the next three years and the decline in wages to a recently agreed minimum reduced the membership by nearly half. Hughes responded with 'An Appeal for Better Unity', and for membership of 'one of the most powerful organisations that was ever known in this country: viz, the Miners' Federation of Great Britain'. There were hundreds of miners in North Wales, he wrote, who were unaware of its existence but were reaping the benefits from it and had done since it was founded 17 years before. 'Pray don't allow anyone to say that we in North Wales "take up that which we have not laid down, and reap that which we did not sow".'

In 1903, with the membership standing at just over 7,200 and short time in several pits causing great hardship to the men and their families, the contribution was raised from threepence per month to sixpence per week, and Hughes put a question to

that selfish creature 'the non-union man' who states that he is always able
to get from the manager what is due to him without the interference of
any third person or 'agitator'. What has he done to assist the women and
children who have been on the verge of starvation owing to the depression
in trade?

In 1908 when the paper membership was over 13,000 he recorded
'about 10,000 good members' and reminded them all of that
£31,000 which had been paid out in various benefits over seven
years. In 1911 'I have warned this Association for years that it was
more of a Friendly Society than a Trade Union.'

In 1913, in common with other areas, North Wales embarked on
a campaign against non-unionists. By March 1914 the secretary was
able to assert that he knew of no non-union man working underground in the coalfield, but there were 'thousands of unfinancial
members who have become non-unionists' and who, he wrathfully
reminded them, had very little understanding of the inescapable
connection between financial resources and trade union strength.
Out of 13,500 men on the books, 4,000 were so far in arrears that
'you cannot pay them benefits—they are members simply on paper'.
The missing contributions amounted to £1,800, and it was barely
two years since the Association had been called on to provide nearly
£12,500 in strike and lock-out pay.

The war years afford only tantalising glimpses of relations
between the North Wales miners and their union. In 1915 some
of the men are reported by the secretary as asserting that 'they will
not join this Association: they will join the Army first'. Large
numbers of them carried out their threat, until the government
made mining a reserved occupation and North Wales, in common
with other coalfields, was forced to recruit men who had no
background in the industry and no true stake in its future
prosperity.

Soon after the end of the war the North Wales Miners' Association was in desperate straits. The national strike of 1920 and the
lock-out of 1921 'not only used up all our savings but caused us to
borrow and mortgage what stocks we had, including the house and
the offices'. The members responded to the crisis by voting to
reduce their contributions by half, a course which put them in
conflict with the national Federation. In 1923, in what proved to be
his last message to them, Hughes tried again to force them to face
facts.

> What good is 6d. contribution and 10 shillings per week to fight an Employer of Labour? What is 10 shillings per week for a family to depend on? It is not enough to provide rent and coal ...
>
> I am told that what we want in North Wales at present is Unity to resist, and not funds. *That is good so far* but go and meet a body of men and tell them about their duty to resist grave injustices at the colliery. The first question that is put to you is 'If we give notice and come out on strike, have you money to support us?' ... My long experience in North Wales [is] that there is any amount of 'Unity to resist' if there is prospect of financial support ... I shall never be responsible for asking any body of men to strike unless there are funds to support them. I have collieries in mind now where I would like to go and tell the men that it was their duty in their own interests and the generation to come to stop work until the manager would learn to treat them as human beings ...

Hughes died in 1925, to be succeeded by his son Hugh, who was no less willing than his father had been to spell out unwelcome truths and told his members plainly in February 1926 where they stood.

> It is not a question of whether the owners of Yorkshire are more generous or more amiable to meet than the owners of North Wales ... Honestly, if it came to that I would much prefer meeting our owners than those of many other districts ... If we had varying district minimum percentages, based on the economic ability of the district to pay, the miners of North Wales would either have to submit to a reduction in wages and the extension of hours or the Government would have to continue the subsidy.

The industrial strife of these years crippled North Wales trade unionism, as Edward Hughes had foretold that it might. Income from contributions in 1925 and 1926 barely exceeded the cost of strike and lock-out pay. Membership fell from 14,000 in 1926 to less than 7,500 in 1928, a figure from which it varied by little more than a hundred or two either way until 1934, the year of Gresford. Similar stories could be told of most coalfields; for example, when Jim Griffiths took on the job of president of the South Wales Miners' Federation in 1934 he found that, of 140,000 miners at work in the coalfield, only 76,000 were members of the Federation, although the position there was complicated by the existence of the rival Spenser Union, whose liquidation brought 20,000 members back into the Federation fold at a stroke.

In May 1928 Hugh Hughes, in a manner reminiscent of his father, tried to rally his dispirited troops with a stirring 'Appeal to Non-Unionists and Unfinancial Members'.

> Times have been so bad that even veterans of Trade Unionism are becoming disheartened and losing faith. To them I say 'You have experienced times just as bad, and even worse, yet you built up a fine organization. You know the dark and terrible past. Have faith; struggle to maintain ideals; continue the fight; you have a clear conscience, better days are coming.' To the young I say, 'You ask what good is the Union. You do not remember the time, not many years ago, when your fathers went home after working six shifts of ten hours per shift on the coal face, with only a shilling or two in their pockets. There is a difference now, is there not? Do you think the kind hearted owners granted the Minimum Wage willingly? No my lads, they fought hard against it and said as usual that the industry could not afford it. *Join up and play your part. Pull your weight in the struggle. Do not let your older comrades carry a heavier burden than they should because you are not playing the game.*' To all I say, shake yourselves out of the apathy and despair into which you have fallen. There is hope yet.

This clarion call seems to have evoked little response. But the figures for total membership, which show a drop of 50 per cent over a period of ten years, also conceal some remarkable variations from pit to pit. In 1928, the year in which Hughes issued his appeal, while membership in eight lodges declined, in six it actually rose. In the following year membership improved slightly in nine pits but continued to fall in others, including Gresford, which always wilted sadly in times of stress. From a membership of 1,355 in 1919 it dropped by 1932 to 401, of whom only 385 were financial members; and this in a pit with a work force of around 1,800. Witnesses at the inquiry might justifiably dismiss Gresford as a non-union pit. By 1934, the year of the accident, after a delusive increase to 749, membership was down again to 548, and years later old colliers could still recall the pitiful little hut by the colliery entrance where lodge officials would try to waylay them and extract their sixpence a week from them.

Writing in 1933, Professor A. H. Dodd referred to 'that exclusive camaraderie and that defiant self-consciousness which have left their marks to this day in the coal mining communities of North Wales',[2] and the contrast between Gresford and some of its neighbours is striking. During the troubles of the early 1920s, when Gresford was slipping back, Hafod increased its membership from 1,396 to 1,658, and throughout the crisis of 1926 and its aftermath never dropped below 1,200. It has been said that Hafod was the 'village' pit of Rhosllanerchrugog, close-knit, largely Welsh-speaking, with deep roots in the community, in the manner of South

Wales or the North East, while Gresford was 'cosmopolitan', 'anonymous', lacking a sense of cohesion, drawing men from dozens of small villages scattered over a wide area and from Wrexham, an impersonal, diversified town. But what of Llay Main, larger and no less cosmopolitan than Gresford? In 1932, the year of Gresford's nadir, Llay Main claimed 2,779 members, all of them financial. Admittedly it was a new and expanding colliery with a larger work force than Gresford's, but this cannot of itself explain so extraordinary a disparity in union loyalty. There is perhaps a clue in the comment of the secretary of the North Wales Miners' Association, Hugh Hughes, that the owners of Llay Main fought hard for their point of view in any negotiations over wages or conditions of employment, but that once an agreement was reached and signed the management could be relied on to carry it out loyally.[3] All the more reason, it might have been thought, for a strong union presence in Gresford, where management notoriously showed itself in a somewhat different light.

Years after the disaster, when little was left of the North Wales coalfield, a strong and natural reluctance remained among old colliers to speak ill of workmates who died, but it was also possible to detect an implied belief that neither Hafod, nor Bersham, nor Llay Main, and perhaps no other pit in the coalfield would have tolerated the conditions which brought disaster on such a scale to Gresford. However grim the times, and however weak the Association as a whole—following the death of Hugh Hughes in 1932 it was without an agent and general secretary until young Edward Jones, from Point of Ayr Colliery, took on the job early in 1934—there must appear something bewildering in the apathy and self-centredness which seem, like firedamp, to have poisoned so much of the atmosphere of the Dennis Section, recalling the unhappiness of periods in the Association's past.

'In a good organised colliery', Edward Hughes wrote in 1908, 'the humblest of men—like the strong and able—can reason with their managers without fear of being victimised.'[4] Time and the coal industry had changed and the outspoken fearlessness of the Gresford workmen's inspectors of 1914 was no longer to be expected, but if Hughes had survived into his seventies, like some of his better-known contemporaries such as Herbert Smith and Peter Lee, and still held office, it is difficult to believe that the world at large would ever have heard of Gresford.

NOTES

1. See Dodd (1929); Rogers (1963–73); Lerry (1968). For a general account: *The History of the British Coal Industry* (1984–93); Arnot (1949, 1956, 1961).
2. See Dodd (1961), p. 399.
3. See Lerry (1968), p. 75.
4. Sir Henry Walker was of the same opinion.

> ... it is, I think, of importance that a large proportion of the persons employed at the Colliery were not effective members of the North Wales Mineworkers' Union [sic] ... I believe that a well organised trades [sic] union, wisely directed, can be as potent an influence for promoting greater safety in mines as it is already in matters, for example, of wages and conditions of employment. (report, p. 89)

The *Colliery Guardian* disagreed profoundly:

> Sir Henry Walker makes the revolutionary proposal that all persons employed at mines should be members of an effective trade union ... With all deference, we submit that no evidence whatsoever can be adduced to support the view that it would be in the public interest to extend the monopoly powers of the trade unions in this way. In making this strange request, the Chief Inspector has surely exceeded his prerogative ... (12 February 1937, p. 314)

CHAPTER 15

The Reports

On 14 December 1934, the twenty-eighth day of the hearing, the last of 185 witnesses, some of whom had appeared more than once, left the witness chair. Henderson thanked the Commission for the patience and consideration it had displayed throughout, and Sir Henry Walker in particular for 'the very tactful, the very skilful way ... in which you have steered us all clear of the rocks of discord that appear from time to time as one makes one's way along the channels of advocacy', and the inquiry was adjourned *sine die*. It had heard much evidence of scandalous incompetence and flagrant flouting of the law, but none bearing directly on the question it was required to answer: what was the cause of the accident? It could move no nearer to a solution of the problem until an inspection could be made of the devastated districts. These were still firmly sealed off and remained so while a bitter campaign was waged by the miners, who staked their reputations on gaining access to them, against the owners, who were just as stubbornly determined to keep them out, and could count on the tacit acquiescence or, as the miners furiously asserted, the active collusion of the Inspectorate in their obstructive tactics.

The basis of the opposition to any attempt to re-enter the Dennis Section was put in early October in a letter to Edward Jones, the miners' agent, from his opposite number in the North Wales branch of the National Association of Colliery Managers: if the places where the fire had occurred were to be exposed to a current of fresh air before they had cooled down, and while the whole Section was full of firedamp, there could well be a renewed outbreak of fires and explosions with further loss of life among men caught below ground at the time.

Those responsible for the conduct of operations were of course fully alive to the danger and agreed that the pit must remain sealed at least until after the inquiry had been concluded. An extreme view, not widely canvassed but gaining ground in some quarters, was that no attempt would ever be made to re-enter the destroyed Dennis Section of the colliery. This would have enraged the miners, who counted on an investigation of the area to substantiate their charges against the management, but it would have come as an even more profound shock to the relatives of the victims, for whom grief at their bereavement would have been deepened beyond bearing if they had known for certain that they would never have the bodies of their loved ones brought out of the pit to be given proper burial. Irrational as it might seem, when the men already lay deep in the earth to which a funeral service could only commit them again, a fierce emotional need, older and more deep-rooted than mining itself, required that the due forms and ceremonies be observed. Without them it was as though the dead could never be at rest. 'In its way', the Duckhams wrote in a striking analogy, 'formal burial was as important to the inhabitants of a colliery village as to the Greeks of the *Iliad*.'[1] Bereavement caused by the Gresford disaster spread far beyond the confines of a single colliery village, but the response to it was no less strong and, with the passage of time and the decline of hope, was intensified rather than diminished, especially when a rumour began to spread towards the middle of 1935 that work was to be resumed in the part of the colliery which had not been affected by the explosion. Petitions bearing thousands of signatures expressed the general sense of outrage and resentment. 'We, the undersigned Widows and Relatives of the entombed at the above Colliery,' a typical one read, 'Feel very strongly that every Possible effort should be made to recover the *Bodies*, Before Proceeding to Produce Coal at the Above Colliery.' Demonstrations were held at the pit and Walker received deputations to whom he talked as kindly as he could, 'but I had to tell them that it would not be honest to let them think that there was any but the slightest chance of the bodies being recovered'.

By this time many of the bereaved would have settled for less than bodies. 'Distressed mothers and widows visit me almost daily,' Jones told a miners' meeting, 'pleading for only a bone or an ounce of their dust.' Many could not come in person but wrote, not always pleadingly.

> Mr Jones
>
> You have meetings to reopen dennis deep. You have people from London, birmingham and anywhere Why dont you as Agent for us insist that at the next meeting the men who worked dennis deep and knew the men, and some of these men are the companys men and if the Company dont call them Why don you! You call men who know nothing about the

place ... You are slow Your time is short in your office We will see to it
There is something wrong.

Some widows of
Gresford Colliery.

Jones may have agreed that there was something wrong but it lay far beyond his jurisdiction to put it right. Until the middle of December everyone had been too much occupied with daily attendance at the inquiry to spare much time for the colliery, but on 4 January 1935 the first of many meetings heard a preliminary report on the problems facing the engineers. In addition to the water which was pouring down the Martin shaft at the rate of many gallons a minute, metal rails and wooden beams, dislodged by the later explosions, had fallen down the Dennis shaft; one was known to be resting on the cage near the top of the shaft and others might be blocking it further down. The temperature at the bottom might be very high. Even if the shafts could be cleared there were no properly trained rescue men who could enter the poisonous atmosphere of the pit and work in it for any length of time. Bonsall admitted to Walker that no rescue practices had been held at Gresford for 'a few years'. A public appeal for volunteers produced 600 applicants, of whom 75 turned out to have some knowledge of the subject and after a course of intensive training were pronounced ready, by the beginning of March, to go down and start a cautious exploration of the area near the pit bottom. The Secretary of Mines made a special appeal in Parliament to the public and the press not to assemble at the colliery and to protect those who were to undertake the dangerous assignment from distracting influences.

Proceeding by carefully worked out stages the rescue teams constructed an air-lock at the top of the Martin shaft, then, wearing breathing apparatus, opened the seal which had been placed over the shaft shortly after the explosion, and finally ventured to the bottom on 10 March. What they found there was later described to the miners' annual conference at Rhyl by Joe Hall who, with Peter Lee, Walker and a representative of the management, was allowed down for a look around when conditions were considered safe enough. The effects of the first explosion had stopped short some distance from the shaft bottom. The second explosion, following the withdrawal of the rescue workers, had produced, in Hall's words, 'for three hundred yards from the pit bottom ... a state of things ... no man could ever have seen. It was indescribable. Iron girders weighing many hundredweights were blown many yards, even heavy cutting machines were removed.' The water, estimated at 20 to 25 million gallons, which had been pouring unchecked into the workings, was reckoned by the management to have submerged the whole area affected by the first explosion, although this was disputed by the miners.

By this time a change had been made in the colliery management. Bonsall had been removed and replaced by the son of the inspector for the division. This provocative appointment led to a question in the Commons, alleging that it had caused dissatisfaction because of a lack of confidence on the part of the men in the work of the inspectors. The Secretary of State rejected the allegation, refused to take any action, but admitted that he had received protests.

In June another prominent figure disappeared from the scene. Peter Lee died[2] and was replaced as the Miners' Federation representative by Herbert Smith, president of the Yorkshire Mine Workers' Association. Smith was of the same generation as Lee, 73 years old, but out of a somewhat different mould. Adopted from the workhouse by a miner and his wife, he first went down a pit at the age of 10, was delegate for his miners' lodge at 30, a checkweighman two years later, and thereafter ascended the trade union ladder by the usual stages, ending as president of the Miners' Federation and leading an equally full life in local government in the Yorkshire coalfield. He was described as 'the most perfect expression of the pitman that ever came to leadership'; he was also the epitome of a certain conception of the Yorkshireman. Jack Lawson, who wrote his biography as he had already written that of Peter Lee, quoted descriptions of him as 'a showman', and 'vain', but also as 'human— hard words, but kindly'. He was also dour and pugnacious; even in old age, Lawson remarks, 'he gave the impression that he would rather fight than talk'. He revealed this characteristic most markedly during the strike of 1926,[3] when his intransigence as one of the miners' leaders, meeting every advance and proposition from the other side with a firm and contemptuous 'nowt doin'', helped to prolong the strike far beyond the point where the miners could hope to win and well beyond the stage at which they could even keep what they had.

Smith was a veteran of many inquiries into pit disasters and, although handicapped by coming late on the scene at Gresford, he entered the fray and harried the opposition with far more tenacity and hard words than the ailing Peter Lee had brought to the task. His direct involvement coincided with the breakdown of whatever agreement may have existed among the parties concerned as to the future course of investigations underground. The miners' representatives accepted that two districts, 14s and 109s, might be too severely damaged by fire, explosion and water to be penetrable to any great depth, but they attached great importance to reaching 29s from which survivors had emerged, and 20s, which had probably escaped physical damage. The body of one rescue worker had been brought out of the airway in which he had died and there was a lingering hope of finding many other victims. But with each visit to the pit the miners saw plainer evidence of the owners' and management's intentions. Preparations were going forward for a resumption of coal-getting from the undamaged area of the pit, but the Dennis Section remained impenetrably sealed off, and any demand that the stoppings should be progressively removed, as had been proposed in a communication from the Mines Department, received a standard response: the time was not yet ripe, there was too much gas, the heat was still too great, the water level had risen too high. Walker, who had at first been critical of the excessive caution shown by the experts and the management, came round to their point of view and was at once attacked by the miners. Tempers were lost, angry letters passed to and fro; Smith, Hall, Jones and Grenfell presented themselves at the mine in their pit clothes, ready to take the risk of entering the sealed areas on their own, but were refused permission by the management; meeting after meeting ended in deadlock; more and more 'obstacles' were found to be preventing progress in making the Dennis Section fit to re-enter.

The stalling tactics of the management had the further effect of postponing a resumption of the inquiry, which in turn delayed the appearance of an official report on the accident. There was talk of an interim report, which came to nothing, and in February 1936 questions in Parliament addressed to the new Secretary for Mines, Captain Crookshank, drew only the familiar reply that despite measures taken to reduce the leakage of air into the sealed-off district and thereby to minimise the risk of fire breaking out when the pit was re-opened, excessive leakages were still recurring and he was advised that there would be undue risk to life in attempting to re-open the area yet.

The Commissioner himself was becoming restive at the delay

and decided to re-open the inquiry. A short and bad-tempered session was held in London on 31 March 1936. Evidence was given of two penetrations of the airway to 20s, which had enabled the body of the remaining rescuer to be brought out, and of measurements made by a team of experts which showed how narrow and inadequate the airway was; this could be attributed in part to deterioration which had taken place in the year-and-a-half since the accident. There were bitter protests because, while the miners had been prevented from exploring the area as far as the Clutch, the management was found to have privately sent some of its own men well beyond it. Questioned by Henderson, one of the party described the route they had taken and conceded that there was no reason why they could not have got to 29s, where many of the victims were lying.

As Edward Jones, the North Wales Miners' agent, had shrewdly foreseen, the resumption of the inquiry really signified that although the struggle might continue, all hope of an inspection of the scene of the accident could be given up. The next session, which was to last for three days, was fixed for 15 April, and was to be devoted to final submissions by counsel and other representatives. Cripps was to speak first and in the event monopolised the entire session.

Much of his speech was devoted to going over familiar ground and reading out long passages from the verbatim transcript of the evidence in support of the miners' case against the management. Mining, he stressed, had undergone great changes in two decades, and it was questionable whether the old Regulations and the old Act itself were now adequate to deal with modern conditions. 'The whole atmosphere of the evidence in this case, and the experience in many mines today, is an atmosphere of driving for output at all costs.' There were, he admitted, no statistics available as regarded Gresford itself to show this increasing pressure for output, but he appeared to take it for granted that if they had been forthcoming they would have supported his thesis. He then moved on to matters that were more fully documented, and to areas where, as with the missing reports, the absence of documentation was in itself an offence.

> That a man should be able to get a banjack pipe and blow away gas in the last minute or two of a shift, and then record it as not being present when it has been present ... seems to me merely a device for misleading both

the management and the Inspectorate ... It would be no exaggeration to say that, so far as this pit was concerned, whether it is ventilation or stone-dusting or firemen's records, there was a complete disregard of the Regulations. Apparently what Mr Bonsall thought convenient was replaced for the Regulations, and a more callous disregard of the provisions which Parliament had laid down for the safety of miners has never taken place in any other pit in this country.

Similarly with shot firing:

> There is not the slightest doubt that the drive for output in 14s led to [a] complete disregard of Safety Regulations so far as shot firing is concerned ... In my submission it is perfectly clear that those shots can only have been fired by not observing the precautions which are laid down, and particularly the inspection for gas ... examinations for gas were never made, or scarcely ever made, in any part of the pit where there was real pressure for production ... the management was absolutely callous about the thing ... allowing this extremely dangerous state of affairs to develop in a pit the ventilation of which was ... seriously defective.

Once again the Inspectorate felt some of the roughest edges of Cripps's tongue. Describing inspection at Gresford as 'an absolute farce', he read out passages from his cross-examination of Dominy, punctuating them with acid comment:

> ... that is either a gross piece of ignorance in an inspector or a very unworthy effort to make an excuse for dereliction of duty—I don't mind which way Mr Dominy has it ... Really, it's pathetic that a person who answers questions like that should be in charge of the inspection of mines in a large area in this country ... Apparently Mr Dominy has to think there's going to be an explosion in a pit before he sees that the Regulations are observed ... It's almost inconceivable that any human being who has the vaguest feeling of responsibility for the safety of mines could conduct himself in such a way.

Dominy's failure to bring to light the amount of illegal overtime being worked came in for particularly grave censure. Reminding the court of the number of men who were 'doubling' on the night of the disaster, Cripps expressed the opinion that:

> whatever the actual incident may have been that caused this gas magazine to explode, it is more likely that that incident would happen when tired men were working, and men with frayed nerves who were working in this awful noise and smoke and dust, than men who were working in the ordinary course of the shift ... I am quite sure that had it been known or ascertained that this regular practice was being carried out in Gresford Mine, it would have been stopped long before this accident happened,

and it may be that the stopping of it would also have meant the stopping of this explosion.

The Chief Inspector, listening in silence in his capacity as Commissioner, must have passed one of the most disagreeable hours of his life, especially when Cripps came to wind up this section of his submission. As far as failure to enforce safety regulations at Gresford was concerned it was not a question of allotting blame to the management or to the Inspectorate: both were equally to blame.

> They both had the responsibility ... Had those Regulations been duly complied with throughout the whole of this pit, it is almost certain that the conditions of danger which must have been there ... would probably have been obviated, and it might be that we should never have had to embark on this Inquiry.

In the absence of direct evidence as to the cause of the explosion, Cripps devoted almost the whole of his third day to a review of the position in 14s, which he described as 'a gasometer', and to which in his view the evidence of all the witnesses who had been examined pointed as the danger spot.

> ... you had conditions in 14s which were absolutely ripe for causing an explosion if anything careless or untoward happened—an accident with the cutter, an accident with a lamp, a shot misfiring—anything that may have happened, all those many things which do happen from time to time in mines, and when they do happen, if the state of the mine is a state of danger, then you get the sort of tragedy which occurred at Gresford.

It was to be hoped that so many lives had not been lost in vain and that, 'as a result of the sacrifice which has taken place in that pit, something really material may be done to safeguard the lives of the hundreds and thousands of miners who are working in this country'.

The Miners' Federation, which had at first been reluctant to accept Cripps as a participant in the inquiry, was filled with so much enthusiasm for his speech that it published a special summary, commending it as 'a masterly analysis and in its complete and utter fearlessness ... one of the most remarkable utterances of our times', and making it the basis of an appeal for a new campaign for membership.

> No mineworker [can] possibly read these revelations without coming to the conclusion that his only real safeguard against such horrible conditions as existed at Gresford is to be a member of a strong Trade

> Union ... Let [the report] be a torch which will light the way to greater
> security—let it be the means which will give our men greater control over
> their own lives, and let it be the precursor of a condition of things which
> will make another Gresford for ever impossible.

The Court of Inquiry still had a good deal of business to conduct but there was consternation when the official letter summoning the participants to a further session on 8 June 1936 at the Institution of Mechanical Engineers in London gave notice that 'Before continuing the addresses from interested parties further evidence will be called in regard to the general arrangements for the ventilation of the Dennis District.' The miners' advisers leapt at once to the conclusion that an attempt was to be made by the management to explain away some of the deductions which Cripps had drawn from the records, and there was resentment at the idea of such a manoeuvre being permitted after he had delivered his closing address. The truth was very different, and no one can have looked forward to the session with greater foreboding than the manager and his assistant.

At some point after the close of the previous session—when and how was never disclosed—it had been discovered that the plan of the mine, drawn up by the company surveyor and certified by him as showing the state of affairs below ground at the time of the explosion, was inaccurate. Some time towards the end of May or the beginning of June 1934 two doors had been built in the return airway from 20s and 61s, near to the point at which the air which had circulated round a large part of the workings was sent up the Martin shaft and out of the pit. The surveyor disclaimed all knowledge of them. Bonsall, asked now by the Commissioner why in all the evidence he had given earlier he had never mentioned them, excused himself on the ground that he had been 'in such a mental state' that he hadn't remembered them. On behalf of the owners Shawcross denied that they had known of the doors and argued that it would have been to their advantage to bring out the fact that they were there.

More to the point was why they had been installed. Bonsall maintained that they were designed to control 'fluctuations' in the air currents passing through 20s and 61s. Cripps insisted that they must have been intended to improve the ventilation in 14s, and that the concealment of their existence was confirmation that the management had known how bad conditions in 14s were. Time and time again he put the argument to Bonsall who, having by now lost some of his earlier dread of him, refused to concede it. Cripps finally gave in, clearly convinced that he had gained his point.

The Commissioner tried his own blandishments on the witness without success, and Bonsall was allowed to stand down; but not for long. A Mr William Idris Cuffin was sworn and the inquiry took the last of its many astonishing turns.

Cuffin was a young man whose job had been to go round the Dennis Section of Gresford measuring the flow of air at designated points, entering the readings in his notebook and compiling from them the records on which Cripps had drawn at such bewildering length during his cross-examination of Bonsall and Williams. Questioned by the Commissioner himself, Cuffin now admitted that the figures were even more unsatisfactory than Cripps had alleged them to be, because some of them had not been arrived at by taking measurements: he had made them up himself.

His story, which was not disputed, was that some weeks before the explosion, when he had a lot of work to do, he was told not to bother taking air measurements for the time being—Bonsall would put someone else on the job. After the explosion, when full records were called for in connection with the inquiry, it was discovered that Bonsall had forgotten or neglected to find a replacement for Cuffin and there were no figures for the weeks in question. When Cuffin asked what he should do about the gaps Bonsall told him to invent some plausible entries and he had done so. Much of the evidence he had given earlier in the inquiry was therefore false.

The Commissioner was appalled by these frank admissions and asked no more questions. Smith said the inquiry should end at that point. Others established briefly that Cuffin was telling the truth this time. Cripps demanded that the relevant papers should be sent to the Director of Public Prosecutions (who subsequently decided for reasons which were not disclosed that no action should be taken). Bonsall, invited to comment and warned that he need not, preferred to say nothing.

With these two embarrassing episodes out of the way, the closing submissions were resumed. Joe Hall restated from the point of view of the working miner many of Cripps's criticisms of conditions in the mines in general, especially those which were the result of mechanisation. He wanted deputies to be government officials not responsible for production, overtime to be restricted in the interests of health and to reduce unemployment, and inspection to be increased and improved. He was also in favour of shots being fired less often and only when the fewest men were in the pit. On 14s and 29s faces in Gresford half the men's time was taken up in getting out of the way of the shot firer, which apart from the question of danger had a bad effect on their wages.

With regard to the accident and responsibility for it, Hall had only one target. The proprietors were on the whole decent men, there had been no shortage of money or materials at the colliery, the inspectors were not particularly blameworthy, Williams, the under-manager, was a man of vision, 'conscientiously working with might and main to get the pit into a decent state of repair ... but the fellow hadn't the time'. The true villain, the sole repository of guilt, was Bonsall. 'Do not think for one moment, sir,' said Hall sententiously, 'that I'm simply trying to thrash this man to death', and went on to explain what he was doing.

> This man ... has come here to get the goodwill and sympathy which you're going to give him. He'll never suffer sufficiently mentally for the disaster he's responsible for. When it's been our own men under his administration he never once extended his sympathy to them; he's told them that they're serfs and slaves under him, and must work according to his command. Now when he's placed in that chair ... as far as the Miners' Federation is concerned, we're asking that he's going to be made an example of, to prevent any repetition of anything of this kind.

Others besides Bonsall must have sighed with relief when Hall sat down. A representative for the National Association of Colliery Managers later produced a resolution allegedly passed unanimously by 'Union men' at Gresford which stated that they resented Hall's attack on Bonsall who, they affirmed, had behaved well to the men and treated them properly.

Charlton devoted most of his speech to the defence of Dominy and the Inspectorate, but he also advanced an explanation of the disaster. The explosion, he suggested, had been caused by a spark from a faulty telephone situated on the main road between the bottom of the shaft and the Clutch. It was a lame theory which did little credit to a man of Charlton's experience and seniority in the Inspectorate. Even if the telephone had given off a spark there was unlikely to have been a sufficiently large concentration of gas for it to ignite at a point so near to where fresh air entered the pit. The Commissioner, members of the management and hundreds of rescue workers had travelled that part of the roadway during the fire-fighting operations and had seen that the damage, though severe, bore no relation to what might have been expected from an explosion in the vicinity. The few victims to be found in the area and brought out of the pit had plainly died from carbon monoxide poisoning and, although badly burned, bore none of the injuries which an explosion so near to them would have caused. The force of the explosion at that point would have travelled by the shortest route down to 29s, which was precisely the route by which the only survivors had escaped.

The representative of the Lancashire, Cheshire and North Wales Colliery Deputies' and Shot Firers' Association used the occasion to attack Cripps bitterly for political bias and to drag in various accusations concerning the miners which had not been heard in evidence. The proceedings degenerated into a tedious squabble, with Hall intervening to spoil the effect of some earlier and uncharacteristically complimentary references to the Commissioner.

So two more days of the inquiry came to an end with the submission by Shawcross on behalf of the owners still to be heard. A further and, as everyone must have hoped, final session was arranged for 14 July.

As he rose to begin his speech Shawcross was in much the same position as a tail-ender in the fourth innings of a test match, when only an impossibly large score could produce victory and only those with an unshakable dedication to the game or a direct personal interest in the outcome could be counted on to see things through to the end. Undeterred by the task facing him he succeeded in speaking for the greater part of four days, longer even than Cripps had needed, and although his handling of some of the evidence moved Dai Grenfell to annotate a copy of the transcript of the evidence with exasperated comment ('this is unmitigated humbug' ... 'what an absurd submission from a learned gentleman!'), he scored some points which might have counted for more in a cause which was less obviously past saving.

He had first to dispose of the inconvenient revelations made at the previous session, which he could hardly deny or excuse. His comment on the forged air measurements, for which it was tacitly agreed that Cuffin was not to be held responsible, might well have been applied to Bonsall's whole performance while in sole charge at

Gresford: it was an act, said Shawcross, 'of one who is a fool, but one of whom it is difficult to believe that he was a knave'.

For the rest his main strategy was one which shrewd and instructed observers had foreseen, taking the form of an attack based on the proposition that 'if witnesses are prepared to lie about major matters ... their evidence in regard to other questions cannot be relied on'. The 'major matter' he had particularly in mind was the use of stone dust in Gresford, where he was, and the other side knew he was, on firm ground.

In the course of his own speech Cripps had noticeably treated this subject cursorily, saying that although he had a very full analysis of all the evidence, 'it would hardly be a valuable use of the time at my disposal to go through the whole of that'. Almost certainly it was not time which influenced his decision but the nature of the evidence. The brief and the proofs of evidence, which Jones, the miners' solicitor, had carefully compiled himself, made it quite clear that whatever the situation near the coalfaces and in the roads leading to them, the main intake roads had been well treated with stone dust for a matter of 1,000 yards from the pit bottom. The Commissioner himself had taken samples of coal dust from this part of the road; when analysed they were found to be well within the limits of combustible matter allowed. When counsel for the miners arrived in Wrexham to interview witnesses before the inquiry opened, Jones's accurately prepared proofs were 'revised' so as to omit all references to stone-dusting which was known to have been done properly, and miners called by the Association gave evidence which was demonstrably untrue, denying that stone-dusting was done anywhere. It was in itself perhaps a small lapse—Grenfell dismissed it as irrelevant—but Jones, a scrupulously fair man, foresaw what the consequence would be. Shawcross made the men's veracity, or lack of it, the test for the reliability of their evidence on other topics, and Jones, knowing that the attacks were justified and were carrying considerable weight with the Commissioner, felt every time stone dust was mentioned 'as though someone was thrusting a knife into my heart'.

With a somewhat lighter touch Shawcross dealt with the evidence given on other matters, such as the behaviour of gas in 14s as described by some of the more imaginative witnesses. Much of this was simply forensic point-scoring—'a farcical performance' Grenfell called it—but some of it seems to have struck home and aroused unease and resentment. 'Be a little kind, Mr Shawcross', pleaded Joe Hall of all people, but Shawcross was not to be deflected.

In the circumstances Shawcross felt that it was not possible to discuss in any detail what had caused the explosion but he put forward, presumably on the instructions of his clients, the possibility that it may have been due to 'the spontaneous combustion of a gob fire'. Near the entrance to 29s district there was a pillar of coal left unworked since the stoppage of 1926. Under pressure the coal had been crumbling, it was suggested, releasing gas which had accumulated in the nearby waste, or goaf, or gob, while air had been leaking in, building up an explosive mixture which had at last ignited by natural heating in the coal.

So, with a final assurance from Hall that if it was the last thing they did the Miners' Federation would demand an inspection of the affected area, the inquiry into the Gresford disaster came to an end, and the Commissioner was left to contemplate the 38 volumes of verbatim evidence running to 1,621,000 words and the mass of other documents which it had generated, and to make what he could of them. Four months later he had completed the first draft of his report,[4] and one month later still he learnt that one of his assessors, John Brass, representing the employers' organisations, was sorry to say that he disagreed with it in many particulars and had therefore prepared a report expressing his own views. The other assessor, Joseph Jones, of the Miners' Federation, differing sharply from both Walker and Brass, contributed a third and shorter report.

Walker had obviously found great difficulty in reconciling the mass of contradictory evidence offered him on almost every aspect of the working of the Dennis Section. Much of it he dismissed as 'inaccurate', and of some he wrote that 'it does not ring true and I do not accept it as true',[5] which was the nearest he came to an accusation of lying. Some of his findings and *obiter dicta* have already been quoted. He spent much time analysing the state of affairs in the various districts and came to some general conclusions, but unlike Cripps and the miners, who had concentrated the weight of their attack on conditions in 14s, he was more disturbed by revelations concerning 95s, particularly a locality known as '24s heading' where a number of well-attested incidents left little doubt that lax inspection, poor ventilation, occurrences of gas and incautious shot firing had created a situation which was in his opinion 'precarious' and 'one of great danger'. Work in this district, as in 14s and 29s, should have been stopped until more adequate ventilation was available. Even if drastic remedies of this kind had been taken there would still have remained 'the initial error',[6] which he considered to have been the failure, 12 or 15 years earlier, to complete the second of two airways originally planned and so to provide adequate ventilation for all the districts.

As was to be expected, he responded vigorously to Cripps's sweeping allegation that the inspectors were, with the management and the deputies, 'directly responsible for the explosion'. He accepted that 'certain inspectors were at fault in their dealings with this colliery over a period of years', but he claimed that Cripps had misconceived the powers available to the inspector,[7] and he made the point that any enlargement of the scope of government inspection 'should have careful regard that the powers of Inspectors are commensurate with their responsibilities'.[8]

Summarising the theories advanced by Cripps, Charlton and Shawcross as to the cause of the explosion, Walker dismissed out of hand the idea of a 'gob fire' on the grounds that there was no history of spontaneous heating in Gresford, and declined to discuss the arguments for and against the other suggestions, contenting himself with the observation that 'for reasons stated earlier . . . in the Report I look with grave suspicion upon the circumstances existing in connexion with 24s airway in 95s district'.

A report which implicates everybody satisfies nobody. To John Brass most of Walker's criticism of the management and the deputies at Gresford was unacceptable and his own report exonerated them. The management were always ready and willing to put right any matter requiring their attention which was brought to their notice. The deputies were an intelligent body of men and had carried out their duties in a manner that was expected of them. If the district had been in the condition described by witnesses called on behalf of the North Wales Miners' Association, work would have been impossible. Brass believed that the deputies reported gas when they found it in 14s and other districts, as required by the Coal Mines Act, and that they had no reason to do otherwise.

He could not concur with the view expressed that the fear of victimisation prevented any workman at the colliery from lodging a complaint if he had a genuine grievance. Men working in 14s had complained not against working conditions but against the heat, with the result that additional payment had been made. Nor did it follow that a stronger trade union would have improved matters: indeed there were cases where strong trade unions had definitely set their faces against the introduction of methods for increasing the safety of workmen; he was thinking particularly of the use of steel supports for the roof, the adoption of which had been continually urged by Inspectors of Mines.

Brass did not agree that 24s airway in 95s should be looked on with suspicion as the point of origin of the explosion. He was in substantial agreement with Charlton that it had occurred in the neighbourhood of the Clutch. The great loss of life in this disaster was not, in his opinion, due primarily to the explosion but to the resulting fire at or near 29s junction.

Finally, leaving no part of Sir Henry's edifice of argument untouched by dissent, Brass insisted that the provisions for inspection were exceedingly wide and fulfilled all requirements.

By contrast Joseph Jones, obviously feeling that Walker's report dealt far too leniently with the sins of the management, went out of his way to underline them, reiterating the familiar charges that the evidence

> revealed glaring instances of indiscipline and complete demoralisation among officials of the mine and conveyed quite definitely the impression that the mine lacked leadership and character, that the officials ... were more concerned with output than with the law or safety precautions, and that flagrant risks were taken ...

Even in the face of the rapidly deteriorating conditions in 109s and 14s, 'the firemen drove their men to work with increasing recklessness and open contempt for the dangers run'.

Rejecting both 95s and the area of the Clutch as the scene of the explosion, Jones stressed once again the miners' preference for 14s with its 'excessive accumulation of firedamp'. It could only be described as a place of grave danger. Aligning himself with Cripps, he concluded that the Inspectorate as it stood was both inadequate and ineffective, and in a final passage—which in places rivalled Cripps for severity and Hall for aggression—he listed at least 14 'flagrant and persistent' breaches of the Coal Mines Act and the General Regulations for which he wanted Bonsall, Williams and the officials to be dealt with as the law directed; accused Harold Thomas of manslaughter in respect of the lives lost by the rescue team; and expressed his considered opinion that the Chief Inspector of Mines or any of his assistants should *not* in future be called upon to conduct formal investigations of this kind. The task should be entrusted to members of the Judiciary with persons of practical experience in mining to assist them.

On reading the three reports, the Secretary for Mines to whom they were addressed may well have reflected that, in the words of Shawcross in a different connection, 'you took your choice'.

Although so much time had elapsed since the disaster, Gresford was still significant enough to engage the attention of Parliament. Time was set aside for a debate in the Commons on 23 February 1937, but interest in the contents of the report was eclipsed for many members by excited speculation about the role to be allotted to Cripps, who was by now at even greater odds with his Party than he had been in 1934. During the interval the threat from abroad, especially from the rise of National Socialism in Germany, had broadened his concept of the class struggle (which owed little to Marx, whom he had never read) and led him to put his considerable influence behind the left-wing argument which, throughout the middle and late 1930s, held that it was of paramount importance to halt the advance of fascism but that since a predominantly Conservative British Government could not be trusted with arms, which it would infallibly use against the working class in an imperialist war, it must at all costs be denied them.[9] The Socialist League, having outlived its usefulness as a ginger group within the Labour Party, was reconstituted as a separate organisation, and Cripps, who had resigned from the National Executive Committee of the party, threw himself energetically into campaigns for unified action along Continental lines with the ILP and the Communist Party. It was at this period that in one of his most notorious speeches he informed an audience at Stockport, according to press reports, that 'he did not believe it would be a bad thing for the British working class if Germany defeated us [in a war]. It would be a disaster for the profit-makers and capitalists but not necessarily for the working class.'[10]

In spite of claiming support from enthusiastic constituency parties, the movement was ultimately doomed to failure through its own inner dissensions. The ILP and the Communist Party, mutually hostile at the best of times, found themselves on opposite sides in the conflict which split the opposition to Franco in the

Spanish Civil War. The solid core of trade unionists in the Labour Party, ideologically committed to opposition to the Communists, would have no truck with Fronts, United or Popular, and Cripps, by identifying himself resolutely with such outlawed causes, strained his links with the party to breaking point and was expecting to be expelled when the debate on Gresford was announced for 23 February, fortuitously giving him an opportunity to throw his political opponents into temporary disarray.

Although virtually an outcast as far as the Labour Party hierarchy was concerned, he had the strongest claims, on the score of his knowledge of the subject and his widely acclaimed performance at the inquiry, to open the debate on the Opposition motion, and it has frequently been asserted that he did so.[11] The party leadership, although obviously embarrassed by the situation, was not so wholly bereft of talent and found a face-saving compromise. Cripps spoke from the back benches and the task of opening was given to David Grenfell, the miner and long-serving member for Gower, who knew as much about Gresford as Cripps did, had acted as his mentor throughout the inquiry, and was, as Cripps later acknowledged in a warm tribute, more responsible for its effectiveness than any other man in England.

The motion asserted that

> This House views with deep concern the conditions revealed by the inquiry into the Gresford Colliery explosion in which 265 lives were lost, and is of the opinion that grave responsibility rests upon the country and Parliament to prevent such disasters by adopting immediate and effective measures for ensuring that the industry is carried on under conditions of maximum safety.

To a House remarkably better attended on the Opposition benches than on the Government side, Grenfell gave a workmanlike summary of the contents of the report and of the story of 'recklessness and demoralisation' which the inquiry had revealed, allowing himself only the occasional rhetorical self-indulgence.

> There is no language in which one can describe the inferno of 14s. There were men working almost stark naked, clogs with holes bored through the bottom to let the sweat run out, a hundred shots a day fired on a face less than 200 yards wide, the air thick with fumes and dust from blasting, the banjack hissing to waft the gas out of the face into the unpacked waste, a space 200 yards long and 100 yards wide above the wind road full of inflammable gas and impenetrable for that reason.

The only mystery was that the explosion had not happened long before.

Apart from those witnesses whom he accused of having deliberately set out to mislead the inquiry, Grenfell singled out for particular attack Charlton and his 'impossible and ridiculous suggestion' that the explosion had been caused by a spark from a telephone, a theory for which there was not a scrap of justification and which, Grenfell claimed, was invented by Charlton and Shawcross when it was too late for Charlton to be cross-examined on it.

> I regret that His Majesty's Inspector has ignored the facts and has resorted to fancy instead. I do not wish to refer to Mr. Shawcross except to say that Mr. Shawcross, much against his will, had to take gas at the inquiry. He swallowed a reservoir of gas and now we find him, on page 169 of the Report, sniffing at a gob stink.

The Secretary for Mines, Captain Crookshank, replied pacifically for the Government, asking the House to accept the motion.

CAPT. CROOKSHANK: I do not want there to be any division of opinion ... on a matter of this kind. It would be easier for us if the Hon Member, instead of saying in his motion 'to prevent such disasters', would say 'to try to prevent' because ... there are things called Acts of God, which cannot really ... (Interruption)
MR GEORGE GRIFFITHS: This is an act of the Devil.
CAPT. CROOKSHANK: I do not press it.

During the undistinguished debate which followed, all interest was centred on the question of when Cripps would speak. He was in his place from the beginning, forming part, as the *Manchester Guardian* observer commented, of a curious picture.

> The silent, watchful, handsome figure of the distinguished lawyer, and one of the four best debaters, whom nobody seemed to want, whom everybody seems to fear, held all eyes. Tomorrow the Labour Party will decide whether it wants Sir Stafford to remain in the Party. Tonight it watched him uneasily and admiringly. When at last he rose to speak the dilemma of the Labour Party became increasingly apparent. It listened to its own case being put vastly more skilfully than it could put it, and vastly more effectively.

Much of the speech covered ground familiar to anyone who had followed the course of the inquiry, but its power lay in the skill with which the disclosures concerning Gresford—the disregard of regulations, the neglect of safety, the ineffectiveness of the Inspectorate, the men's fear of victimisation—were used with deadly effect to reinforce the simple message: private enterprise could no longer be tolerated in the coal mining industry.

> The accusation against profit-making in industry is not that every employer is bad and inhuman ... but every mining employer must have profits made for him somehow or another out of the enterprise of mining if that enterprise is to continue within a profit-making society ... Always the main drive is for production at a low cost, and in that drive there is always the liability for a disregard of safety measures to arise in particular instances.

An obvious temptation was to avoid the cost of putting new ventilation into a district which would shortly cease production.

> That is precisely what happened in the case of Gresford Colliery, and I am perfectly certain that the management at Gresford honestly thought that they would get through the job without an explosion. They took that risk and that risk had the tragic results which we know.

Referring to specific examples from Gresford of men being taken away from the completion of new airways and sent to work on the coalface, Cripps asked, of the management,

> Is it to be imagined that these people were such inhuman monsters that they did that just for the sake of doing it, without any motive to drive them and force them to that most undesirable end? The only conceivable purpose can have been to save money and in order to keep down the cost of production ...

Cripps agreed that it was necessary to increase the efficiency of the Inspectorate, and have more inspections by workmen, but why was it necessary? 'If the drive for profits doesn't increase the dangers to safety, why are these precautions necessary?' The problem was not confined to the mining industry: why had the State had to legislate as regards the conditions of labour of men, women and children continuously for the last hundred years? 'It's not from wanton inhumanity that the workers have had to be protected by legislation, it's from the necessities of the drive for production coming from the profit-making system itself.'

He was, he made it clear, not attempting to exonerate those responsible for the events at Gresford. There had been 'a complete disregard for the law of the safety of mines in that pit' which he hoped would be punished, to show that such laxity could not and would not be allowed to persist. He hoped also that the House would take into account, and act on, the lessons to be learned,

> as indeed it must if it is to be faithful to the duty that it has to protect this large section of the community from dangers which we ourselves impose upon it in order that we may derive the vast wealth that we do from the coal mines.

But in his view, although he admitted that it was something that could not be immediately accomplished, the problem of safety in mines would not be solved

> until the miners are made wholly responsible for their own safety by having the control of the mining operations. In other words, the conflict between profits and high production on the one hand, and safety and decent working conditions on the other, will never be solved until the whole industry is taken out of the hands of private ownership.[12]

NOTES

1. Duckham and Duckham (1973), p. 30.
2. Peter Lee died 16 September 1935.
3. See Lawson (1941), pp. 183, 203.
4. Cmd. 5358. The comment of the *Colliery Guardian* (12 February 1937) was that 'this mountain in labour has produced a very *ridiculus mus*' (p. 313).
5. Report, p. 36.
6. *Ibid.*, p. 62.
7. *Ibid.*, p. 90:

> ... I find no justification in the evidence for imputing any general neglect or incompetency on the part of the Inspectors concerned, and I feel that a large part of the general charge of complete failure made against them and more particularly against Mr. Dominy was based on an erroneous idea of the duties of the Inspectorate under the present system and practice of Government inspection in this country. That misapprehension on the part of Counsel was, I think, shown by a reference in his address to 'the over-riding [sic] power of supervision of the Inspectorate' and by a question which he put to Mr. Dominy—'Of course, it is part of your job, is it not, to supervise generally the whole circumstances of the mine so far as ventilation and safety are concerned?' Mr. Dominy's reply, 'Yes I have to see that they have adequate ventilation', lent colour to Counsel's misconception.

8. *Ibid.*, p. 91.
9. Cripps was at pains to make his own position clear. Cooke (1957, p. 168)

described him as 'a strong pacifist'. Cripps made no such claim. In *The Struggle for Peace* (1936) he wrote: 'I personally am not a pacifist in the sense that never under any circumstances would I fight … I cannot close my eyes to the fact that a straightforward pacifist programme today is not practical politics.' He was therefore prepared to sanction armaments in a State 'where the government has attained economic control', the safeguard being that 'the armaments will be controlled by the common people, and that should provide an assurance that they will not be used for capitalist or imperialist exploitation' (p. 118). Even after the socialist revolution, every nation would always require forces 'to maintain internal order against the attempts of the capitalist class to win back by force the power and privileges that have been taken away from them by the will of the people' (*ibid.*, p. 137). Events moved so quickly in the 1930s that it is difficult at times to keep up with Cripps's response to them. David Marquand (1963, p. 173) sums him up as being 'in a state of dialectical schizophrenia … although he wanted Fascism to be resisted he was not prepared to give the British Government the wherewithal to do so'. At one period his earlier support for the League of Nations gave place to an assertion that, the League itself being 'a capitalist creation', the British Labour Party should 'undertake to resist a war entered by the National Government by every means in its power, including a general strike' (Cooke (1957), p. 169).

    10. *Manchester Guardian*, 16 November 1936.

    11. See for example Estorick (1949), p. 158.

    12. See Appendix A. Addison (1994, p. 192) points out that following Cripps's expulsion from the Labour Party in 1939 for advocating a Popular Front, he 'came down to earth with a vengeance', omitting reference to nationalisation from his campaign literature, although there is no indication that he had personally lost faith in it. The course of his public life changed remarkably between the outbreak of war in 1939 and his death in 1952, but that takes the story beyond the limits of the Gresford disaster.

CHAPTER 16

The Last Rites

Cripps's speech was heard in almost total silence. It was so brilliant, the *Manchester Guardian* commented, that both friends and foes disliked it, but he had earned himself a reprieve, unlike Bonsall and his colleagues, whose troubles were about to enter their next stage. Towards the end of March 1937 it was announced that proceedings were to be taken under the Coal Mines Regulations Act against the owners, manager and other officials of Gresford Colliery.[1]

An almost inevitable consequence of the undisciplined manner in which the inquiry had been conducted was confusion in some minds between alleged breaches of the Regulations and actions which could be shown to have caused the accident and for which there was no evidence. The Solicitor General, for the Director of Public Prosecutions, took special care to make it plain at the outset that there were 'no allegations that any of the defendants were responsible, by the acts with which they were charged, for the explosion'. The alleged breaches were of a technical nature, carrying small penalties even if proved, and there is no truth in the assertion made by two of Cripps's biographers that as a result of the revelations under Cripps's cross-examination of witnesses, a manager of the mine was imprisoned.[2]

There were in all 42 summonses, some against the manager, the under-manager or firemen individually, others jointly against United Westminster and Wrexham Collieries Ltd and the manager; the charges, in various combinations and permutations, concerned failure to provide adequate ventilation, failure to cause air measurements to be taken, failure to keep records, allowing shot firing without treating with stone dust, firing shots in a manner likely to endanger the safety of persons employed in the mine, and so on. The hearings began at Wrexham County Petty Sessions on 20 April 1937 and continued for some days. Many of the *dramatis personae* from the inquiry reappeared and went through their lines again, but this time within the normal legal restraints on the admissibility of evidence: for example Sir Patrick Hastings, appearing for the defence, successfully objected to the hearing of evidence dealing with the explosion. In this formal atmosphere, without the emotional drive and forceful personality of Sir Stafford Cripps to boost them, the explosive power of the charges was damped down to the point at which it seemed hardly worth while having gone to the trouble of laying them. On 23 April summonses against three men in relation to alleged failure to keep records were withdrawn and the defendants were discharged; on 26 April further summonses were dismissed and five more defendants were discharged, leaving only the company and the manager in the dock; on 27 April summonses relating to ventilation were dismissed and convictions were secured on the remaining eight summonses, which related to keeping records. Fines totalling £140 were imposed and the defendants were ordered to pay £350 costs. The reverberations which this result set going throughout the mining industry are not recorded.

Meanwhile the aggression which was held in check in the presence of the Wrexham magistrates had been finding an outlet in London, where relations between the Miners' Federation and the Department of Mines had deteriorated almost to breaking point.

When, after more months of delay, it became known that once the circulation of air had been restored in the pit and the accumulation of gas had been flushed out, the management proposed to put a permanent stopping on the road leading to the wrecked districts, Hall defiantly informed the press that the sealed portion of the pit would be entered by a party of miners in an effort to recover 81 bodies from 29s district. This move was frustrated by the discovery that the men concerned would not be covered by insurance against the risks involved.

It was the beginning of the end. In an increasingly acrimonious three-cornered contest, the miners accused the Inspectorate of always supporting the owners against them. The Inspectorate, which took its cue from an expert from the University of Birmingham who was in charge of the operation, asserted that the stoppings would not be opened until he gave the word. The miners retorted that they were perfectly capable of judging whether it was safe to re-enter the pit. The North Wales Miners' agent let it be known that he was not going to be dictated to by the Mines Department; Joseph Jones announced that the men would go through the stoppings no matter how long the delay lasted; Joe Hall declared that they were being fooled and the fooling must stop.

All this bluster and attempted show of bravado was put into perspective when three Gresford rescue teams, lining themselves up with the Inspectorate, were reported to have decided not to enter the Dennis Section until it was pronounced safe by the expert; and revealing for the first time a lack of patience with the domination of North Wales by Yorkshire, they expressed resentment at the part being played by Smith and Hall and stated firmly that they would be competent to enter the affected area when the time came without assistance from any other coalfield.

The necessity did not arise. On 31 May 1938 the Member for Wrexham, Mr Robert Richards, asked the Secretary for Mines when the sealed part of Gresford mine was last tested for gas and what the result was. In a written reply the Secretary informed him that air samples were last taken on 17 May and that the results indicated that the air inside the stoppings was still such that it was unsafe to remove them. There the matter was allowed to rest and Gresford withdrew into welcome obscurity for nearly 30 years.

The General Election of May 1945, held within a few weeks of the ending of the war with Germany, returned Labour to power for the first time with an overall majority. Before the year was out, a Bill for the nationalisation of the coal mining industry had been introduced in Parliament. In 1946, after fierce battles, it became law. On 1 January 1947 the coal mines of Britain passed from private hands into national ownership.

In contrast with the fears of some and the hopes of others, the former owners were to be compensated for the properties which the State had acquired from them. An independent tribunal fixed the basic value of the industry for compensation purposes at £164 million, which did not include the value of other property, such as houses, railways, coke ovens, and so forth. The total compensation payments in cash or Treasury stock brought into the accounts of the National Coal Board amounted to nearly £390 million. The Board was to be responsible for redeeming the capital value of the stock and paying interest on it. In 1958 the sum set aside for payment was £32 million, of which the shareholders of United Westminster and Wrexham Collieries received their allotted portion; in the same year their links with the company were finally severed after complicated, protracted and wearisome negotiations with the liquidator appointed to wind it up.

United Westminster and Wrexham Collieries formally ceased to exist on 22 July 1958, and one year later, in accordance with the undertaking he had given, the liquidator destroyed all the company's books, accounts and documents.

In July 1936, while the inquiry was still stumbling through its closing stages, a Royal Commission chaired by Lord Rockley,[3] with Sir Henry Walker and David Grenfell among its members, had been instructed to review the whole subject of safety in coal mines and to make recommendations for changes in the law. It reported in 1938 but events on a wider stage, including a world war and the calls on parliamentary time made by the extensive programme of social reform undertaken by the Labour Government of 1945, postponed consideration of new legislation, and it was not until 1954 that a revised Mines and Quarries Act reached the statute book.

Among its provisions were several which had their origins in the revelations elicited by Cripps and others during the long and heated exchanges of the inquiry. Some were straightforward: for example, managers would no longer be able, like Bonsall, to plead ignorance of what was going on in any particular part of the mine.

> 10.   It shall be the duty of the manager of every mine, with respect to each report, record or other item of information which ... is entered in a book which ... is required to be provided for that purpose by the owner of the mine, either to read it himself forthwith, or to secure that it is read by some other competent person, and that there is promptly brought to his attention any matter disclosed ... which is of abnormal or unusual nature or ... may necessitate the taking of steps.

Less easy to resolve was the apparent ambiguity in the role of the fireman, or deputy, which had provoked such fierce dispute during the inquiry. Should a fireman be required to concentrate solely on the safety of his district and the men working there or could his sphere of responsibility be widened to include, for example, maintaining the output of coal from the faces under his charge? It was a topic which had occupied the minds of experts and legislators over a long period and the Rockley Commission reviewed the various changes of emphasis which had occurred.

From the earliest times down to 1911 no restrictions had been placed on the duties which a deputy might undertake, and an earlier Royal Commission, reporting in 1909, while expressing the opinion that 'where practicable the fireman should be enabled to give his whole time and attention to the duties concerned with the safety of the workmen under his charge', had conceded that in practice this might not always be possible. The Coal Mines Act of 1911 which followed, and which was still in force at the time of Gresford, went in Rockley's view a good deal further than the preceding Commission had intended, making it a legal requirement that the fireman devote his whole time to safety except that he might also be employed in the additional duties of 'measuring the work done by persons in his district, and firing shots in his district . . .'.

While coal was still being got by hand, no serious problems had arisen, but with the changes consequent upon the introduction of mechanisation, conflicts of interest became apparent. As the Rockley Commission put it, 'there is serious and increasing difficulty in reconciling the requirements of the law with the exigencies of production'. Evidence given to the Commission highlighted the differences of view on the subject. Charlton thought it was not a practical proposition for a deputy to confine himself to safety matters; spokesmen for the deputies stressed the clash of loyalties which resulted from dividing safety and output into watertight compartments; the Mineworkers' Federation stood firmly by the concept of the fireman as above all a safety official.

The Commission came to the conclusion that 'efficient management and safety go hand in hand' and saw

> no reason why [the deputy's] duties should be limited to safety or why it should be assumed that there is some difficulty which prevents the official who is most closely and continuously in contact with the progress of work from paying due regard to both the safety and the production aspects of the art of mining.

This, the Commission affirmed,

> should not diminish the importance to be attached to the influence of the deputy on the safe conduct of the operations of which he is in charge. It rather puts it on a higher plane, by giving him a greater authority and status.

Men from the Dennis Section of Gresford Colliery who had avoided the fate that overtook the night shift on 22 September 1934 might have been forgiven for taking a less sanguine view of the advisability of conferring greater authority and status on some of their erstwhile overlords in 14s and elsewhere. They would perhaps have been reassured when Parliament, framing the new Act of 1954, settled as it had done in 1911 for more explicit restrictions on the fireman's job description than a Royal Commission had proposed.

12. (1) Provision may be made by regulations
  a) for imposing, in relation to a mine, such requirements with respect to the carrying out, by competent persons appointed for the purpose ... of inspections of the mine as it may appear to the Minister ... expedient for the purpose of securing the safety and health of the workmen ...
  (2) Regulations ... shall be so framed as ... to secure that ... those persons shall give preference to the securing of the safety and health of the workmen employed at the mine over the securing of any other matter.

In one further area which had aroused acrimonious controversy at the inquiry the Rockley Commission pointed the way towards what amounted to the rejection of the philosophy which had largely prevailed since the days when Seymour Tremenheere had embarked on his first timid dealings with Lord Londonderry and his kind. The official view, quoted at the inquiry by a witness from the Mines Department, had been firmly opposed to any system of inspection 'which would involve an inspector in performing the duties which should naturally fall on the officials of the colliery'; any change which would have the effect of extending the authority and enlarging the powers of inspectors 'appears to us alien to the objectives of governmental inspection'. The essence of the situation, as Charlton had complained bitterly in response to Cripps's equally savage criticism, was that '[the inspector] can advise—he cannot order'. The Rockley Commission demolished this barrier in one brief paragraph.

480.   That part of the Mines Department which is directly responsible for the administration of the law relating to safety and health should be further strengthened and given a status and authority corresponding to the importance of its work ... the authority and position of the inspectorate should be enhanced ... in particular by greater devolution of responsibility ... and by improved conditions of service.

These terse recommendations were translated in the Act of 1954 into an equally forthright and, as some must have thought, revolutionary provision.

146.   (1) If an inspector is of opinion that a mine ... or any matter, thing or practice ... connected with the control or management is or is likely shortly to become dangerous to the safety or health of the persons employed ... he may serve on the responsible persons a notice stating he is of that opinion and imposing ... such prohibitions or restrictions (of whatsoever kind) as appear to the inspector necessary ...

The substitution of 'shall' for 'may' would have strengthened the clause but the legislature perhaps felt it had already gone far enough in an industry in which it might be presumed, however mistakenly, that there would never again be private owners to be appeased.

NOTES

1. See Appendix D. For details of the proceedings see *The Times*, 21 April 1937 and subsequent days.

2. See Strauss (1943), p. 80; Estorick (1949), p. 135; Bryant (1997), p. 140. All accounts by Cripps's biographers of the Gresford inquiry and its aftermath should be treated with caution.

3. Appointed on 14 December 1935 to inquire

> whether the safety and health of mine workers can be better ensured by extending or modifying the principles or general provisions of the Coal Mines Act 1911, or the arrangements for its administration, having regard to the changes that have taken place in organization, methods of work, and equipment since it became law, and the experience gained; and to make recommendations.

Epilogue

In 1948 a young man from Rhosllanerchrugog, who was at the time reading chemistry at Bangor University, decided that on taking his degree he would 'go in for mining', which meant that instead of simply working in the pit he would also study to become a manager. There were by this time six collieries still operating in North Wales, and the obvious one for him to enter as a beginner would have been Hafod, the village pit at the foot of the hill, where his father, starting work at the age of 13, had risen to be underground manager; but the young man wanted to go where he would not be known and applied to Gresford Colliery, which by then employed 1,600 men. Even Gresford had some associations for him because his father, as captain of a rescue team, had been the first man to set foot on the pit bottom when exploration of the gas-filled area was begun in 1935.

As a newcomer he spent six months on a training face.

> We worked stripped to the waist in stifling heat and dust, and Peter [the supervisor] never cured me of my habit of drinking water from my tin every quarter of an hour or so ... I sweated profusely and each shift I weighed 10 or 12lb less at the end than I had done at the start.

At the end of his training he was sent to work in the Slant District, on a face two-and-a-half miles from the pit bottom. 'The district was a hot one, much warmer than the training face, which was itself uncomfortably warm, and we all stripped to the waist and wore football shorts at our work.'

In due course he achieved his ambition and became a manager at Bersham Colliery on the outskirts of Wrexham. Later still he fulfilled his earliest dream by becoming manager at Hafod, but the dream had turned sour on him. Hafod, the aristocrat of North Wales pits, was to close and his melancholy duty was to supervise the closure.

The North Wales coalfield, proving more and more uneconomic, had continued to shrink. Of its six remaining pits the first to be closed, in March 1966, was Llay Main, which had been

210

opened with high hopes as recently as 1923. Hafod, after strenuous attempts to save it, succumbed in March 1968. When he had finished presiding over its dissolution the manager, Tom Ellis, turned to politics and at the general election of June 1970 entered Parliament as the Labour member for Wrexham. A third colliery, Brynkinallt and Ifton, closed in November 1968.

There were now three collieries left, Bersham and Gresford near Wrexham and Point of Ayr 35 miles to the north on the Flintshire coast. Of these, Bersham seemed to have the least promising future because it supplied coking coal to the steel-making plant at Shotton on the Dee estuary which was also threatened with closure, but it was Gresford which, like the weak member of the herd, began to show signs of ailing, falling behind the rest and attracting the attention of the predators. The colliery was placed on the National Coal Board's 'jeopardy list' in November 1969 because of 'heavy financial losses and the doubtful prospects of [its] future viability'. By December 1970 it had recovered strength sufficiently to be taken off the list and was breaking its own output records, but the revival was short-lived. By February 1973 the colliery was being 'singled out for special attention' and in May the axe fell. The mining position at Gresford, it was explained, had been difficult over recent years because of the intensity of major and minor faulting which interrupted the smooth progress of face-working. Geological conditions in the remaining reserves of the Main Seam coal were unlikely to improve, and an attempt to exploit another seam, the Quaker, had failed at a cost of £400,000. Everyone at the colliery had cooperated in trying to keep down costs but in the past year, even with a subsidy of £2 per ton on the selling price of industrial coal, the pit had lost £1.5 million, or more than £5 on every ton produced. The North Wales Area Director of the Coal Board could therefore see no justification for continuing production at Gresford after 1973.

The news was received as might be expected. The North Wales Area of the National Union of Mineworkers appealed to the Coal Board, the local authorities of Denbighshire and Wrexham appealed to the Secretary of State for Wales, each with the same message: half the work force of the coalfield had already been lost in the recent closures; the area had lost heavy industry of other kinds and was likely to lose more; unemployment was already high and a thousand more jobs would be lost if Gresford closed. The union asked for 12 months' grace in which to try for even greater efficiency and drive new headings in search of better conditions, but the logic of the situation was inexorable. An official of the NUM visited the Quaker seam, noted the naturally weak and friable nature of the rock and was left in no doubt that exploitation of the seam would be 'an abortive exercise', and that he had no technical case to make against the proposed closure. Tom Ellis came to the same conclusion, and regretfully told the men that he did not honestly think the government could be persuaded to underwrite further losses in order to prevent the social hardship that would arise if the colliery closed.

Deprived of support, the men capitulated. Coal winding at Gresford ceased on 23 October 1973 and the colliery closed on 10 November.[1] Some months were spent in bringing out of the pit everything worth salvaging. One set of pit-head winding gear was left standing as a memorial to the mine and the disaster.[2] Then, far below the farmland of Cheshire and Clwyd and the streets of Wrexham, the relentless pressures of the earth were left to destroy the Slant District, as they must long ago have crushed the deep recesses of the Dennis Section, the roads and conveyors, the scourings and headings, of 20s and 61s, 109s and 95s, 14s and 29s; leaving the men who died there on 22 September 1934 to lie in the most impregnable of tombs.

NOTES

1. The *Wrexham Evening Leader* of 6 November 1973, under the headline 'After 62 years it's the end of the mine', noted 'On Friday the last coal will be hauled to the surface ... The colliery officially closes on Saturday, but it is unlikely that the miners, superstitious as they are, will be working that final shift.' Bersham Colliery, the last in what had been Denbighshire, did not long survive Gresford, and with the closure of Point of Ayr, in the former Flintshire, in 1996 coal-mining in North Wales came to an end.

2. To accommodate the reconstruction of the main road from Wrexham to Chester, now carried on a flyover, the pit-head gear, which stood in the way, was dismantled, and a smaller memorial, consisting of a single wheel resting on a plinth, was erected to one side on an unobtrusive site screened by trees. A plaque commemorating the events of 22 September 1934 records that the memorial was unveiled by His Royal Highness the Prince of Wales on 26 November 1982.

Nationalisation (see p. 69)

The history of the conflict between the government, the colliery owners and the miners during the decade following the end of the First World War need not be described in detail here, but in view of Sir Stafford Cripps's consistent advocacy of nationalisation as the solution to the mining industry's problems, and the use he made of Gresford in support of the policy, a brief summary of the main stages of the campaign which preceded his appearance on the scene may put his own attitude and endeavours into perspective.

Closely bound up with the issue of nationalisation of the mining industry, by which coal was extracted from the ground and sold, was the issue of royalties, the payment made to owners of land, not necessarily mine owners themselves, from beneath which the coal was extracted. State ownership of royalties was broadly favoured by owners and wholly so by miners, the chief difficulty being how to unravel the extremely complex legal and other problems in which the subject was enmeshed.

Consideration of the factors generally accepted as contributing to the unsatisfactory state of the industry was for the most part pushed to one side during the war when the mines, because of their vital contribution to the prosecution of the conflict, were brought under government control. It was the suggestion, following the end of hostilities, that control was to be handed back to the owners which brought nationalisation to the fore as one of a package of reforms demanded by the miners which also included a substantial increase in wages, to meet a steady rise in the cost of living, and a reduction in the eight-hour day to six hours. Faced with the prospect of a crippling strike, which would have involved the railwaymen and the transport workers, the government offered to set up a Commission under Mr Justice Sankey, a High Court judge. This was accepted by the miners on the understanding that the Commission would produce an interim report on the question of wages and hours of work within three weeks, and that, in the words of Sydney and Beatrice Webb (*History of Trade Unionism*, 1920):

> the [Miners'] Federation should be allowed to nominate to the Com-
> mission not only three of its own members, to balance the coal owners
> who had been informally designated by the Mining Association ... but
> also three out of the six professionally disinterested members, so as to
> balance the three capitalists whom the Government had already chosen as
> representing the principal industries depending on the supply of coal at a
> moderate price.

This demand was accepted. Although the Webbs do not name the
miners' three 'disinterested members', Sydney himself was one of
them; another was R. H. Tawney. One of the miners' professional
representatives was the Yorkshire leader Herbert Smith; one of the
government's chosen neutrals was Arthur Balfour.

According to the Webbs' account (written within a year of the
event) the sessions of the Commission, which were held in public,
created 'an immense sensation. Instead of the Trade Union it was
the management of the industry that was put on trial.' The results
of its deliberations were rather more predictable.

There were in fact three reports. Mr Justice Sankey and his
three 'independent' colleagues recommended increases in pay for all
workers and a seven-hour day for underground workers, to be
reduced to six at the end of 1920 if conditions permitted. As to
nationalisation:

> Even upon the evidence already given the system of ownership and
> working in the coal industry stands condemned, and some other system
> must be substituted for it, either nationalisation or a method of
> unification by national purchase and/or by joint control.

No schemes of this kind had yet been submitted, and the Commissioners (or this section of them) were not prepared to give at that
time 'a momentous decision upon a point which affects every citizen
in this country ...'. They were prepared, however, to report that 'it
is in the interests of the country that the colliery worker shall in the
future have an effective voice in the direction of the mine'.

The remaining Commissioners were divided as might have been
expected. The three colliery owners were prepared to concede an
increase in wages and a reduction in working hours, but in each case
only half of what the miners had asked for. They made no proposals
for overhauling the structure of the industry. The three miners and
their three supporters recommended full acceptance of the demands
relating to wages and hours of work. On nationalisation, while
agreeing that the Commission had not yet had time to consider

the subject in detail, they echoed the sentiments of, among others, Sir Richard Redmayne, 'the Government's principal Coal Official', in whose opinion there was general acceptance of the view that 'the present system of individual ownership is extravagant and wasteful, whether viewed from the point of view of the coal industry as a whole or from the national point of view'. They therefore stressed the miners' claim for a more efficient organisation of their industry and thought that 'in the interests of the consumer as much as in that of the miners, nationalisation ought to be, in principle, at once determined on'.

The conflicting opinions of the mine owners and the mine workers to some extent cancelled each other out, but the declaration of the Chairman of the Commission and his three colleagues carried considerable weight, and the Chancellor of the Exchequer, Bonar Law, pledged the government to implement the interim report (i.e. Mr Justice Sankey's) 'in the letter and in the spirit'. The miners as a body were unimpressed but agreed to drop further opposition on the understanding that the Commission would continue to investigate and report on the question of national ownership of the industry and the practical issue of how to give miners 'an effective voice in the direction of the mine'.

Some weeks later a 'second stage' report was published, signed by all the members of the Commission. They were unanimously in favour of royalties becoming the property of the State, they were unanimous in agreeing that miners should be given some share in the management of the mine, but that was as far as their unanimity went. The Chairman, drafting his report somewhat unexpectedly in the first person singular, declared his hand unequivocally.

> I recommend the continuance of the Coal Control Order for three years from the date of this Report ... I recommend on the evidence before me that the principle of State ownership of the coal mines be accepted ... I recommend that the scheme for local administration hereinafter set out ... be immediately set up ... and that Parliament be invited to pass legislation acquiring the coal mines for the State, after the scheme has been worked for three years from the date of this report, paying fair and just compensation to the owners.

For the rest, the members of the Commission aligned themselves according to their various allegiances, which, since they all proved ultimately to be irrelevant, are of interest only to the specialist in the subject. Broadly speaking the miners favoured a complex scheme of nationalisation. The three 'independent capitalists' believed that the nationalisation of the coal industry in any form would be detrimental to the development of the industry and to the economic life of the country. The attitude of the coal owners, as reported by Sankey, was expressed by one of their number who, giving evidence to the Commission, had stated: '... if owners are not to be left in complete executive control they will decline to accept responsibility for carrying on the industry ...', and although they regarded nationalisation as disastrous to the country, 'they would in such event be driven to the only alternative—nationalisation on fair terms'.

The essence of the government's response to the report was that State ownership of royalties would be proposed but the report itself would not be adopted. The Miners' Federation accused the government of reneging on its promise to adopt the report 'in the letter and in the spirit'; the reply was that Bonar Law's pledge related only to the interim report. With nothing significant achieved apart from some modest improvements in the matter of wages and hours of work, the two sides returned to their previous positions. Control of the mines was handed back to the owners, and the miners, with the support of the Labour Party and the trade union movement, began a campaign in favour of nationalisation.

When, by 1925, the situation had again become explosive, the government set up a Royal Commission, chaired by Sir Herbert Samuel, 'To inquire into and report on the economic position of the Coal Industry and the conditions affecting it and to make recommendations for the improvement thereof'.

The Commission's remit covered every aspect of the industry including proposals for nationalisation, which it dealt with in Part II chapter 6 of its report. There were, it said, many other considerations not peculiar to coal mining which bore upon the general question of State action in trade and industry. These would certainly not have precluded the Commission from recommending nationalisation if the case for it had been proved, but 'we have seen ... no scheme that will withstand criticism; we perceive grave economic dangers; and we can find no advantages which cannot be attained as readily, or more readily, in other ways'. The Commission's last words were unambiguous: 'We contemplate the continuance of the industry under private enterprise but we make a number of proposals for its reorganisation.'

Far from submitting to reorganisation, the industry plunged shortly into the strike of 1926 with all its consequences, and it was left to the Labour Government of 1929 to bring in the Coal Mines Bill of 1930 (see above, p. 30). Introducing the second reading in the House of Lords, the Lord Chancellor, Lord Sankey, claimed that since the publication of his report (in 1919) he had not written or spoken a word on the subject of coal mining. He had not changed his mind: he still believed in nationalisation. He had had good grounds for believing that his suggestions would be accepted, but it was not to be. Some might say, if he believed in nationalisation why was he supporting the present Bill? 'The answer is simple. I am a member of a Minority Government. In my view no Minority Government is entitled to put forward so sweeping a measure as nationalisation' (Hansard, Lords, 29 April 1930).

That was the position when in 1930 Sir Stafford Cripps joined the Labour Government, and was still the position when in 1934 he accepted the invitation of the North Wales Miners' Association to represent them at the inquiry into the Gresford disaster.

APPENDIX B

The Davy Lamp (see p. 157)

One of the earliest reported uses of the Davy lamp occurred in North Wales. Among his papers Davy preserved a letter, dated 27 January 1817, from Mr John Morris of Plas Issa, a colliery near Acrefair, to John Simmons Esq., Paddingtonhouse. Following an explosion of firedamp in one of Simmons's mines, 'by which several of the men were dreadfully burnt and bruised', Morris ordered some lamps. Neither he nor the colliers had any experience of them and in the absence of instructions Morris read out an account from the *Edinburgh Review*. The men, who had previously 'secretly treated them with some contempt', were now ordered to take the lamps into the pit for a trial, but their wives, Morris wrote, 'made so much noise and lamentation that it was with some difficulty that I could keep them off'. The experiment was concluded without mishap, all the men in the district being 'astonished and amazed that so simple-looking an instrument should destroy and defy an enemy heretofore unconquerable'. The reference to 'destroying' firedamp suggests that the principle of the lamp had not been fully grasped (*Davy's Collected Works*, Vol. 6, 1825, p. 99).

Inspectors' reports for North Wales later in the century refer frequently to accidents allegedly due to breaches of the regulations concerning safety lamps. Higson described an explosion which occurred in 1862 at Gardden Lodge Colliery near Ruabon, killing a miner. The colliery was served by only one shaft, 'the downcast pit being only 3 feet in diameter separated from the upcast by a brick wall only 9 inches thick'. Higson had secured from the management an undertaking that only safety lamps under proper regulations would be used in the workings, but this promise had not been fulfilled when the explosion occurred, 'and against this general use, which efforts have since been made to enforce, the men have actually struck, and still positively refuse to work with any other than open lights ...' (Higson's Report, 28 February 1863).

More than a decade later Hall reported similar obstinacy,

218

following the deaths of three men in an explosion at Westminster Colliery, Wrexham.

> The accident arose through the use of naked lights. I have impressed upon the manager the necessity of using safety lamps but have to report that no change has been made. Indeed so strong is the feeling against safety lamps both among managers and workers in North Wales that I feel it is almost hopeless to suggest their introduction. It is asserted, perhaps with some degree of truth, that the light from the safety lamps does not enable them so well to examine the roof of working places and guard against falls. (Hall, 26 March 1877)

Another defence put forward on behalf of the miners is that North Wales and Lancashire were the only two coalfields in the country in which the men were required to buy their own lamps (Dodd, *The Industrial Revolution in North Wales*, p. 196).

There is also the possibility that, like the manager at Plas Issa, at least some of the men had not fully grasped the function of the safety lamp. An incident at Vron Colliery near Wrexham in 1869, as reported by Higson, reads like a scene from a Buster Keaton black comedy. James Thomas, a horse-keeper working below ground, had frequently been told not to go to a certain place without a safety lamp because of gas which gathered in a hole in the roof. 'So on the day in question he was going along with a safety lamp in one hand and a naked light in the other.' The resulting explosion killed him, and thus, Higson sternly comments, 'he sacrificed his life as a penalty for his disobedience'; or perhaps because no one had thought to explain the situation to him.

APPENDIX C
Butties (see p. 158)

Nothing perhaps indicates more clearly how the progress of events had in some respects passed the North Wales coalfield by in the 1920s and 1930s than the persistence there in however residual a form of the subcontracting or 'butty' system of employment among underground workers after it had died out in every other coalfield, chiefly in the Midlands, where it had once been the norm. (According to the *History of the British Coal Industry*, Vol. 1, p. 417, the subcontractors were known as 'charter masters' in Shropshire and Derbyshire, 'chalter' in North Wales and 'butties' in South Yorkshire and Staffordshire. Ashton and Sykes, writing of the eighteenth century, describe the 'chalter' as 'the remuneration of the group'. In North Wales the terms seem to have been interchangeable.)

The system had its roots in the geological and economic conditions of the areas in which it developed—broadly, a terrain rich in minerals, especially coal and iron, but not in wealth on a scale necessary to promote and sustain a well-organised industry, except perhaps during the reign of John Wilkinson in North Wales in the eighteenth century. Both minerals were found not far beneath the surface and were mined together—coal, as one observer put it, being 'subservient' to iron—and with no regard for the environmental consequences. Readers of *The Old Curiosity Shop* will recall the industrial landscape through which Little Nell and her grandfather passed on their journey north. A less emotional but no less striking description of the scene was given by Thomas Tancred, a Commissioner sent 'to conduct a special inquiry into the condition of the persons employed in the mines in the counties of Worcester, Warwick, Stafford and Shropshire ... and generally into the circumstances which affect their social position'. Tancred's investigations were confined chiefly to South Staffordshire, where a strike and associated rioting had paralysed the coalfield during the summer of 1842, but from other evidence it seems likely that he would have found similar scenes if he had crossed into parts of North Wales at the same period.

The whole country might be compared to a vast rabbit warren ... the traveller appears never to get out of interminable villages. In some directions he may travel for miles and never be out of sight of numerous two-storied houses, for the most part not arranged in continuous streets but ... interspersed with blazing furnaces, heaps of burning coal in process of ironstone calcining, forges, pitbanks and engine chimneys ... and the small remaining patches of the surface soil occupied with irregular fields of grass or corn, intermingled with heaps of the refuse of mines or of slag from the blast furnaces.

Tancred's unexpected conclusion was that in spite of the squalor of their surroundings, the unrest among the mining population was due not, as had been claimed, to the influence of Chartist agitators who were active in the area, nor even to a recent reduction in wages, but to 'the abuses of the butty system of employing labour' which were 'the standing subject of grievance and dissatisfaction among the colliers and miners of South Staffordshire' (First Report of the Midland Mining Commission, 1843 [Cmd 508]: a second Report was projected but not published).

The system arose because of the shortage of capital among landowners and others who could, singly or jointly, afford to sink a fairly shallow pit on their property but not to equip it or pay the wages of the work force. This task would therefore be undertaken by a butty, usually an experienced collier who, having amassed some capital of his own, 'engaged with the proprietor of the mine to deliver coal or ironstone at so much a ton, himself hiring the labourers requisite, using his own horses and supplying all the tools necessary for working the mine'. Opinions of the system varied according to the perceptions and experience of the observer. James Mitchell, reporting to the Children's Employment Commission (1842, Vol. xvi), saw the butty as 'generally a steady, well-doing man, who has risen from being a common workman by his good behaviour and power of self-restraint'. This was an unusually favourable assessment. One of the first inspectors of mines appointed under the Act of 1850 dismissed the butty as

a generally uneducated and unskilful person raised a step above the ordinary miner and to whom a remuneration derivable from the proprietors on the one hand and from labourers on the other is the chief object, regardless of the permanent welfare of both. (Morton, 1st report, September 1851)

A Select Committee reporting in 1853 took a similarly censorious view.

Among the evils of the system, according to Tancred and most other commentators, was that

> the butty has become the middleman or taskmaster ... The man of property, who possesses or rents the royalty, sinks the pits and erects the machinery: whose position therefore in society would insure [sic] general humane and liberal treatment of his labourers, is by the intervention of a butty entirely disconnected with them.

As was to be expected, the emphasis on getting out as much coal as possible for the greatest profit relegated questions of safe working to the background.

Little progress towards mitigating the abuses of the system was made until the passing of the Coal Mines Regulation Act of 1872 which, by requiring every mine to be under the control of a certificated manager, was intended to put an end to the 'big butty' system as it came to be called, leaving only a 'little butty' system under which the power and independence of the butty were severely curtailed. In this the Act is usually held to have succeeded and it is therefore all the more surprising to find a distinguished authority providing a Royal Commission as late as 1907 with evidence suggesting that although even the little butty system had effectively died out in North Staffordshire, in the southern part of the county the butty's wings appeared to have suffered little clipping. W. A. Atkinson was Superintending Inspector of the Swansea and Cardiff Division, and his 'Report on the Charter-Master System in South Staffordshire and East Worcester' was published as Appendix XIV to the Commission's Report of 1909 (Cmd 4820). According to Atkinson, 'Where a certificated manager is required or an undermanager employed, the owner pays them as required by the Act, and they look after his interests *as against the Charter Master*' (author's italics). The system, Atkinson asserted, 'conduces to the working of the pits in an unskilful way, and to the neglect of discipline and measures of safety'. Questioned by members of the Commission, he cited an extraordinary anomaly apparently sanctioned by the law. The Act of 1872 prohibited a contractor from himself examining a pit and reporting on its safety but there was nothing to prevent him from giving the job to one of his employees, often a member of his own family. The Royal Commission expressed modified doubts about the situation.

> While we think that the system of contracting for special purposes may be advantageous we are of opinion that the practice by which a contractor employs a large number of men in getting coal is not always conducive to safety and that it should be carefully watched and discouraged except where it can clearly be adopted with safety. (para 21)

Concerning North Wales there is little reliable information; most authorities (e.g. Rowe, 1923, p. 63) content themselves with noting the existence there of the butty system and the general similarity to the position in other coalfields. As the complaints from Hall's reports at the turn of the century reveal (see above, p. 157), the system was open to the same criticism in North Wales as elsewhere. That it not only survived but was officially recognised as late as the 1920s is confirmed by the opening words of a document setting out 'terms for employment' which applicants for jobs with the Westminster and Acton Collieries Company were required to sign: 'Any person employed on or about the Works, and whether employed directly by the Company or by Charter-master or other person ... etc.'.

The question which is probably unanswerable after this lapse of time and foiled even the inquisitorial skills of Sir Stafford Cripps is how much power the charter master, chalter or butty still exercised in Gresford in 1934. Was it perhaps reflected to some extent in Bonsall's acquiescence in the breach of the overtime rules 'because the men liked it'? Or in the pressure put on reluctant shot firers by the colliers to fire more than one shot at a time? Was the 'drive for output', on which Cripps laid so much stress, maintained solely from the management side? Rowe, writing in 1923, when the butty was almost an extinct species, quoted the comment of 'a well-known trade unionist' that many former butties had 'never ceased to hanker for the fleshpots of the system, and the employer encouraged it, because of the fact that many of the butties were bullies, and to put it mildly they did undoubtedly supervise, spur and speed up' (1923, p. 64). Was this still true of a few survivors of the breed in Gresford 11 years later?

Section 96 (2) of the Coal Mines Act, 1911 provided that 'The wages of all persons employed in or about any mine shall be paid weekly ... and there shall be delivered to each such person a statement containing particulars of how the amount paid to him is arrived at.' This was still the law on the subject in 1934. If the first-hand accounts of relations between charter master and worker given to the present author are to be believed (see above, p. 159), this requirement was, like so many others, regularly being contravened in Gresford, where the management turned a blind eye to it, relying either on the men's ignorance of their legal rights or on their apathetic acceptance of the flagrant denial of them in the face of the sheer impossibility, in current circumstances, of asserting them.

Owners (see p. 72)

Michael Foot was presumably speaking metaphorically of coal owners in general when he referred to Cripps having put them in the dock at Gresford, but observers may have wondered why the owners of Gresford succeeded in avoiding penalties of some kind in respect of breaches of the law revealed at the inquiry. One answer is that since no conclusion was ever reached as to the cause of the explosion, no charges could be brought on that account; but the question also overlooks the obstacles in the way of securing a conviction against an owner for anything found to have been amiss in his mine.

From the early nineteenth century the law had been so framed as in effect to protect owners from being successfully prosecuted. Ashley's Act of 1842, designed primarily 'to prohibit the Employment of Women in Mines and Collieries [and] to regulate the Employment of Boys ...', also made 'other Provisions relating to Persons working therein', the last of which stipulated that:

> if any Offence shall be committed against this Act for which the Owner of any Mine or Colliery is hereby made responsible, and it shall be made to appear, to the satisfaction of any Justices or Sherriff, that the offence has been committed by or under the authority of some Agent, Servant or workman of such Owner, it shall be lawful for such Justices or Sherriff to summon such Agent, Servant or Workman ... to answer such offences [and to convict them] in lieu of such Owner.

As time went by and Act succeeded Act, this provision was easily extended to mean that an owner, having appointed an agent or manager to supervise the operation of his mine, had by implication delegated all responsibility to the man or men in question, and was therefore to be exonerated from blame for any mishap or breach of regulations occurring in or about his property. In 1878 one of the General Rules had not been complied with in certain mines. The Home Office unsuccessfully instituted proceedings against the owner who, the defence claimed, had in fact taken no part in the management of the mine. Giving judgement, Baron Cleasby asked:

> Is not a man who has a share in a mine justified in leaving the management to a person who has the daily supervision of the mine, and who, the Act [of 1872] says, *shall* have the control of it? ... A proper person, a certified manager under the Act, had been appointed to see that everything was done that ought to have been done.

This interpretation was confirmed in the Act of 1887 which provided that in certain specified circumstances 'the owner of the mine shall not be liable to any fine if he proves that he had taken all reasonable means ... to prevent the mine being worked in contravention of this section'. In 1906 the prosecution of an owner failed in a case brought in Scotland concerning allegedly defective ventilation. The Sheriff, while convicting the manager of the mine, dismissed the complaint against the owner on the ground that 'The owner may dissociate himself from the mine by appointing a certified manager.' These and other cases were quoted in Section IV—'Supervision and Management'—of the report of the Royal Commission of 1909.

The Coal Mines Act of 1911, Sections 75 and 90, reaffirmed the owner's right to immunity from prosecution if he could prove that he had taken 'all reasonable means' to prevent breaches of the Act, but it seems to have been felt that some more stringent definitions of responsibility were called for. These were laid down in Part VIII of the Act under the heading 'Legal Proceedings'. Section 102 (1), dealing with proceedings taken against 'the owner, agent or manager or each of them', stipulated that the owner or agent should not be liable to any penalty 'if he proves to the satisfaction of the court':

> (a) that he was not in the habit of taking and did not in respect of the matters in question take any part in the management of the mine;
> (b) that he had made all the financial and other provision necessary to enable the manager to carry out his duties; and
> (c) that the offence was committed without his knowledge, consent or contrivance.

The next subsection blocked off part of the escape route previously offered to owners.

> (2) Save as above provided, it shall not be a defence in any proceedings brought against the owner or agent ... that a manager has been appointed in accordance with this Act.

A further subsection (3) suggests that someone may possibly have had some slight acquaintance with the works of Macchiavelli: an owner, agent or manager would not be liable to a penalty if he could prove that any contravention of or non-compliance with the provisions of the Act 'was due to causes over which he had no control and against the happening of which it was impracticable for him to make provision' (see the epigraph to the present work).

The first serious test of the new statement of the law came in October 1913 with the explosion at Senghenydd Colliery in Glamorgan, the worst disaster in British coal mining history, in which 439 men lost their lives. After a delay of nine weeks, attributed by the Home Secretary to his inability to find a colliery owner willing to serve on the court, an inquiry was opened, with Richard Redmayne, then Chief Inspector of Mines, as Commissioner, the North Wales agent, Edward Hughes, as one of the representatives of the Miners' Federation, and Mr (later Lord Justice) Sankey representing the owners, Lewis Merthyr Consolidated Collieries Ltd. The proceedings lasted for over three weeks, and it was a subject of much adverse comment that no director of the company was called to give evidence to show, as a Welsh MP put it, that they had taken reasonable steps, as proprietors of the colliery, to see that there had been no breaches of the Act and no non-compliance with the Regulations. The solicitor for the company, presumably with Section 102 of the Act in mind, responded by arguing that the purpose of the inquiry was to discover the causes of the explosion and the circumstances surrounding it. How, then, could a director of the company have been of assistance to the court? 'The directors, as we know, have no practical knowledge of the working of the mine', and therefore to have called Lord Merthyr or any other director 'would have been wasting the time of the Court'. As Lord Merthyr, otherwise Baron Merthyr of Senghenydd, had been among other things President of the Mining Association of Great Britain, President of the Institution of Mining Engineers, and a member of numerous Royal Commissions on mining matters, it was felt in some quarters that he might have been able to throw at least a little light on the working of his own colliery.

The detailed conclusions of the Senghenydd inquiry are not relevant to this discussion except in so far as they were described by Clement Davies MP in terms echoed 20 years later at Gresford: 'A more amazing, more flagrant, more culpable violation of an Act of Parliament I do not recall.'

Two months after the end of the inquiry the manager of the colliery was prosecuted for 17 minor breaches of the Coal Mines

Act. Seven charges were dropped, others dismissed; convictions were secured on the remaining five. The fines imposed totalled £24. Four charges were brought against Lord Merthyr and the other owners of the colliery. All were either dropped or dismissed.

With this precedent to guide them it is hardly surprising that the authorities, faced in 1937 with a similar situation, should have decided that Section 102 of the Act of 1911 provided the owners of Gresford with so impenetrable a defence that a prosecution was hardly worthwhile. As at Senghenydd, the managers and other officials escaped with convictions for a few minor breaches of the Act; whatever charges may have been brought against United Westminster and Wrexham Collieries seem to have got lost along the way.

(For the Commissioner's report on the inquiry into the explosion at Senghenydd, see British Parliamentary Papers 1914 [Cmd 7346], xxiv 435. For a more partisan narrative see R. P. Arnot, *South Wales Miners* (1967); this also includes a list of 'Examples of Penalties for Offences against the Coal Mines Act 1911'. For a contemporary (i.e. 1938) discussion of the responsibilities of owners under the 1911 Act, see the report of the Royal Commission on Safety in Mines, pp. 148 ff.)

Bibliography

A NOTE ON SOURCES

This book was conceived primarily as social rather than mining history. Technical and other information provided is intended to serve as background to an understanding of the remarkable though not always typical circumstances, both local and national, which produced the disaster at Gresford.

The principal sources of information on the disaster are the reports of the Chief Inspector of Mines and his two assessors (Cmd 5458) and the verbatim transcript of evidence given. The latter was not published but survived in typescript in 38 volumes, one for each day on which the inquiry held a session. I am grateful to the committee of the then North Wales area of the National Union of Mineworkers for giving me the opportunity to consult their copy. Very full accounts of the daily proceedings were carried in the *Wrexham Leader*, copies of which are held on microfilm in the public library in Wrexham.

All records and correspondence relating to the operations of United Westminster and Wrexham Collieries appear to have been destroyed, except for a handful of financial statements held at Companies House under the index number 85251. The correspondence concerning Welsh-speaking inspectors of mines is filed in the Public Record Office under POWER 10/44.

From the middle of the nineteenth to the middle of the twentieth century, the coal industry was the subject of a succession of Acts of Parliament, Select Committees, Royal Commissions and specific sets of official instructions, many of which bear directly on the subject of Gresford. Volumes 3 and 4 of the *History of the British Coal Industry* (Oxford 1984–93) deal with the period in detail, with full bibliographies. The Second Report of the Royal Commission on Mines (Cmd 4820), issued in 1909, includes a useful 'Short Sketch of Mining Legislation' covering the years from Ashley's Act of 1842 down to the time of the Commission's own sessions. The report as a whole and the associated volumes of evidence discuss comprehensively, but of course from the contemporary point of view, many of the topics raised or referred to in connection with the Gresford inquiry, e.g. inspection, firemen's duties, ventilation, managers' qualifications, the butty system and so on. The Coal Mines Act of 1911, much of it based on the Commission's recommendations, was in the main the legislation by which the industry was still governed in 1934 at the time of the Gresford explosion. For the subsequent period see the report of the Royal Commission on Safety in Mines (Cmd 5890), 1938. The Acts of most significance to Gresford, together with the principal reports which inspired or influenced them, are listed in the bibliography to the present work.

For the rest, a specific reference is usually not given where the source of a statement or a quotation is either cited in the text or may be deduced and located without difficulty from the information supplied. The following is either a guide to some of the less easily identifiable sources, or an amplification which may be of help or interest in the investigation of a subject in greater depth.

SELECT BIBLIOGRAPHY

Addison, P., *The Road to 1945* (Pimlico, 1994).

Arnot, R. P., *The Miners*, Vols I–III (Allen and Unwin, 1949, 1956, 1961).

Arnot, R. P., *South Wales Miners: A History of the South Wales Miners' Federation* (Allen and Unwin, 1967).

Ashton, T. S., *Iron and Steel in the Industrial Revolution* (Manchester, 1968).

Ashton, T. S. and Sykes, J., *The Coal Industry in the 18th Century* (2nd edition, Manchester, 1964).

Beazley, E. and Brett, L., *Shell Guide to North Wales* (Faber, 1971).

Beazley, E. and Howell, P., *Companion Guide to North Wales* (Collins, 1975).

Boyd, R. N., *Coal Mines Inspection: Its History and Results* (W. H. Allen, 1879).

Branson, N., *Britain in the 1920s* (Weidenfeld and Nicolson, 1975).

Branson, N. and Heinemann, M., *Britain in the 1930s* (Weidenfeld and Nicolson, 1971).

Bryant, C., *Stafford Cripps* (Hodder and Stoughton, 1997).

Bullock, A., *Life and Times of Ernest Bevin*, Vol. I (Heinemann, 1960).

Challinor, R., *The Lancashire and Cheshire Miners* (Frank Graham, 1972).

Challinor, R. and Ripley, B., *The Miners' Association* (Lawrence and Wishart, 1968).

Chaloner, W. H., 'John Wilkinson, Ironmaster', *History Today*, 1951.

Citrine, W., *Men and Work* (Hutchinson, 1964).

Colliery Year Book 1934.

Condry, W., *Exploring Wales* (Faber, 1970).

Cooke, C. A., *Life of Richard Stafford Cripps* (Hodder and Stoughton, 1957).

Court, W. H. B., 'Problems of the British Coal Industry between the Wars', *Economic History Review*, Vol. XV, 1945.

Cripps, R. S., *Can Socialism come by Constitutional Methods?* (Socialist League, undated).

Cripps, R. S., *The Struggle for Peace* (Gollancz, 1936).

Cripps, R. S., *God in Our Work* (Nelson, 1949).

Dalton, H., *The Fateful Years* (Muller, 1957).

Davies, P., 'Gresford Colliery Explosion 1934', *Denbighshire Historical Society Transactions*, 1973.

Davies, W. W., *A Wayfarer in Wales* (Methuen, 1930).

Davy, H., 'On the Safety Lamp', *Collected Works*, Vol. 6 (1825, 1840).

Dodd, A. H., 'The North Wales Coal Industry during the Industrial Revolution', *Archeologia Cambrensis*, 1929.

Dodd, A. H., 'Welsh and English in East Denbighshire', *Transactions of Cymmrodorion Society*, 1940.

Dodd, A. H., *Life in Wales* (Batsford, 1972).

Dodd, A. H., *The Industrial Revolution in North Wales* (University of Wales Press, 1951).

Dodd, A. H. (ed.), *History of Wrexham* (Hughes, Wrexham, 1957).

Duckham, B. and Duckham, H., *Great Pit Disasters* (David and Charles, 1973).

Ellis, T., *Mines and Men* (Educational Explorers, 1971).

Engels, F., *Die Lage der arbeitenden Klasse in England* (German edition, 1845).

Estorick, E., *Stafford Cripps: A Biography* (Heinemann, 1949).

Evans, E. W., *The Miners of South Wales* (University of Wales Press, 1961).

Fishbourne, E. A., *An Architectural History of the Parish Church of All Saints, Gresford* (Chester, 1924).

Fishbourne, E. A., 'The Church of All Saints, Gresford', *Journal of Chester and North Wales Architectural, Archeological and Historical Society*, Vol. XV, 1908/09.

Foot, M., *Aneurin Bevan*, Vol. I (MacGibbon and Kee, 1962).

Fox, C., *Offa's Dyke* (Oxford, 1956).

Fraser, M., *Wales* (Hale, 1957).

Fraser, M., *Welsh Border Country* (Batsford, 1972).

Galloway, R. L., *Annals of Coal Mining and the Coal Trade, 1898 and 1904* (reprint, David and Charles, 1971).

Geological Survey
   Geology of the Country around Liverpool and … Part of Flintshire Coalfield, 1923.
   Geology of the Country around Flint etc., 1924.
   Geology of the Country around Wrexham, 1927/28.
   North Wales, 1969.

Griffin, A. R., *The British Coal Mining Industry: Retrospect and Prospect* (Moorland Publishing, 1977).

Griffiths, J., *Pages from Memory* (Dent, 1969).

Harris, K., *Attlee* (Weidenfeld and Nicolson, 1982).

The History of the British Coal Industry, 5 vols (Oxford, 1984–93).

Jarman, S. G., *The Village of Gresford* (4th edition, Jarman, 1912).

Jarman's North Wales Guardian Year Book, 1898–1934.

Jenkins, R., *Nine Men of Power* (Hamish Hamilton, 1974).

Jenkinson, H. I., *A Practical Guide to North Wales* (1878).

Jevons, H. S., *The British Coal Trade* (Kegan Paul, 1915).

Johnson, S., *Diary of a Journey into North Wales* (1774).

Jones, J., *Wrexham and its Neighbourhood* (1859).

Jones, J., *The Coal Scuttle* (Faber and Faber, 1936).

Jones, J. I., *A New Geography of Wales* (Hughes, Wrexham, 1969).

Keynes, J. M., *The Economic Consequences of Mr Churchill* (Hogarth, 1925).

Lawson, J., *Peter Lee* (Hodder and Stoughton, 1936).

Lawson, J., *The Man in the Cap: The Life of Herbert Smith* (Methuen, 1941).

Leland, J., *Itinerary*.

Lerry, G. G., 'Henry Dennis', *Denbighshire Historical Society Transactions*, 1952.

Lerry, G. G., *The Collieries of Denbighshire* (2nd edition, Wrexham, 1968).

Lewis, *Topographical Dictionary of Wales* (1833, 1838, 1843).

The Listener, 1934.

Lovett, R., *Welsh Pictures* (Religious Tract Society, undated).

Marquand, D., 'Stafford Cripps' in *The Age of Austerity,* ed. Sissons, M. and French, P. (Hodder & Stoughton, 1963).

Marquand, D., *Ramsay Macdonald* (Cape, 1977).

Miners' Federation of Great Britain, *The Position of the Coal Miner* (Miners' Federation of Great Britain, 1933).

Ministry of Fuel and Power, *North Western Coalfields: Regional Survey Report* (HMSO, 1945).

Morrison, H., *An Autobiography* (Odhams, 1960).

National Coal Board, *Accidents and Disasters in Coal Mines* (National Coal Board, 1978).

Nef, J. U., *The Rise of the British Coal Industry* (Routledge, 1932).

Neumann, A. M., *Economic Organization of the British Coal Industry* (Routledge, 1934).

North, F. J., *Coal and Coalfields in Wales* (National Museum of Wales and University of Wales, 1931).

Palmer, A. N., 'Offa's and Wat's Dykes', *Cymmrodorion Society,* 1891.

Palmer, A. N., *History of the Town of Wrexham* (1893).

Palmer, A. N., *John Wilkinson and the Old Bersham Ironworks* (1899).

Palmer, A. N., 'History of the Old Parish of Gresford', *Archeologia Cambrensis,* 1903–05.

Pennant, T., *A Tour in Wales* (1778–81).

PEP, *Report on the British Coal Industry* (Political and Economic Planning Industries Group, 1936).

Pimlott, B., *Labour and the Left in the 1930s* (Cambridge, 1977).

Playfair, Lyon, *Memoirs and Correspondence,* ed. W. Reid (1899).

Pryce, W. T. R., 'Approaches to the Linguistic Geography of North Wales 1750–1840', *National Library of Wales Journal,* Vol. 17, 1971/72.

Rawson, R. R., 'Coal Mining Industry of the Hawarden District', *Archeologia Cambrensis,* 1941.

Redmayne, R. A. S., *Men, Mines and Memories* (Eyre and Spottiswoode, 1942).

Reports of Commissioners of Inquiry into the State of Education in Wales, 1847.

Reports of Inspectors of Coal Mines 1852–.

Reports of Secretary for Mines 1919–.

Roberts, D., *Victorian Origins of the Welfare State* (Archon Books, 1969).

Rogers, E., 'The History of Trade Unionism in the Coal Mining Industry of North Wales to 1914', *Denbighshire Historical Society Transactions,* 1963–73.

Rowe, J. W. F., *Wages in the Coal Industry* (P. S. King, 1923).

Royal Society, *Philosophical Transactions,* No. 136, 25 June 1677.

Safety in Mines Research Board, *What Every Mining Man Should Know* (Safety in Mines Research Board, 1934).

Schoss, D., *Methods of Industrial Remuneration* (Williams and Norgate, 1898).

Shinwell, E., *I've Lived Through It All* (Gollancz, 1973).

Stewart, W. D. H., *Mines, Machines and Men* (King, 1935).

Strauss, P., *Cripps, Advocate and Rebel* (Gollancz, 1943).

Sylvester, D., *Rural Landscape of the Welsh Borderland* (Macmillan, 1969).

Taylor, A. J., 'The Sub-contract System in the British Coal Industry' in *Studies in the Industrial Revolution*, ed. L. S. Pressnell (University of London, The Athlone Press, 1960).

Tremenheere, H. S., *Reports of Mining Districts*, 1844–53.

Tremenheere, H. S., *I Was There* (Shakespeare Head Press, 1965).

Webb, B., *Diaries 1924–32* (Longmans Green, 1956).

Webb, S. and Webb, B., *History of Trade Unionism* (Longmans Green, 1920).

Williams, C. R. (ed.), *History of Flintshire* (Gee, Denbigh, 1961).

Williams, D. T., 'Linguistic Divides in North Wales', *Archeologia Cambrensis*, 1936.

Williams, E. T. and Palmer, H. M. (eds), *The Dictionary of National Biography: 1951–1960* (Oxford University Press, 1971).

Williams, G., 'Language, Literacy and Nationality in North Wales', *History*, Vol. 71.

Wyatt, W., *Confessions of an Optimist* (Collins, 1985).

Young, G. M., *Stanley Baldwin* (Hart Davis, 1952).

The Times
Manchester Guardian
Daily Express
Daily Herald
Daily Mirror
Daily Telegraph
Daily Worker
News-Chronicle
Observer
Sunday Times
Chester Chronicle
Wrexham Advertiser
Wrexham Leader
Colliery Guardian
Hansard

LEGISLATION

1842 5 and 6 Vict C 99.

An Act to prohibit the Employment of Women and Girls in Mines and Collieries, to regulate the Employment of Boys, and to make other Provisions relating to Persons working therein.

1850 13 and 14 Vict C 100.

An Act to provide for the Inspection of Coal Mines in Great Britain.

1855 18 and 19 Vict C 10.

An Act to amend the Law for Inspection of Coal Mines in Great Britain. (Repealed the Act of 1850: provided for the establishment of seven General

Rules, and Special Rules for every colliery, to be posted in a conspicuous place at the mine.)

1872   35 and 36 Vict C 76.

An Act to consolidate and amend the Acts relating to the Regulation of Coal Mines ... ('The Coal Mines Regulation Act 1872').
('26 ... A person shall not be qualified to be the manager of a mine to which this Act applies unless he is for the time being registered as the holder of a certificate under this Act.')

1878   Instructions for H.M.'s Inspectors under the Coal Mines Regulation Act 1872 (Cmd. 1987), lxi 221.

1887   50 and 51 Vict C 58.

An Act to consolidate with amendments the Coal Mines Acts 1872 and 1886 ('The Coal Mines Regulation Act 1887').
(General Rules increased to 39.)

1896   59 and 60 Vict C 43.

An Act to amend the Coal Mines Regulation Act 1887 ('the principal Act') ('The Coal Mines Regulation Act 1896').

1908   8 Edw 7 C 57.

An Act to amend Coal Mines Regulation Acts 1887 to 1905, for the purpose of limiting hours of work below ground ('The Coal Mines Regulation Act 1908').
(See above, p. 27.)

1911   1 and 2 Geo 5 C 50.

An Act to consolidate and amend the Law relating to Coal Mines and certain other mines.
Regulations and Orders made under and supplementing the provisions of the Coal Mines Act 1911 ('Regulations and Orders relating to Safety and Health') General Code of 10 July 1913.

1913   Explosives in Coal Mines Order of 1 September 1913.

1920   10 Geo 5 C 4.

An Act to make temporary provision on account of the emergency arising from the war as to the profits and control of wages in, and advances in respect of, colliery undertakings, and for the purposes connected therewith.
11 (1) ... may be cited as the Coal Mines (Emergency) Act 1920.
        (2) ... deemed to have had effect as from 1st April 1919 and continue in force until 31st August 1920.

1920 10 and 11 Geo 5 C 50.

An Act to provide for the better administration of mines, to regulate the coal industry, and for other purposes connected with the mining industry and the persons employed therein (Mining Industry Act 1920).

1 ... there shall be established a department of the Board of Trade (to be known as the Mines Department) under a Parliamentary Secretary of the Board ... referred to as 'the Secretary for Mines'.

4 His Majesty in Council may by order make such consequential and supplemental provisions as may appear necessary or expedient for the purpose of giving full effect for any transfer of powers or duties under this Act, including the transfer and vesting of any property, rights, liabilities held, enjoyed or incurred by any Government Department ... and may make such adaptations in the Acts or regulations relating to such powers or duties as appear necessary.

1930 20 and 21 Geo 5 C 34.

An Act to provide for regulating and facilitating the production, supply and sale of coal by owners of coal mines; for the temporary amendment of the Coal Mines Regulation Act 1908; for the constitution and functions of a Coal Mines National Industrial Board; and for the purposes connected with the matters aforesaid.

1954 2 and 3 Eliz 2 C 70.

An Act to make fresh provision with respect to the management and control of mines and quarries and for securing the safety, health and welfare of persons employed thereat ...

PARLIAMENTARY PAPERS

1843   Report of the Midland Mining Commission (508) xiii 1.

1852/53   Reports from the Select Committee of the House of Commons on the Causes of the Numerous Accidents in Coal Mines and the Best Means for their Prevention (691) xx 2, (740) xx 179, (820) xx 278.

1854   As above.
          (169) ix 1, (258) ix 63, (277) ix 219, (325) ibid.

1865   Report from the Select Committee on the Operation of the Act for the Regulation and Inspection of Mines 1867 (496) xiii I.

1878   Instructions for H.M.'s Inspectors under the Coal Mines Regulation Act 1872, C 1987 lxi 221.

1886   Final Report of the Royal Commission appointed to inquire into Accidents in Mines, and the possible means of preventing their recurrence or limiting their disastrous consequences (Cmd 4699), xvi 411.

1890/91 First Report of the Royal Commission on Explosions from Coal Dust in Mines (Cmd 6543), xxii 555.

1894   Second Report as above [Cmd 7401], xxiv 583.

1909   Report of the Royal Commission on Mines [Cmd 4820], xxxiv 599.

1919   Reports of the Royal Commission on the Coal Industry (Sankey).
    a) ... interim report by Mr Justice Sankey, Mr Arthur Balfour, Sir Arthur Duckham and Sir Thomas Royden (Cmd 84), xi 263.
    b) ... by Messrs Robert Smillie, Frank Hodges, Herbert Smith, R. H. Tawney, Sydney Webb and Sir Leo Chiozzo Money (Cmd 85), xi 277.
    c) ... by Messrs R. W. Cooper, J. T. Forgie and Evan Williams (Cmd 86), xi 297.
    d) second stage: reports by Mr Justice Sankey etc. (Cmd 210), xi 305.

1926   Report of the Royal Commission on the Coal Industry (1925, Samuel) (Cmd 2600), xiv 1.

1938   Report of the Royal Commission on Safety in Coal Mines (Cmd 5890).

Reports of Commissioners
(on circumstances attending Explosions and other Accidents)

1914   Senghenydd Colliery, Glamorgan (Cmd 7346), xxix 435.

1924/25 Llay Main Colliery, Wrexham (Cmd 2365), xii 509.

1936/37 Gresford Colliery, Wrexham (Cmd 5358), iii 733.

Index